HATRED
HAS
NO FUTURE

HATRED HAS NO FUTURE

New Thinking on Relations with Japan

Ma Licheng

Based on the Japanese Translation by
Oikawa Junko

Japan Publishing Industry Foundation for Culture

PUBLISHER'S NOTE
This book follows the Hepburn system of romanization of Japanese words. All personal titles and ages of the public figures mentioned in this book are as of the publication date of the Japanese hardcover edition in 2014.

Hatred Has No Future: New Thinking on Relations with Japan
Ma Licheng. Translated by the Japan Institute of International Affairs (JIIA).

Published by
Japan Publishing Industry Foundation for Culture (JPIC)
2-2-30 Kanda-Jinbocho, Chiyoda-ku, Tokyo 101-0051, Japan

First English edition: September 2020

仇恨沒有未來：中日關係新思維 © 2013 Ma Licheng
Japanese translation © 2014 Oikawa Junko

English translation © 2020 The Japan Institute of International Affairs (JIIA)

Originally published in Chinese in 2013 by Hong Kong Open Page Publishing Co., Hong Kong.
Japanese translation published under the title *Nikushimi ni mirai wa nai: Chunichi kankei shin shiko*, translated by Oikawa Junko and published in 2014 by Iwanami Shoten, Publishers, Tokyo.
This English edition was translated based on the Japanese edition. Publishing rights arranged with Iwanami Shoten, Publishers, Tokyo.

This publication is the result of a collaborative effort between the Japan Institute of International Affairs (JIIA) and the Japan Publishing Industry Foundation for Culture (JPIC).

Jacket and cover book design: Miki Kazuhiko, Ampersand Works

Printed in Japan
ISBN 978-4-86658-123-1
https://www.jpic.or.jp/

CONTENTS

NOTES FOR READERS

- Because different governments and different speakers use different names for some of the territories mentioned, and because changing the name depending upon the speaker can easily be confusing, we have used dual names—e.g., the Daioyu/Senkaku Islands—to avoid confusion.

- Chapter 10 of the Japanese has been omitted with the author's approval.

- Some of the "quotations" in this book are not really quotations. Sometimes they are summations. Sometimes they are amalgamations of things the speaker said at different times. When they are real quotations, and when it has been possible to find the original (or an official translation of the original), that has been used. When this has not been possible, the source text has been translated as is and the passage has been represented as a quotation in keeping with the source text's intent.

- Personal names are given in the order preferred in that person's language. This means Chinese, Japanese, and Korean citzens' names are given family name first.

- Apologies in advance, but some of the hyperlinks may no longer be working by the time you read this.

Preface to the English Edition

When China's Deng Xiaoping met Japanese Prime Minister Nakasone Yasuhiro in Beijing on March 25, 1984, he told him: "We must look to develop the Sino-Japanese relationship from a long-term perspective and build a lasting, ongoing friendship between our countries. This is more important than any of the issues that exist between us." (*Deng Xiaoping Nianpu* [Chronicles of Deng Xiaoping], vol. 2, Zhongyang Wenxian Chubanshe [Central Party Literature Press], July 2004.)

Despite the differences of opinion that have arisen over various issues from time to time, reconciliation is the most important thing for the relationship between China and Japan. From a long-term perspective, whether China and Japan are at peace or in conflict will have a decisive effect on China's ability to accomplish its modernization objectives, as well determining the success or failure of the Asian unification process. It will also affect whether the wider world is at war or at peace. The Sino-Japanese relationship is an issue of primary importance whose repercussions will be felt worldwide. It is only by addressing the relationship from this broad perspective that one can properly understand the pulse and needs of the times. This is the essence of Deng Xiaoping's perspective on Japan.

A skillful wrestler is able to use his opponent's strength to achieve victory. In Chinese, the expression *si liang bo qian jin* (four ounces can move a thousand pounds) expresses how a relatively small force can be used to achieve great results. If we put this wisdom to use in our foreign policy, the results will be clear indeed. The New Thinking on Relations with Japan is a new approach to the development of the Sino-Japanese relationship. The New Thinking involves a conceptual change and will help us resolve longstanding problems at no great cost. To strengthen this new approach, both countries will need to control their respective nationalisms, rise above their squabbles over the good and bad of history, and achieve reconciliation. Reconciliation between China and Japan will benefit both countries and can make a major contribution to the development and prosperity of Asia and the world.

Feng Zhaokui, a Japan specialist and former deputy director of the Chinese Academy of Social Sciences (CASS) Institute of Japanese Studies, has described the New Thinking as the linchpin of a new system of thought that will develop with the times. History shows that it is often difficult for major new streams of thought to be accepted by all sections of the population right away. The New Thinking sparked a major response in both China and Japan as soon as it was published in 2002 and started a debate that continues to this day. The New Thinking and the debate surrounding it have followed a tortured path over the past decade. It has been gratifying to see that people in all areas of society have shown greater understanding of the New Thinking as time has passed, and I am particularly pleased to see that increasing numbers of young people now support the New Thinking. Whenever I travel, particularly along the southeastern coastal regions of the country, I hear expressions of support. One example is the many comments on the popular Weibo blogging site by ordinary people reflecting critically on the outrageous actions by some people at the height of the anti-Japanese demonstrations in September 2012. This book looks back at the uneven trajectory that the New Thinking has taken over the past ten years and reflects on the many changes that have characterized the Sino-Japanese relationship over the course of the past decade. In these discussions of the developments and in the ups-and-downs of the bilateral relationship during this period, my emphasis is on looking forward with optimism for the future. I hope the book will help to commemorate forty years since the normalization of diplomatic ties between China and Japan. Deng Xiaoping once described himself as "someone who is passionate about Sino-Japanese friendship and cooperation. (Pei Hua, ed., *Zhong-Ri waijiao fengyun-zhong de Deng Xiaoping* [Deng Xiaoping Amid the Currents of Sino-Japanese Foreign Relations], April 2002.) I believe that this is also the wish of the great majority of Chinese people, myself included. Of course, part of the process of making this hope a reality includes the need to guard against and remain critical of the discourse and actions of the Japanese right wing, which can damage the relationship.

Harvard University professor emeritus Ezra F. Vogel, who is fluent in both Japanese and Chinese and has published major works including *Japan as Number One: Lessons for America* and *Deng Xiaoping and the Transformation of China*, was invited to speak at the Fudan Development Forum at Fudan University in 2012. He made the following remarks.

> China's foreign policy focuses on its relations with Japan and the United States. Deng Xiaoping was a great leader . . . in 1978 he visited Japan. He said that Japanese literature deserved to be read by Chinese people and that Japan's movies and TV programs should also

be shown to Chinese audiences. Exchanges like this helped to give the Chinese people a relatively positive view of Japan at the time. Naturally, they had not forgotten the devastation and damage that Japan inflicted on China during World War II. But they looked at Japanese people in a way that was quite different from the view that prevails today. We cannot deny that Japan committed many atrocities during the war. But other factors are also important to Sino-Japanese relations. That's why I believe that China can learn a lot from Deng Xiaoping on the best way to handle its relationship with Japan. (*Shehui Kexue Bao* [Social Sciences Weekly], Shanghai, November 29, 2012)

I discuss Deng Xiaoping in more detail later in Chapter 3.

Niwa Uichiro, a popular Japanese ambassador to China, made the following remarks at a press conference when he stepped down from his post on November 26, 2012.

It is a source of great regret that the relationship between China and Japan is going through such a tempestuous time. The relationship is a bit like a marriage—with the exception that, although a married couple can choose to separate, Japan and China are stuck with each other. Even at its longest, a human life only lasts around 100 years, but Japan and China share a history as neighbors that goes back thousands of years already."

He also said: "Through my contacts with various influential people in China, I am convinced that the future of the relationship is bright."

Contrary to many people's expectations, even in the midst of the continuing dispute over the Diaoyu/Senkaku Islands, negotiations got underway in November 2012 for a free-trade area encompassing China, Japan, and South Korea. In my view, close and indivisible trade and economic relations between China and Japan had positive influences. There is a line in a poem by Wang Anshi, a poet of the Northern Song dynasty: "I fear not the clouds that may block our view." Numerous times in the past the outlook for Sino-Japanese relations has been clouded by storms and tempests. But every time the relationship has encountered difficulties, it has been possible to break through the impasse and forge a new path forward thanks to thorough-going efforts from both sides. In the context of an evolving environment as globalization progresses, I am confident that leaders and intellectuals in both countries will succeed in finding a peaceful solution to the current stand-off. This hope for the two countries is shared by the whole world and was the initial inspiration for writing this book.

On May 31, 1979, Deng Xiaoping met future prime minister Suzuki Zenko, then a member of the House of Representatives on his first visit to China, for talks that included a discussion of the Diaoyu/Senkaku Islands. The record of this conversation as published by the Central Party Literature Press in *Deng Xiaoping Amid the Currents of Sino-Japanese Foreign Relations* offers useful insights and wisdom still today.

With an austere expression, Deng Xiaoping touched on the subject of the Diaoyu/Senkaku Islands. He said: "Your side has recently been causing excessive fuss by talking loudly about this issue. Our two countries should not get entangled in this issue at present. When I visited Tokyo, I suggested that we shelve issues of territory and sovereignty for the time being. The views of Foreign Minister Sonoda we can accept. He said we should not let this issue become prominent for the sake of the bilateral relationship."

Deng Xiaoping said that he could not accept the views expressed by Japan's chief cabinet secretary, who had said: "The government has recently expressed its position on this issue, and this is a subject on which we cannot remain silent."

Following on from this, Deng Xiaoping offered up a suggestion. "I repeat that we should shelve this issue and should consider jointly developing the resources of the region. Is it not possible to consider this issue together? . . . Both sides should refrain from propaganda, have discussions with a view to joint development, and agree not to touch on questions of territory and sovereignty. Of course, the Japanese side would supply the technology. We would carry out joint development in the Bohai Gulf and form a company to do so together." He asked Suzuki to pass this suggestion to Prime Minister Ohira.

Suzuki said: "You have suggested a very original idea, which I will pass on to the prime minister for his consideration."

Deng Xiaoping said he had been considering possible methods of joint development during his visit to Japan. It would be the oil and other resources in the seabed around the islands that would be jointly developed, with a company to be managed by joint investment and profits accruing to both sides. The same formula could also be adopted for the Spratly Islands.

The report to the 18th National Congress of the Communist Party of China

(CCP) says: "We will improve and grow our relations with developed countries by expanding areas of cooperation and properly addressing differences with them; and we will strive to establish a new type of relations of long-term stability and sound growth with other leading countries. We will handle relations with neighboring countries appropriately and continue to promote friendship and partnership with our neighbors, to consolidate friendly relations and deepen mutually beneficial cooperation with them, and to ensure that China's development will bring more benefits to our neighbors." All these objectives have a close connection to Sino-Japanese relations. Successfully building a new relationship between two leading powers is something unprecedented, and the road will surely not always be smooth. But if China and Japan strive with wisdom and courage to find a way forward and work to overcome the obstacles in their way, I believe we can walk together down a path of peace and mutual benefit. This is my hope, and the hope of the entire world.

Ma Licheng
December 8, 2012

Introduction by the Japanese Translator

i

This book is a translation of my translation of Ma Licheng's *Chouhen mei you weilai: Zhongri guanxi xin siwei*. Ma's book was originally published in Chinese by Hong Kong's Zhonghe chuban youxian gongsi in January 2013, with my Japanese translation published by Iwanami Shoten a year later. That said, the Chinese and the Japanese are somewhat different, Ma's original fifteen chapters dropping to fourteen with the deletion of Chapter 10 and with Chapter 6 being revised to an extent, both changes made with the author's approval. As a result, this English translation from the Japanese is obviously not the same book as its Chinese grandparent.

Ma was born in 1946 and grew up in Chengdu, Sichuan Province. After serving for many years as deputy chief editor at *China Youth Daily*, the official organ of the Communist Youth League of China, and as senior editorials editor at the *People's Daily*, he worked as a news commentator for Hong Kong's Phoenix Television. Having spent many years researching and writing on the changes in Chinese social modalities and nationalism, he currently provides insightful analysis and commentary from his home in Beijing.

His distinguished career notwithstanding, it was his "New Thinking on Relations with Japan"—essentially the ideas recounted in Chapter 2—that catapulted Ma to national attention. This treatise was written in 2002 in part drawing upon his experiences during his first visit to Japan, is sharply critical of fanatical nationalism in both China and Japan, and argues that China needs to rethink its Japan policy.

Coming about a decade after his "New Thinking on Relations with Japan" essay, the Chinese-language *Hatred Has No Future* anthology was an intriguing text with the potential to further discussion on Ma's thesis in light of subsequent developments in Sino-Japanese relations. The major ramifications that his New Thinking argument had for Sino-Japanese relations are documented in Chapter 1. Chapters 3 and beyond provide historical background for understanding the New Thinking as well as discussion of the comments of other specialists in the field. As such, they demonstrate clearly that his ground-breaking essay has been and continues to be a significant contribution to the policy debate.

Sino-Japanese relations have had numerous ups and downs, and Chapter 9 sets out the most prominent developments from the "ice age" to the "warm spring." Chapter 10 follows up with discussion of relations in the wake of the Great East Japan Earthquake of 2011 and the hope the empathy shown then would engender further progress in the relationship. However, as noted in Chapter 11, the next year, 2012, was marked by friction and turmoil over the Senkaku (Chinese name: Diaoyu) Islands, and there were fears as noted in Chapter 12 that the two nations would come to blows. Yet Ma held fast to his New Thinking thesis and to the hope that the relationship can be forward-looking.

Ma's essential message is encapsulated in this volume's title: Hatred Has No Future. Sino-Japanese relations are fraught with difficulty, yet it is imperative for East Asia, all of Asia, and indeed the whole of the global community that this bilateral relationship develop smoothly. I hope the publication of this English translation can contribute to that process.

ii

I first met Ma in the spring of 2010 when he was doing research at the University of Tokyo. I knew even then that he had authored the seminal "New Thinking on Relations with Japan," but I was more interested in his research on political reform in China and remember being impressed by his admonition that it is essential we think in half-century or even century-long terms and consider how reform emerges from within over the longer term.

At the time, my research was focused on the reformist intellectuals within the Chinese Communist Party and elsewhere. Ma and I having many mutual friends and acquaintances, I had numerous opportunities to talk with him in Beijing and Tokyo over the course of the decade. Yet it was not until the July 7, 2013, international symposium in Tokyo on resolving territorial issues and creating an East Asian sea of tranquility that I gave serious thought to translating his "New Thinking on Relations with Japan" into Japanese.

This symposium was organized by an array of volunteers who were concerned that the stand-off between Japan and China over territorial issues was being played out against a background of deep-seated historical issues and that the two countries were in serious danger of getting sucked into a vicious spiral of accelerating animosity. Many of these people had been involved in drafting the earlier (September 28, 2012) Japanese citizens' appeal to end the escalating conflict over territorial issues. Chapter 13 introduces and discusses both the citizens' appeal and the symposium presentations from Japan, China, Korea, Taiwan, and

Okinawa on transforming this ocean of animosity into a sea of peace.

Although I was only a very interested observer when these Japanese public figures took the initiative in announcing their citizens' appeal seeking an end to the widening dispute over territorial issues, I was nonetheless very interested in Sino-Japanese people's diplomacy. What with one thing and another, fate decreed that I be on the symposium executive committee and act both as moderator during the symposium and as interpreter during the post-symposium press conference. Fate also had Ma, then at Hokkaido University, agree to deliver the symposium keynote, all of which gave me many welcome chances to talk with him again.

Titled "The Diaoyu/Senkaku Dispute in the Context of Sino-Japanese Relations," Ma's keynote address first explained the structural changes and transformations in East Asia underlying the Diaoyu/Senkaku dispute and then took up the question of how to resolve this dispute, offering the following four suggestions.

1. Work to avoid an accidental contingency situation,
2. Have both Japan and China control their nationalistic fervors,
3. Compromise to create a climate conducive to settlement, and
4. Discard old animosities and build a shared future.

These suggestions show up repeatedly in this book. Ma has long argued that the big-picture priorities for both China and Japan should be the pursuit of strategic mutual interests, the structuring of a win-win relationship, and the promotion of development and prosperity in East Asia and all of Asia. In short, he has implored the two countries to learn from the postwar Franco-German relationship.

Listening to his keynote speech gave me a far clearer understanding of his assertion that hatred has no future and why he is so insistent on this point. His plea for discarding old animosities and building a shared future made a profound impression on symposium participants, and I hope it will resonate equally with readers of this English translation.

iii

The structure of Sino-Japanese relations has changed on many levels between the time the original Chinese text was published and the present, with both sides acknowledging that their diplomatic relations have returned to normal. The two leaders have exchanged visits and achieved remarkable improvement. High-level talks have been held on security, economic relations, cultural exchanges, and a number of other areas and there is increasing talk of a new era in Sino-Japanese relations.

Major changes have also taken place tangential to Sino-Japanese relations. To cite a few examples, Hong Kong had its umbrella movement in 2014 and then the protests that started last year and continue even now; and Taiwan had its sunflower movement and Democratic Progressive Party (DPP) of Tsai Ing-wen's re-election in January. These events in Hong Kong and Taiwan are essentially over how to engage China and how much distance to maintain from the Chinese government. People are clearly conflicted between the desire to preserve popular sovereignty and liberty and the desire to promote development, which conflict extends beyond governance to the more universal sphere of values.

Sino-Japanese relations have been very significantly impacted by the structural shift in Sino-American relations, where the discord is not limited to trade friction or science and technology competition but is more importantly jousting for global primacy in human rights, national security, and a host of other areas of concern to the international community. With these changes in the multi-dimensional structure, Japan has aspired to the stable development of its relations with China while being fully aware of the need to keep a watchful eye on Chinese influence in both the immediate region and the international community at large.

Given that it is of crucial importance that not just Japan, but the whole of the international community understand the Chinese reality objectively and assess it calmly, what are the primary takeaways from this book? One that I would stress is the existence of alternative voices within the Chinese linguistic sphere. My "alternative voices" are not dissenting voices in frontal opposition but are rather voices other than the official position of the Chinese Communist Party and Chinese government. They are not the radical public opinion that both encourages and feeds off the rise of unhealthy nationalism but are rather critical voices like Ma's that persist in taking an independent stance and advocating liberal thought. While they may not be a very conspicuous presence in China as a whole, they are undeniably present in the current political structure. Ma's hatred-has-no-future advocacy was definitely such an alternative voice on Sino-Japanese relations when the relationship grew heated over historical narratives and territorial issues.

What is such an alternative voice saying? What is it like to be an alternative voice? What awareness enables such a voice to persist in the Chinese commentariat, and what difficulties does it encounter? These are all questions that will be answered for readers as they turn the pages of this alternative tome.

One of the things that I particularly admire about Ma's determination to make his voice part of the public discourse and that deserves mention here is that this book was originally published not on the Chinese mainland but in Hong Kong. Despite, or perhaps because of, his having been senior editorials editor at the *People's Daily*, the official organ of the Chinese Communist Party, and intimately familiar with intra-party politics and propaganda tools, he recognized that it would be difficult to publish this book on the mainland. So it happened in Hong Kong. This too is a Chinese reality.

It is essential we preserve open linguistic spaces if these alternative voices are to be heard. It is essential we constantly and steadfastly resist those powers that would seek to isolate and extinguish these alternative voices within society. Article 35 of the Chinese Constitution explicitly provides for freedom of speech, but the fact that it is expressly guaranteed is no guarantee that it can be expressed. It is now about seven years since Ma's Chinese original was published, yet freedom of speech is increasingly restricted in China. Looking at the situation today, I am not at all sure that the same freedom to publish such an alternative voice still exists even in Hong Kong.

Just as I am critical of the unfreedom of expression in China and Hong Kong, I am also seriously concerned about the very real threats to Japan's linguistic space despite its claim to be free and open. Is Japan's linguistic space really that open to a diversity of alternative voices? Or is it becoming increasingly difficult to speak out in Japan, not just in the face of political repression but also given the equally repressive social climate and the unspoken deference afforded those in positions of power, as well as the priority of market forces and financial considerations? China and Japan have very different political and class structures, but Ma's observations on the formation and maturity of civil society are also very relevant to the self-censorship evident in Japan.

Likewise in the international community where authoritarian government systems, me-first nationalism, and the like are at sharp odds with internationalist cooperation, it is clear that a diversity of alternative voices needs to be respected if we are to achieve the shared imperative of sustainable development. Now in early 2020, there is a novel coronavirus rampaging in China and drawing heightened attention from Japan and worldwide. Arousing grave concern, this is yet another event illustrating the extent of China's regional and global impact. With all countries everywhere scrambling to contain the pandemic, it is all the more important we understand the Chinese reality and make this an opportunity for rethinking China's relations with Japan and the whole of the international community.

When I asked Ma about the social impact of this novel coronavirus, he responded quickly with this insightful comment:

> Emerging in early 2020, the novel coronavirus COVID-19 has spread with explosive force throughout China, starting in Wuhan and going rapidly nationwide to engulf the public in a tsunami of fear. Recognizing the danger, the Japanese government has on numerous occasions voiced support for China's efforts to cope with this pandemic and has airlifted masks, disinfectants, and other medical supplies to China. At the grassroots level, there have been signs in Tokyo storefronts lauding the Chinese efforts and it is fully possible for Chinese in Japan to get the assistance they need at Japanese medical facilities. This Japanese solidarity has been a major encouragement to the people of China in their battle with this medical threat and a clear indication that Sino-Japanese relations have unquestionably grown closer.

While there are still numerous issues outstanding between China and Japan, including historical issues, territorial issues, and more, the common danger posed by this novel coronavirus has moved the two countries to reaffirm their interdependence and highlighted the need for further bilateral cooperation.

How are we to spread the hatred-has-no-future message that pervades this book? While there are numerous troublespots in the Sino-Japanese relationship, surely it should be possible to develop specific solutions to specific issues, thereby enhancing mutual understanding and mutual trust. Can China and Japan find the shared values they need as neighbors coexisting in the same era? What lessons does the course of Sino-Japanese relations hold out for the international community in seeking to better understand an increasingly influential China? Nothing would please me more than to have this book serve in some small way as reference and inspiration for concerned readers.

In closing, I would like to express anew my gratitude to Ma Licheng for authoring the Chinese original, to Iwanami Shoten's Baba Kimihiko and Morikawa Hiromi for shepherding the Japanese translation production process through to publication, and to the many people involved in producing this English translation,

Oikawa Junko
Spring of 2020

CHAPTER
ONE

An Earth-Shaking Controversy

In essence, the New Thinking was that China's rise to great power status had led to a change in the balance of power between China and Japan and that the gap was steadily growing. Given these conditions, using the great overarching framework of encouraging the move toward a united Asian community as our departure point and based on the premise of always staunchly maintaining China's sovereignty, we should overcome the resentments of history, suppress nationalism in both countries, and achieve reconciliation between China and Japan. In order to pursue development and prosperity together in a spirit of equality and mutual benefit, we must resolve those contradictions and problems that exist in a calm and rational manner, and this includes the issue of the Diaoyu/Senkaku Islands.

The year 2012 marked the fortieth anniversary of the normalization of diplomatic relations between China and Japan. This ought to have been an occasion for renewed celebrations after previous high-level visits had already "broken the ice," "melted the ice," "welcomed spring," and created a "warm spring" between the countries.[1] But the dispute over the Diaoyu/Senkaku Islands plunged Sino-Japanese relations into the doldrums again. There were some similarities with the situation that had prevailed ten years earlier on the occasion of the thirtieth anniversary of the normalization of relations between the two countries in 2002. At that time, Japanese Prime Minister Koizumi Jun'ichiro had repeatedly visited Yasukuni Shrine while in office and relations between the two countries had cooled rapidly. The heaving ups and downs of the bilateral relationship were causing widespread unease for both countries and for people at all levels in societies around Asia.

How are we to respond to this situation? Surely no one wants an armed clash. As globalization continues and Asia moves inexorably toward unity as some form of community, China and Japan are indivisibly joined together in their economic and trade relations. Informed opinion in both countries is unanimous that the path of conflict, which would inevitably lead to mutual destruction, is not an option. We need a new kind of evolutionary thinking that can resolve the contradictions between the two countries and help us build a future in which China and Japan can cooperate.

Ten years ago, I proposed a new way of thinking about China's relationship with Japan building on Deng Xiaoping's view of Japan.

In essence, the New Thinking was that China's rise to great power status has led to a shift in the balance of power between China and Japan and that the gap between them is steadily widening. Given these circumstances, starting from the departure point of the major framework of promoting the integration of Asia and with the basic proviso of strict maintenance of China's state sovereignty, we should work to overcome the resentments of history, rein in nationalist feelings on both sides, and aim to achieve Sino-Japanese reconciliation. This new approach holds that, in order to pursue development and prosperity together in a spirit of equality and mutual benefit, it is essential the two countries solve the existing contradictions and problems in a calm and rational manner. This includes the issue of the Diaoyu/Senkaku Islands. As some readers may be aware, the publication of these ideas prompted a fierce debate that has continued nonstop to the present day, taking in a wider spectrum of society in both China and Japan than I could ever have predicted. Considering the complexity of Sino-Japanese relations, it is perhaps inevitable that opinions should differ on how best to proceed. It may be that the debate will continue for another twenty or thirty years. But I remain convinced that the two major currents of our times—globalization and Asian unification—will help to build a favorable path forward for this New Thinking. Will my readers agree with this opinion? Since Sino-Japanese cannot be divorced from the feelings of the Chinese people, readers may be interested in looking back at how the debate has developed over the past few years and what this shows us about the changes in the Sino-Japanese relationship. And then I hope we can think together about how to resolve the problems that remain.

The December 19, 2002, *Zhongwen Daobao*, Tokyo's biggest-circulation Chinese newspaper, had an oversized front page headline that read: "Ma Licheng's Earth-Shaking Proposals for Relations With Japan." This headline was followed by a long editorial by Zhang Shi, a *Zhongwen Daobao* journalist.

> This year marks the thirtieth anniversary of the normalization of diplomatic relations between China and Japan, but relations between the two countries are currently at a low ebb owing to conflicts over a number of different issues. On an official level, plans for Koizumi Jun'ichiro to visit China in October have been canceled because of the prime minister's visit to Yasukuni Shrine in April. At the non-governmental level, a recent survey by the *Yomiuri Shimbun* newspaper showed the proportion of people in Japan with positive feelings about China has fallen to the lowest level since 1978. Only 37 percent of respondents said they feel they can trust China. In another survey, published by the CASS Institute of Japanese Studies in November, a mere 5.9 percent of Chinese people said they felt affinity and affection for Japan. In this climate of frosty relations, Ma Licheng, a senior editor at the *Renmin Ribao* (*People's Daily*), has published an article in the latest edition of *Zhanlue yu guanli* (*Strategy and Management*) with the title "Duiri guanxi xinsiwei" (New Thinking on Relations with Japan). In it, he criticizes the anti-Japanese feelings common in the Chinese media and public opinion and writes perceptively about some of the most pressing issues in Sino-Japanese

relations. It surely can be no accident that a leading commentator for the *People's Daily*, the official mouthpiece of the Party, should suddenly have released an earth-shaking piece like this.

The argument runs as follows. First Ma Licheng argues that Japan, despite its small size and lack of natural resources, has risen to become the world's second-largest economy and that this should make it the pride of Asia. This marks a remarkable departure from the us-vs-them view of the relationship held by many people in China, and its contemplation of the idea of China and the rest of Asia belonging to a single community together also marks something new. Second, the article rejects the view held by many in China for nearly half a century warning against a revival of Japanese state militarism. The article argues that it is important to maintain a distinction between Japan's wish to rebuild its armed forces as a "normal country" and any possible return to being a military state. Third, the article proposes for the first time that the question of Japanese apology for the war has been already resolved. In his article, Ma Licheng notes that former prime minister Murayama Tomiichi and others have visited Marco Polo Bridge, Shenyang, and other places with particular association with the war and have expressed feelings of remorse, and he says that Japan has expressed regret for its war of aggression and invasion. Therefore, he says, the question of a Japanese apology has been already resolved and there is no need to insist on a particular form or wording. This goes to the heart of a central problem in Sino-Japanese relations. If this article truly represents the thinking of the organ as the "throat and tongue" of the Party,[2] it is fair to say that Sino-Japanese relations may have reached a historic turning point.

The editorial continues:

Some Chinese academics in Japan have expressed support for Ma Licheng. Zhu Jianrong, a professor at Toyo Gakuen University, said: "I went back to China again in early December. There's a widespread awareness in diplomatic and intellectual circles in China of the need for a new understanding of Japan at the moment. Understanding of Japan has deepened across the board as a result of the exchanges that have taken place over the past ten or twenty years, while economic growth has given the Chinese people new confidence. Developing our relationships with Japan and Southeast Asia would allow us to stop the slide toward a unipolar world under American control and also help us deflect American criticism of and pressure on China."

Ye Qianrong, assistant professor at Tokai University, said that since Ma Licheng published *Jiaofeng* (*Crossing Swords*) and *Huhuan* (*Calling*),[3] he has been following his writing with great interest and has felt that his views are essential for China . . . Without showing any weakness in his attitude to the right-wing forces that can be seen objectively to exist in Japan, his essay warns that China needs to abandon its habit of looking at the world through the prism of narrow nationalism. As the situation develops, his arguments will only become more important over the years to come, as subsequent developments are likely to prove. We have seen on numerous occasions in Chinese history over the past 100 years that this kind of argument often helps China stand invincible and gain respect internationally.

A Mr. Wang, an author resident in Tokyo, said: "Ma's essay says exactly what I have been arguing for many years, but as someone living in Japan, I can't speak my mind like this. I'd probably be criticized as a traitor to the Chinese people." One Chinese professor who specializes in Sino-Japanese relations said that the anti-Japanese sentiment common in China today is not based on an understanding of the reality of today's Japan but results from a tendency to automatically equate the militarism of fifty years ago with Yasukuni Shrine today.

The article being discussed in this report was a piece I published under the title "*Duiri guanxi xinsiwei*" (New Thinking on Relations with Japan) in the bi-monthly *Strategy and Management*, issue 6, in December 2002, published in Beijing. In addition to this editorial by Zhang Shi, the *Zhongwen Daobao* also carried the complete text of my article.

What were the circumstances that led me to write this essay? To answer that question, let me begin with a visit I made to Japan in January 2002. That year happened to mark the thirtieth anniversary of the restoration of diplomatic ties between China and Japan. Normally these decade anniversaries would be marked by a mood of celebration, but at this time the political relationship was chilly and subdued. As if to make matters worse, there was widespread alarm among commentators in newspapers, magazines, and Chinese Internet forums about the rebirth of Japanese militarism. The situation was so dire that some people were advocating military action.

During my two weeks in Japan, I visited Tokyo, Kyoto, and Osaka. Nowhere did I discern the slightest sign of any renascent militarism. I saw Chinese people wherever I went. At that time, more than 10,000 people on average were traveling between the two countries every day. I was reminded of the lines from Sima Qian: "Jostling and joyous, the whole world comes after profit." It was difficult to be sure, but as far as I could see no one seemed very interested in the thirtieth anniversary of the restoration of diplomatic ties. There seemed to be a reluctance to speak of the fact that relations between the countries had been tense since the early 1990s. I was reminded of the verse from "Zhaojun yuan" by the Song poet Zhu Dunru: "I keep the things of the past in my heart as hidden resentments/When will my resentment come to an end?"

In this context, I'd like to mention a piece written a little later by Shi Yinhong, a professor at Renmin University of China. His article "Sino-Japanese Rapprochement and the Diplomatic Revolution" was published at the beginning of 2003. The grave tone of his piece seemed to tell the story of my own state of mind when I wrote my article. He wrote: "The widespread and deep tensions that have beset Sino-Japanese relations over the past several years have become a worrying problem that requires mature consideration." In particular, he was concerned about one of the most striking and dangerous characteristics of the relationship, namely the mutual dislike and animosity that have rapidly increased among a majority of the population in both countries.

I continued to consider these issues for nearly a year after my return to China. In early December, I published my conclusions in *Strategy and Management*. Normally, I spend my time thinking about reforms and development in China; Sino-Japanese relations are not my area of expertise. But I felt I couldn't ignore my own humble sense of patriotism. I felt it was vital to look widely at a range of useful research on Sino-Japanese relations and consider opinions from all areas of society. It was this that led me to write the article in which I did my best to delineate the problems that had resulted from the continuing deterioration of relations between the people of the two countries and proposed a new thinking that I hoped would go some way toward dispelling the tensions that had come to bedevil the relationship. I wanted to try to step away from the ill-feeling and the lingering shadow of history and move toward reconciliation between the two countries.

Many scholars in both countries thought my article had torn through a screen that had formed a barrier to better relations between the two countries. As I have mentioned, the *Zhongwen Daobao* is a Chinese-language newspaper published in Tokyo. But the regular Japanese media responded even more promptly to my essay. The *Yomiuri Shimbun*, which boasts the highest circulation of any newspaper in the world (at the time around 12 million copies a day), was a week ahead of *Zhongwen Daobao* in reporting my thesis. On December 12, 2002, under a large eye-catching headline on its main news page, the newspaper carried a commentary running to around half the page, summarizing the most important points of my New Thinking on Relations with Japan. This immediately met with a major response in Japan.

Let me give a small example of the kind of thing I mean. On December 13, the day after the *Yomiuri Shimbun* reported on my article, the Itochu trading company head office in Tokyo placed an urgent call to its Beijing subsidiary instructing the staff to buy a copy of the current issue of *Strategy and Management* and air courier it to Japan as soon as possible. The people at the Beijing office had never heard of the journal before, and none of the newspaper stands on the streets around the city of Beijing carried a specialized academic journal like this. Someone from Itochu Beijing called me to ask where they could obtain a copy. I told them it was available at SDX Joint Publishing close to the National Art Museum of China.

On February 21, 2003, another major Japanese newspaper, the *Asahi Shimbun* (which then had a daily circulation of around 8 million) carried an article summarizing my article and commenting on its most important points. By coincidence, the respected monthly opinion journal *Chuo Koron* and the influential journal of books and ideas *Bungei Shunju* both included a Japanese translation of my article in their March 2003 issues. The journal *Sekai Shuho*, published by the Jiji Tsushinsha press company, published a serialized translation of my article from January 28 to February 18, 2003.

Takahara Akio, then professor at Rikkyo University (now professor at the graduate school of the University of Tokyo) commented on my article in several places. He said that the article showed China's mettle as a proud major power, reminiscent of China as it was at the height of the Tang dynasty. "Ma Licheng's article," he wrote, "shows that China has regained its confidence."

One aspect of the reaction that came as a surprise was that my article seemed to confound Japanese nationalists. Online, a number of Japanese commentators said they had been moved and gladdened to read my article. They noted that the right wing in Japan had always insisted that the Chinese people nursed such strong feelings of resentment and hatred toward Japan that any attempt at reconciliation was a waste of time. Whatever Japan did to apologize or help Chinese development, relations between the countries were doomed to failure and the Japanese should give up expecting anything better from the Chinese. Hearing this kind of argument being repeated again and again inevitably made many people start to despair of any rapprochement, but this new article showed that China was capable of dealing with Japan in a reasonable and rational manner and showed a good understanding of Japan.

One Chinese scholar who lives in Japan sent me an email saying, "When

I saw your article, tears came to my eyes. The article expresses my feelings exactly, but living in Japan I am not able to express these ideas myself."

Another Chinese-language newspaper published in Tokyo, the *Ryuga-kusei Shimbun* (newspaper for students living in Japan) also ran a complete translation of my article and a discussion of the main points in its March 1, 2003, issue. The paper featured an article by Guan Jianqiang critical of my proposal, with the title "New Thinking on Relations with Japan: An Analysis of the New Thinking about the Gloomy Relations between the People of China and Japan." In it, Guan Jianqiang accused me of insisting on a see-no-evil attitude, deliberately blind to the presence in Japan of unscrupulous types who continued to plan for war, and claimed that my article had failed to take into account these forces within Japan. He claimed that the Japanese government's apologies were insincere and did not go far enough. And since Prime Minister Koizumi continued to visit Yasukuni Shrine, it was incorrect to say that the problem of Japanese apology and remorse for its war crimes had been resolved. Furthermore, the deployment of the Japanese Self-Defense Forces was an infraction of Article 9 of the Japanese Constitution. Guan argued that it was wrong to think that Japan could ever "reestablish itself as a normal country militarily." The article also argued that my criticism of the rising tide of nationalism in China itself was a mistake.

On March 6, 2003, an article in the *Zhongwen Daobao* reported expressions of support for the New Thinking had been made at three recent symposiums in China. Let's look a little more at the reaction in China. On February 27, 2003, the *Nanfang Zhoumo* (*Southern Weekly*) newspaper carried a long interview with me by Yang Ruichun, a staff journalist. The article was titled "Looking for a Solution to the Problems Facing Sino-Japanese Relations" and carried the subtitle "An exclusive interview with the author of New Thinking on Relations with Japan." I responded to seventeen questions put to me by the journalist and also spoke about all the things I had felt since my visit to Japan. Japan was already home to a mature democratic system, and it was unrealistic to think that there would be any revival of its former militarism. We should put down the burden of history and turn over a new page. With a radical change taking place in the balance of power between China and Japan, it was time to shake off our historical complexes. And, I said, when the New Thinking was published in Japan, it was greeted by many Japanese nationalists with something close to despair. Why? Because they had always depicted Chinese people as something to be afraid of, but my article had shown normal people in Japan a different image of the reality in China. This was something that most Internet users in China had not expected.

That day's *Southern Weekly* also carried two articles about the New

Thinking: one in support by Wang Ping, a member of the CASS Institute of Japanese Studies faculty, and the other arguing against my ideas by Liang Yunxiang, professor at Peking University.

Wang Ping wrote:

> The publication of Ma Licheng's article is timely. We are at a moment in history when we need to reconsider Sino-Japanese relations. It is essential we not be swayed by emotions when choosing the direction of our strategy for dealing with Japan. There is a strong tendency to dismiss everything Japanese as evil in mainstream society in China, and in some cases even among research institutions and government bodies, and it is difficult or impossible to say anything positive about Japan. Of course, there is much evil in Japan's past, and these acts should be discussed. But there are also many aspects of Japan that we could learn from. Why has it become impermissible to say so? If you speak in defense of Japan, you are likely to be dismissed as pro-Japan at best, and often wind up criticized as a traitor to your country. How severely this popular thinking damages China's national interest! In this sense, I am truly in agreement with Ma Licheng's argument that we need to think strategically about our relations with Japan.

Liang Yunxiang argued that first of all it was essential that Japan never again injure China. Was it really true that relations between the two countries would become friendly if China tolerantly made a gesture by taking the first step? China had already given way twice, and this had not led to any fundamental change toward a correct understanding of history in Japan.

The same issue of *Southern Weekly* also featured several criticisms of my thesis that had appeared online, these in a section headed "Online Voices." The summary of these criticisms goes as follows. Some net users started by discussing my nationality and identity and position. If my article had been written by a Japanese author it might have been only to be expected, but it deserved particular censure because it had been written by a respected scholar and senior editor at the *People's Daily*, the party organ. Some of the more extreme opinions criticized me as a "traitor to the people." Others tried to blame the problem on the Japanese, claiming that the national character of the Japanese made friendly relations between China and Japan impossible. Some online commentators claimed that the Japanese character only respects strength and power. Some people felt that the New Thinking was out of step with reality, as if my view were that the Chinese had to console themselves as best they could and trust in the good faith of the Japanese, while the Japanese look down on China as a pathetic third-world country always trying to extort money out of Japan. Others argued that the essential element of trust, which was vital for any friendly relations, was missing between China and Japan and that there were massive conflicts of interest. My arguments, it was said, were simply unreciprocated hopes; without trust there could be no true friendship.

On March 4, an event was held to mark the foundation of the East Asia Peace and Strategy Forum, which had been organized by the CASS Institute of Japanese Studies. Scholars from the CCP Central Party School, CASS, the China Foreign Affairs University, and the PLA Academy of Military Science attended and exchanged views on Sino-Japanese relations. I was one of the speakers. There was a roughly equal proportion of scholars who supported the New Thinking and those who were skeptical about it.

At the conference, it was decided to appoint me deputy chair of the East Asia Peace and Strategy Forum. The area was not one in which I felt I had any real expertise, and I expressed my reluctance to take up a position of responsibility within the forum. But my friends at the Academy refused to listen to my refusals and insisted I take up the post. As it happened, however, when a report on appointing me for the position was officially submitted, one or more of the senior figures at the Academy disapproved of the New Thinking, my name was removed from the list of directors, and I became a regular rank-and-file member. My friends could only smile wryly. In July that year I moved to Hong Kong to start work at Phoenix Television and no longer maintained regular contact with the Forum.

In April, issue 2 of the magazine *Strategy and Management*, which had played the pioneering role, carried an important article by Shi Yinhong, professor at Renmin University of China, called "Sino-Japanese Rapprochement and the Diplomatic Revolution." In it, he came out in support of the New Thinking. Professor Shi said that the risk of any further deterioration and animosity between the peoples of China and Japan represented a serious danger for China. "The Chinese homeland is often at odds with the United States and is in a position of enmity with Taiwan. India is another potential foe. We cannot possibly cope with all these and deal with an antagonistic Japan at the same time." Building his analysis on the overall situation, Shi argued that China needed to improve its relationship with Japan and achieve a rapprochement. "In fact, China needs an improvement in the Sino-Japanese relationship even more than Japan does." Shi also proposed five important measures that China could take to improve its relationship with Japan. In an article in the *Southern Weekly* of June 12, 2003, Sun Yafei pointed out that in its essentials "Shi Yinhong's article resembles the article by Ma Licheng." Shi subsequently published several other articles about Sino-Japanese relations, which I will introduce in more detail later and which resulted in his also becoming a target of online insults and scorn.

On June 9, 2003, *Zhongguo Xinwen Zhoukan* (*China Newsweek*) printed an article by journalist Hu Kui with the title "Overcoming the Deep Fog of History," introducing the main points of my article and Shi Yinhong's article and expressing support for the New Thinking.

The *Southern Weekly* covered the debate again in its June 12 issue, but this time its attitude had undergone a slight change. Its article titled "Do We Need a New Thinking in our Relations with Japan?" by journalist Sun Yafei introduced doubts and criticisms of my article from a number of different angles and perspectives. Some said that this article reflected the resistance that the New Thinking had met since it had been published.

In June, the journal *Shishi Baogao* (*Reports on Current Affairs*), edited by the Party Central Committee Publicity Department, held a symposium to discuss relations with Japan. Four people spoke at the event: Shi Yinhong, Sun Shulin, Lu Shiwei, and myself. Remarkably, this magazine, aimed at party management, has a circulation in the 500,000 range. All four speakers agreed that new thinking was necessary for China's relationship with Japan. The July edition of the magazine devoted ten pages to our remarks and came out strongly in support of the New Thinking. It was no easy matter for the Publicity Department to support the New Thinking this way. At the time the magazine was edited by editor-in-chief Cao Fentian and deputy editors Cao Boya and Deng Naigang. In our remarks, Shi Yinhong and I both praised Hu Jintao's insistence on the need to take a long-term strategic view of China's position in world affairs.

On July 18, I was invited to appear as a guest speaker on Phoenix Television's *Shiji Dajiangtang* (*The Forum*) program to speak on the subject of my New Thinking on Relations with Japan. I discussed the most important aspects of the New Thinking and answered questions from university students. As soon as the program was broadcast, it drew fierce argument. Around the same time, a website calling itself the Patriots' Alliance started a petition collecting signatures from people opposed to the idea of introducing Japanese bullet train technology into China.

On July 28, the Chinese Association for Japanese Studies in Beijing held a meeting to debate Sino-Japanese relations. Three people spoke about the pieces Shi Yinhong and I had published. Our essays were subjected to harsh criticism (our "positions were mistaken" and we had "been used by the Japanese") and we were attacked as "proxy representatives of the Japanese." On the other hand, one scholar from the Institute of Japanese Studies said that he disapproved of this scapegoating, also asking why no one from the Institute had produced any new ideas as significant as these two articles for breaking through the current impasse.

In July, issue 14 of *Chinese Times* published Lin Zhibo's article "Nine Questions regarding the New Thinking on Relations with Japan." This argued that the real reason Chinese people did not feel well-disposed to the Japanese lay in Japan's mistaken stance, its refusal to show proper remorse for its wars of aggression, and its generally unfriendly attitude toward China. Lin argued that Japan had become rich as a result of pillaging and war and had unleashed a chaos of disaster and tragedy on Asia. It was unreasonable to think that Japan could seek an ordinary position as a major economic and military power. Japan was a hindrance and obstruction to economic integration in East Asia. There was no such thing as narrow-minded nationalism in China. Lin argued that the New Thinking on Relations with Japan was impractical. On August 15, he published a further article in the *People's Daily Online*, "Further Questions and Doubts on the New Thinking on Relations with Japan," a point-by-point critique of the arguments made by Shi Yinhong in his essay. Lin believed that there was no room for any major improvement in Sino-Japanese relations. If China did attempt rapprochement with Japan, Japan would become the object of a squabble for influence between China and the United States and this would inflate Japan's status and possibly increase American suspicion of and animosity toward China. Ultimately it would end up strengthening American attempts to isolate and contain China. In the worst-case scenario, it might even result in a change in American thinking on neutrality and could easily lead to a rash outcome in regard to the situation in Taiwan.

Lin Zhibo's views met with a substantial reaction on Internet chatboards, including one response on August 19 by a user using the name Xiaoguo Guamin (country small, people few) who pointed out that the Japanese government had already repeatedly expressed remorse and apology for the war and that a small number of rightists should not be allowed to represent the whole of the Japanese government and people. "Lin has written an article that is akin to a declaration of cold war. This is part of a tendency to which we should pay close attention. With Sino-Japanese relations currently at a turning point, thinking like this threatens to have a negative impact on that relationship and on China's international image. In a context where China is developing with the times and is making progress toward greater freedom of thought, this argument is backward and regressive."

On August 1, issue 15 of *Shijie Zhishi* (*World Affairs*), edited by the Chinese Ministry of Foreign Affairs, published a number of articles debating Sino-Japanese relations. The first of these was an article entitled "Who Is Really in the Greatest Need of New Thinking?" by the Singaporean Toh Lam Seng, a professor at Ryukoku University in Japan. This article dismissed the New Thinking on Relations with Japan out of hand, insisting that Japan today was more dangerous, more fearsome, and more aggressive than it had been in the 1950s or the 1960s and that it was going back on its acknowledgement of historical issues. What was needed was "not the emergence of some kind of new thinking from the peoples of Asia, but for the Japanese government to come up with some new thinking of its own." Toh Lam Seng argued that my article was merely an attempt to flatter Japan and curry favor.

The article by Jin Xide at the CASS Institute of Japanese Studies criticized Prime Minister Koizumi Jun'ichiro for his visits to Yasukuni Shrine but also said "I do not believe that we should cut off political and military exchanges between China and Japan simply because of the Yasukuni problem."

Wang Xinsheng, professor of history at Peking University, wrote that while cultural differences were certainly one aspect of the Yasukuni problem, Japan needed to give more consideration to the feelings of Asian countries. He also wrote that Chinese and Japanese economic and trade links had a strong reciprocal effect such that it should be possible to continue to develop these relations even if there were friction.

The essay by Jiang Ruiping, professor at China Foreign Affairs University, said the factors making the Japanese economy dependent on China were growing stronger all the time, while Japan's importance to Chinese development was fading. If this continued, he wrote, a change would soon take place in the balance of real power between the two countries.

On August 7, the *Cankao Xiaoxi* (*Reference News*) newspaper carried a four-page special report to mark the twenty-fifth anniversary of the signing of the Treaty of Peace and Friendship between China and Japan. This feature included a piece by Cheung Mong, a young scholar at the Chinese University of Hong Kong, that was called "Dealing Correctly with a 'Normal' Japan" and balanced traditional views on Sino-Japanese relations with some aspects of the New Thinking, arguing that China should face up calmly to the fact that Japan was becoming a "normal nation" while at the same time insisting that it must not compromise on the question of historical issues.

The bi-weekly *Nanfengchuang* (*South Reviews*) carried an article in its edition for the first half of August by Cheng Yawen titled "How Can We Make China Essential to Japan?" The article argued that Japan did not see itself as an Asian nation. "It is in Asia but its spirit is not of Asia," and this made it difficult for the country to build close relationships with Asian countries. Only by first increasing the distance from Japan, the article argued, will it be possible to inspire Japan to acknowledge Asia and move closer to rapprochement with China.

On August 16, *World Affairs* printed the speeches given at a round-table forum discussion jointly sponsored by the magazine and by *World Economics and Politics*, a monthly journal published by CASS. In his speech, Wang Yizhou, who was then vice chair of the CASS Institute of World Economics and Politics, emphasized the importance of reasonableness and tolerance and indirectly expressed understanding and support for the New Thinking. He said that as China rose to prominence, the country should not only develop a constructive attitude and image as a responsible nation but should also cultivate the dignity and gravitas befitting a major power and should deal with conflicts between states with an attitude of rationality and tolerance. In a follow-up statement, Shi Yinhong emphasized the importance of strategic principles and suggested that historical issues could for the most part be put aside without serious problems for China.

Feng Zhaokui, former vice chair of the CASS Institute of Japanese Studies, said that China should strengthen its economic cooperation with Japan to achieve industrialization in China. In his remarks, he said, "In considering relationships between one country and another, we must look chiefly at the strategic interests of the states involved" and quoted a dictum by Deng Xiaoping to the effect that we should not argue about the hatreds of history or worry too much about various aspects of the differences between social systems or ideologies. Feng said this should be our diplomatic strategy for dealing with Japan.

Ling Xingguang, director of the Sino-Japanese Relationship Institute, said that since it was Japan that was responsible for the historical understanding issues, China could not simply shelve the issue even if it wanted to. If the Chinese side minimized major problems and ignored small ones altogether in a desperate attempt to cooperate with Japan, it would only have the effect of slowing down cooperation between the two countries.

Nankai University Professor Pang Zhongying said that history, facts, and the future are all connected. Without history, he asked, how could there be a future for Sino-Japanese relations? Talk of "overcoming history" is vague and deliberately obfuscating, and the state is likely to pay a high moral price for this kind of behavior in the end.

Yang Yanyi, deputy head of the Ministry of Foreign Affairs Policy Planning Department, made the following observation. The Japanese right wing denied history and tried to legitimize aggression and invasion. Their ability to act this way had a malign influence and needed to be resisted. The purpose of this struggle should be to establish Sino-Japanese relations on a healthy foundation and to encourage their development in a correct direction. But we cannot solve the problem by ourselves alone. In a situation where the Japanese right wing is growing in strength and authority, there was little hope that Japan would succeed in achieving an appropriate solution to the problem of understanding historical issues.

Zhang Tuosheng was head of the China Foundation for International Strategic Studies at the time. He started by remarking that it was a good thing that the recent papers by Shi Yinhong and myself had attracted so much attention in both China and Japan. The fact that they were being widely discussed was a positive development, the relationship with Japan was one of the most important of all China's international relationships, and a wide-ranging debate on the issues would help to clarify the best way forward for the relationship in the future. Zhang argued that it was necessary to improve the relationship from three perspectives: (1) changes and developments within the trilateral relationship between China, Japan, and the United States, (2) the aim to move toward economic community and unification in East Asia in the future, and (3) the importance of pushing the Sino-Japanese relationship forward.

He went on to say that the Japanese side has shown some progress in terms of its understanding and position with regard to historical issues over the past few years. The Chinese should be prepared to abandon some of their pessimistic assumptions about the situation and assume a little more of the confidence befitting a major power. For a long time now, the way people in China discussed Japanese militarism has no longer matched the Japanese reality and has not been supported by the people in Japan. Now that the end of the war is decades in the past, it is inevitable that Japan should gradually become a normal country.

On August 16, a special commemorative program on China Central Television (CCTV) Channel 9 to mark the twenty-fifth anniversary of the signing of the Treaty of Peace and Friendship between China and Japan included interviews with Shi Yinhong and me. I might mention in passing that Shui Junyi, a journalist with CCTV, had published an article critical of the New Thinking, but I had a friendly relationship with CCTV dating back many years and it was clear that many of the people at the channel understood and appreciated my ideas.

On August 25, the Chinese-language website *Duowei News*, headquartered in New York, released an article titled "Ma Licheng's New Thinking on Relations with Japan Creates a Stir." The article noted that I had recently been invited to discuss my article in detail on Phoenix Television's *The Forum*, where I had explained the main points of my argument in detail. The main points of the article were as follows. Over the years, Japanese governments have already apologized twenty-one times to China for their war of aggression and the legal problems of the war had been resolved in trials more than fifty years ago. It is time for China to turn a new page in history. Between 1979 and 2001, Japan offered China 2,667.9 billion yen in low-interest loan aid, thereby demonstrating a degree of goodwill. Both China and Japan should work to suppress the nationalism that exists in their countries. Shi Yinhong, a Renmin University of China professor, responded to these points. Shi said that improving relations with Japan would give China more leverage in its relationship with the United States. However, Zhang Chengjun, Secretary General of the Foundation for Research into the War of Resistance to Japanese Aggression and Peace Education in Beijing, criticized these arguments as inadequate and argued that Shi Yinhong and I were in practice both demanding China alone become more tolerant and seek Sino-Japanese friendship. Zhang said that these views ignored the lessons of history and cast aside principles that ought to be defended. Wang Xuan, head of a group suing the Japanese government for damages sustained during the war, said that my arguments fundamentally failed to make sense. The crimes of bacteriological warfare and use of poison gas were not punished at the International Military Tribunal for the Far East.

In August, issue 4 of the bi-monthly publication *Strategy and Management* carried no fewer than four articles about Sino-Japanese relations, which attracted great attention. Feng Zhaokui's "A Discussion of the New Thinking on Relations with Japan" was a long piece of some 30,000 characters. He opened by asking if we need new thinking on relations with Japan and went on to provide clear answers to the question. Essentially, he argued that some kind of new thinking is indeed necessary if Sino-Japanese relations are to break out of their current impasse and push the relationship forward. He wrote that it was only natural that the publication of the New Thinking had provoked such lively debate. He went on to argue about five principles and nine characteristics of New Thinking on relations with Japan and criticized the insults and name-calling that had come out in the course of the debate, with people dismissing the argument and its proponents as traitorous, as being Japanese mouthpieces, or as attempting to curry favor with Japan. But even this long piece could not contain everything Feng had to say, and he went on to publish no fewer than nine further essays on the subject in the course of the following year, attacking the subject from a variety of different angles in a series of impressively argued pieces. I will explain Feng's points in detail later.

Zhou Guiyin of the University of International Relations (now the National University of Defense Technology, College of International Studies) in Nanjing wrote an article called "Understanding Diplomatic Policies with Relation to Japan," a response to Shi Yinhong. Citing examples of "diplomatic revolutions" such as Nixon's sudden visit to China and Egyptian President Anwar Sadat's decision to discard past animosity and achieve reconciliation with Israel, Zhou went on to say: "Diplomacy like this that takes the initiative is an organic element of the countries involved. Its basic aim is to maximize the country's position of security within the international community or to fundamentally improve that security environment." In our current circumstances, Zhou continued,

> we must be proactive in taking the lead and taking that first step. This means building mechanisms of trust within the Sino-Japanese relationship by encouraging mutual trust between the two countries. This must become an organic, fundamental element of China's broad, overarching strategy toward the outside world centered on relations between China and the United States. If the rapprochement between China and Japan becomes more stable and more far-reaching and develops into a sense of trust similar to the deepening China-US relationship, it will be possible to avoid the coming battle for hegemony that is already being widely discussed within the international relations world.

Cheung Mong's "Is Japan on the Road to Militarism Again?" analyzed the political, military, and social conditions in Japan today, concluding that a return to the path of militarism was not realistic in today's Japan and that the country had not reverted to its old ways. In this paper, Cheung argued that the theory of a revival of Japanese militarism, such a frequent part of mainstream discourse in China, was a groundless misinterpretation based on extreme belief in the persistence of cultural traits that only served to strengthen anti-Japanese feelings in China and the reaction against this among young Japanese. This was used, he said, by extreme nationalists in both countries for their own purposes.

Xue Li of the Tsinghua University Institute of International Relations wrote an article titled "Can Sino-Japanese Relations Overcome the Problems of History?" This article analyzed the changing perceptions of the problem of the Japanese view of history within East Asian and ASEAN countries and argued that Sino-Japanese relations were intimately linked to the Chinese national interest. "Should China be considering further measures to overcome historical issues? For the sake of the state as a whole and the country's long-term interests, this may be bitter medicine that China simply has to swallow." In sum, Xue continued, "for the present and future national interest, we need to put the past aside. From the short-term perspective, it may look like a bitter pill to swallow, but this will probably be the best strategy for China in the long term."

In September, Nihon Kyohosha's Duan Press in Tokyo published a book in Japanese by Jin Xide and Lin Zhibo titled *What Is the New Thinking on Sino-Japanese Relations? A Critique of Recent Essays by Ma Licheng and Shi Yinhong*. Jin Xide, a researcher at the CASS Institute of Japanese Studies, criticized the New Thinking and the Japanese right wing. Jin argued that the New Thinking sent a wrong signal to Japan and had been well received by elements in the Japanese right wing because it supported the Japanese right, made clear the victory of Japan's hardline position against China, and accelerated Japan's rightward shift. Lin Zhibo argued that Japan had earned money through its wars in Asia and that a flourishing and prosperous Japan meant not prosperity and peace but disaster and misery for the rest of Asia. Lin dismissed the idea that there existed narrow-minded nationalism in China. He continued by suggesting that the right wing control of Japan is now no longer a possibility but is already the reality. It is fascinating to reflect that this same Jin Xide who criticized the New Thinking so vehemently in this book was later arrested as a Japanese spy and sentenced to fourteen years in jail in 2010. That such a person should march under a flag of patriotism and condemn other people as traitors is ironic indeed.

The debate about the New Thinking continued into 2004. The January 8 *China Newsweek* carried a compilation of comments on the controversy under the title "Where to Start on Understanding the New Situation in Sino-Japanese Relations?" The magazine printed comments from Renmin University of China Professor Huang Dahui, Rikkyo University Professor Takahara Akio, Newcastle University Professor Rheinhard Drifte, *People's Daily* critic and columnist Lin Zhibo, Peking University Professor Li Qiang, and *Asahi Shimbun* Beijing correspondent Isogawa Tomoyoshi, along with excerpts from my essay and pieces by Feng Zhaokui and Shi Yinhong, in which each writer expressed his perspectives on the problem of Sino-Japanese relations.

On January 24, the *People's Daily Online* published a list of the ten biggest Sino-Japanese news stories of 2003, as chosen by the Japan correspondents of more than ten media outlets, including the *People's Daily*, Xinhua News Agency, *Guangming Daily*, *Economic Daily News*, China News Service, China Radio International, *Wenhui Bao*, and *People's China*. In fourth place was "the Internet debate provoked by the New Thinking on Relations with Japan."

In January, the Tokyo-based Duan Press published *A Critical Consideration of The New Thinking on Relations with Japan: In Search of a New*

Framework for Dialogue by Takai Kiyoshi, a professor at the Hokkaido University Graduate School of International Media, Communication, and Tourism Studies. The book claimed that Jin Xide and Lin Zhibo, in arguing that the New Thinking had been welcomed by the right wing in Japan, told only one side of the story, and pointed out that the *Asahi Shimbun* and *Mainichi Shimbun* newspapers, universally regarded as being to the left, had also welcomed the New Thinking and covered it prominently. Speaking of the attention garnered by the New Thinking, Kato Chihiro, an *Asahi Shimbun* editorial committee member, said that the new arguments represented an attempt to build a constructive partnership to improve Sino-Japanese relations for the sake of the future of Asia. Takai wrote that the "Japanese prosperity" discussed in the New Thinking referred to the prosperity of the present time and not the prosperity of the period before the war. Lin Zhibo had argued that when Japan became prosperous and strong it brought misery and disaster to the rest of Asia, but this referred only to the time of World War II. The New Thinking recognized the truth that Japan had walked the path of peace and achieved success and prosperity since the war by developing its industries and science and technology and did nothing to approve Japan's wartime pillaging. The book also noted that many ordinary Japanese people do not approve of the denial of history and that it was important to distinguish between the right wing and the majority.

On February 16, the biweekly *South Reviews* carried an article by Liu Ning titled "One Year on from the New Thinking on Japan Controversy." Liu wrote as follows. A major debate on the New Thinking on Relations with Japan started at the end of 2002 and continues to the present day. The only other comparable phenomenon that could stand comparison with it since the beginning of the period of reform and opening up is probably the Culture Boom.[4] These are only rough statistics but, even if we do not count all the articles and comments written online, the number of articles published by media both in China and overseas already numbers in the hundreds after just one year, and at least five compilations of articles have been published in book form in China and Japan. Along with SARS, the New Thinking has become one of the key terms of 2003. The term has become a vogue phrase in diplomatic circles and the international relations community and is used to refer not only to Japan but also to "new thinking" relating to China's relations with the United States or India, for example.

The March 1 edition of the biweekly *South Reviews* carried an interview with me by the magazine's journalist Guo Yukuan under the title "Ma Licheng Returns to the New Thinking" which contained new details about my ideas. In the article, I was quoted as follows.

If China does not build a constructive relationship with Japan, the greatest winner will be the United States. Both China and Japan are held in equilibrium by the United States, which is able to use the disagreements between them to its own advantage. China is therefore in a relatively weak position within the trilateral relationship. It is only by developing its relations with both Japan and the United States that China can strengthen and improve its position within the trilateral relationship. China should work to build mutual trust with Japan; there are those within Japan too trying to develop better relations with China, and China must understand this point and use it carefully. China's leaders should be proactive in leading public opinion and encouraging greater understanding and exchanges, and must not allow public debate on this issue to remain emotional and undiscriminating.

I continued:

In the thirty years since China and Japan normalized relations, Japan's leaders have expressed remorse to China twenty-one times, have clearly acknowledged that Japan carried out a war of invasion and colonial rule, and have expressed their deep regret and remorse. I believe that we can afford to draw a line here. Of course, we might hope that Japan's leaders, like the German chancellor, might get down on their knees in apology if such a thing were possible.[5] But is such a thing really possible? If we reflect a little, we will surely have to acknowledge that we too have some of the traditional Asian culture of introversion, and there is nothing in terms of international law that would require a head of government to kneel in apology. But that does not mean that the two sides should glare angrily at each other forever. That is why I personally believe that we should not insist on a particular form of apology. Foreign policy issues should not be emotional or sentimental issues but should be considered from a long-term and comprehensive perspective. As China rises, it should aim to become a rational, responsible, and well-balanced major power, not a country filled with hatred and longing for revenge. Deng Xiaoping once said that the only way to deal with the small number of people who dislike the idea of Sino-Japanese friendship is to continually strengthen our friendship and develop our cooperation. This was a fine thing for Deng Xiaoping to have said, wasn't it?

The March 31 edition of the biweekly *South Reviews* carried an article by Lei

Zhiyu titled "The Difference between the Masses in Great and Small Countries," supporting the New Thinking. Then in August, the East China Normal University Press published a collection of essays criticizing nationalism titled *Qianliu: Dui xia'ai minzuzhuyi de pipan yu fansi* (*Undercurrents: Criticisms and Reflections on Narrow Nationalism*). The summary noted that

> Nationalism is a subject that is constantly the focus of attention in Chinese society and has always caused serious discord. Often the subject has been marked by extreme and narrow-minded discourse and behavior. For the past ten years, there has been no systematic, comprehensive, logical, and substantial critique of narrow nationalism. This book is the result of an attempt to provide a thorough-going critique and reflection on narrow nationalism from the three perspectives of foreign policy, war, and globalization.

This collection included my two essays "New Thinking on Relations with Japan" and "Ma Licheng Returns to the New Thinking" in addition to critical essays on nationalism by authors including Xiao Xuehui, Xiao Gongqin, Xu Jilin, Yang Zhizhu, Liu Junning, Wang Yi, Qin Hui, Xu Ben, Li Shenzhi, Ge Hongbing, and Zhu Xueqin. The back cover carried endorsements by Yu Shicun and Wang Xiaoshan. Yu Shicun wrote: "Narrow nationalism has been a prominent presence over the last decade but until now no responsible thinker has stepped forward to present his views from his own perspective. This kind of book has been late in coming, but thankfully it has arrived at last." Wang Xiaoshan said: "Patriotism should not be a veil to cover ugliness, and must not become a refuge of outlaw nationalists. We must awaken to the danger now!"

In 2007, Professor Yuan Weishi of Sun Yat-sen University in Guangdong published a series of long articles in the bi-monthly journal *Changjiang* (*Yangtze*) published in Hebei Province under the title "Observations on the Current Adverse Flow of Nationalism." In this, he wrote:

> In December 2002, Ma Licheng published an essay in Beijing called "New Thinking on Relations with Japan." Any reasonable person who reads this essay seriously will surely be impressed by the discernment and vision of the author's proposal for the future. His views were certainly different from those of many passionate people at the time, but in many points his arguments were either identical or similar to the points made by Wen Jiabao in his speech to the Japanese House of Representatives on April 12, 2007.

Professor Yuan organized my arguments into four categories, compared them with the points made by Wen Jiabao in his speech, and explained what they had in common. Regarding the criticism I had received, Yuan said: "Ground-breaking arguments are probably destined to not be understood by the mass of ordinary people right away, but they are extremely important for the development of the state and society."

On May 25, 2007, the Taiwan-based *Zhongguo Shibao* (*China Times*) newspaper published an article by Zhu Jianling titled "Can Beijing's New Thinking on Japan Be Adapted to the Cross-Straits Relationship?" The article began with an assessment of the "ice-breaking" visit to China by Abe Shinzo, who had just taken office as Japanese prime minister in September 2006, and the "ice-thawing" visit to Japan by Wen Jiabao in April 2007. The author went on to say that before China decided to improve its relationship with Japan, the following developments were likely to have happened:

> On the continent, two figures recently published in the media the idea that a New Thinking was needed in Sino-Japanese relations. One was Ma Licheng, a commentator with the *People's Daily*, the other was Shi Yinhong, a professor at Renmin University of China. As soon as the two men published their proposals for a new approach to China's relationship with Japan, they were widely attacked online by commentators calling them traitors and running dogs. But since the Chinese Communist Party shifted its policy, these insults have already faded from view. According to Ma Licheng and Shi Yinhong's argument, the reasons why a New Thinking is needed for Sino-Japanese relations are: First, for the Communist Party to work with all its energies and strength toward economic development, the strategy of *taoguang yanghui* [6] is vital. Second, the relationship is extremely important for both sides and neither side can afford to cut itself off from the other. Third, it would be extremely dangerous for the future for both sides to leave the animosity and enmity unhealed into the future. Based on these points, Ma Licheng argues that the problem of Japanese apology has already been resolved and that Beijing does not need to insist on a fixed form of apology. Shi Yinhong suggests that Beijing should be satisfied with the remorse and apology that the Japanese government has already expressed with regard to its crimes in invading China in the course of its history.

The *China Times* article suggested that "For now, thinking based on the proposals made by Ma Licheng and Shi Yinhong is likely to form the crux of the Party's thinking on developing relations with Japan." The article also expressed the hope that a similar new thinking might emerge in trans-Strait relations.

In 2011, the March issue of *Kaifang Shidai* (*Open Times*), a magazine issued by the Guangzhou Academy of Social Sciences, carried a long article by Liu Jianping titled "An Analysis of the Post-Colonial Conditions in the Tides of Chinese International Politics Since the 1990s: A Case Study of the New Thinking on Relations with Japan." The article argued that there was nothing "revolutionary" in the New Thinking, that it merely acknowledged the contemptuous view of China and market-China view by which Japan refused to shoulder responsibility for the war and sought only economic gains, and it was merely propagating this view in academically argued form. This was merely most intuitive and enlightened demonstration of the post-colonial situation in the trends of international politics.

Published in April 2012, cumulative issue 45 of the magazine *Lingdaozhe* (*Leaders*) carried a long article by Lei Yi of the CASS Institute of Modern History: "Ambiguous Views of Japan and Public Diplomacy." This article developed its argument from the perspective of public diplomacy and supported the New Thinking. In the article, the author wrote about those who had criticized and insulted the New Thinking:

> The various opinions of the masses and their expression must be fully secured. If one type of opinion was allowed but obstructions were placed in the way of expressing an opposing opinion, the "view of the popular opinion" available to the political decision-making apparatus will be one-sided and unreflective of the whole picture. It is only when the debate is carried out openly, calmly, and rationally that it is possible to produce public diplomacy. Foreign policy decision making based on manipulated public opinion and the pressure of exclusive consensus is not true public diplomacy at all.

These are just a few examples of articles that caught my eye in the course of this debate. But they are sufficient to demonstrate the intensity of the debate and how long it lasted.

The debate also provoked a reaction in Western countries. On July 30, 2004, KTSS-TV based in San Francisco, California, carried out a special telephone interview with me as part of a report on the New Thinking. I responded to the host's questions, summarized my ideas, and answered several questions from ethnic Chinese living in California. This television station expressed support for the New Thinking.

In the spring of 2005, the London-published *China Quarterly*, an authoritative Chinese studies journal, ran a long 20,000-word piece by Peter Hays Gries, then teaching at Colorado State University in the United States, titled "China's 'New Thinking on Relations with Japan.'" This article summarized the New Thinking in detail and commented on the debate the New Thinking had provoked in both China and Japan.

In April 2005, East China Normal University Press published a Chinese translation of *Japan Unbound: A Volatile Nation's Quest for Pride and Purpose* (Chinese title *Wuyueshu de Riben*) by John Nathan, a professor at the University of California, Santa Barbara, and a Guggenheim Fellow, originally published by Houghton Mifflin Harcourt in the United States in 2004. Nathan touched on the New Thinking, commenting that it "represented a startling change in tone."

Whenever I met friends and scholars from the West, the first thing they say is "Tell me about this New Thinking on Relations with Japan." Among prominent scholars to express an interest was Ezra Vogel, professor emeritus at Harvard University, whose publications include *Japan as Number One* and later a major biography of Deng Xiaoping titled *Deng Xiaoping and the Transformation of China*. Without exception, all my friends and all the Western scholars I have met have expressed support for the New Thinking.

NOTES

1. "Breaking the ice" refers to Prime Minister Abe Shinzo's visit to China in October 2006, "melting the ice" to Prime Minister Wen Jiabao's visit to Japan in April 2007, "welcoming spring" to Prime Minister Fukuda Yasuo's visit to China in December the same year, and "warm spring" to President Hu Jintao's visit to Japan in May 2008.

2. The phrase "throat and tongue" is often used to refer to the fact that the Chinese media is aimed at spreading Party propaganda. Here the reference to "the organ" means the *People's Daily*, the most representative of the Chinese media.

3. A reference to two earlier pieces by the same author: Ma Licheng and Ling Zhijun, *Jiaofeng: Dangdai Zhongguo sanci sixiang jiefang shilu (Crossing Swords: Records of the Three Thought Revolutions of Contemporary China)*, Jinri Zhongguo Chubanshe, 1998 and Ma Licheng and Ling Zhijun, *Huhuan: Dangjin Zhongguode wuzhong shengyin (Calling: Five Voices in Present-day China)*, Guangzhou chubanshe, 1999.

4. Under the policy of reform and opening up (*gaige kaifang*) China in the 1980s, not only the economy but also culture and thought became much more liberal. The policy led to some remarkable results in the fields of literature and art, for example. The term "culture boom" refers both to the concrete cultural circumstances at the time and to the debate that developed regarding the position of the arts in society. In the 1980s, the Cultural Revolution was still a recent memory and lively debates took place about reevaluations of traditional Chinese culture, the proactive introduction of foreign cultures, and the idea of *Zhongti xiyong* (grafting Western practical knowledge onto a fundamentally Chinese foundation).

5. In 1970, during a visit to Warsaw, West German Chancellor Willy Brandt fell to his knees in front of a memorial on the site of the Jewish ghetto and apologized for the massacre of European Jews by Nazi Germany. Photographs of Chancellor Brandt on his knees were widely used by the Chinese media, who praised Germany's attitude as a model to be followed in apologizing for war crimes. The image is familiar to most people in China. When Sino-Japanese relations deteriorated around 2005 following Prime Minister Koizumi Jun'ichiro's visits to Yasukuni Shrine, the Chinese media often criticized Japan's view of history by contrasting the image of a Germany that knelt in apology with that of a Japan that continued to glorify its wartime conduct.

6. The phrase *taoguang yanghui* (hide one's talents and cherish obscurity) summarizes the fundamental strategy behind Deng Xiaoping's foreign policy. China was isolated internationally after the Tiananmen Square incident in 1989 and faced a chaotic international situation amid the collapse of the Soviet Union and the upheavals in the formerly Communist countries of Eastern Europe. It was thought that the best response was to avoid drawing attention internationally and work on building up strength. A debate is now underway about what looks like a shift away from this policy, as seen by the friction with Japan over the Diaoyu/Senkaku Islands and the more aggressive marine patrols and incursions into other countries' territorial waters.

CHAPTER TWO

What Was My "New Thinking on Relations with Japan"?

China and Japan are crucial hubs in Asia, and the people of both countries must look more introspectively at their own nationalism and work to overcome their narrow-mindedness in the cause of greater unity and community. For China, our mission must be to move toward the early ratification of a free-trade area between China and ASEAN and to make progress toward signing a three-country free-trade agreement involving China, Japan, and South Korea. This is the direction in which the hearts of people in Asia are tending and the unmistakable tendency of the times.

In the previous chapter, I gave an account of the long and lively debate that followed the publication of my article "New Thinking on Relations with Japan." A decade has now passed since the article appeared, and even today people continue to reflect and discuss the rights and wrongs of the proposals outlined therein. I think this was probably the first time in modern Chinese history that a piece of critical writing caused such a prolonged and heated debate. Lively discussions about the issues laid out in the article seem likely to continue for several decades.

But what was my "New Thinking on Relations with Japan"? The magazine *Strategy and Management*, in which my article appeared at the end of 2002, ceased publication some time ago. Young people today often approach me to ask about the article. I would therefore like to take the opportunity presented by the publication of this book to put the article before the public again and share it with readers of this book.[1] Some critics have said that the article and its arguments are part of a fundamental shift in the theory of international relations and reflect the question of how our ancient and mighty nation can successfully integrate into an increasingly globalized world. I leave it to my readers to decide for themselves the truth of this claim.

New Thinking on Relations with Japan:
The malaise that exists between the peoples of China and Japan

1

I set out for Japan in January 2002, the very coldest time of year in Beijing. But a recent development in the news made me feel the chill even more than usual. The event I am referring to was the "Japanese flag" incident involving the prominent young actress Zhao Wei.

Zhao Wei had been hired to wear a dress whose design resembled the Japanese military flag. I had seen photographs of her wearing the dress in a magazine. Perhaps because the photographs were not very clear, I might not have noticed anything amiss if it hadn't been for the caption underneath explaining her clothes' purported resemblance to the Japanese military flag.

Zhao Wei soon came in for massive and widespread criticism for wearing the dress. Her critics did not care what Zhao Wei had or had not known about the circumstances behind the dress, or what her own intentions might have been. They showed no consideration for her own rights or reputation. In the print media and online they cursed her and threw a hail of abuse in her direction, accusing her of being a traitor to her people, a geisha who had whored herself to "little Japan." They swore: "Rape her! Dig up the graves of her ancestors!" People superimposed Zhao Wei's face on nude photographs, which soon circulated widely over the Internet. The situation escalated until eventually someone pushed her to the ground in front of a crowd and smeared her with excrement. According to a report in the April 3, 2002, *Beijing Qingnian Bao* (*Beijing Youth Daily*), the man responsible for this attack, a man by the name of Wu, had learned that Zhao Wei was due to appear in Changsha on December 28, 2001, and had bought a ticket and gone to the venue carrying a plastic bottle filled with excrement. "I got up on stage behind her, pushed her to the ground, and emptied the contents of the bottle over her," he said.

The criticisms and insults leveled at the actress took place on a nation-wide level; in addition, her image rights were abused and her physical safety put at risk. Subjected to pressure on this scale, Zhao Wei had no choice but to issue an apology to the nation. But in fact, Zhao Wei had a perfect right to wear whatever clothes she chose. Just as other people, of course, had the right to express an opinion about her choices, and even to criticize those choices harshly and urge her to reflect on what she had done. But that is the limit of what is permissible. To be subjected to a national frenzy of insult and abuse on this level, to have her image rights invaded, and to be subjected to criminal assault—all these things represented a humiliating slander on her character and reputation. This mistaken conduct invades the rights of the citizen and can by no means be described as healthy behavior. Even more distressing was a report carried in the April 3, 2002, *Beijing Youth Daily* according to which the thirty-one-year-old "Wu" responsible for the attack continued to display an ignorant and remorseless attitude after the incident, apparently insisting that he had not done anything inappropriate.

When will our people succeed in breaking free of this kind of unreasonable behavior? As Gandhi once said: "Man as animal is violent, but as spirit is non-violent. The moment he awakens to the spirit within, he cannot remain violent." He also wrote: "The first principle of non-violent action is that of non-cooperation with everything humiliating." (Quoted from *Chinese Reader for University Students in the Humanities: People and the World*, Guangxi Normal University Press, July 2002.)

What is particularly disheartening is that after this man carried out his attack, many parts of the media jumped on the bandwagon to support him, saying that "although his position was low, he did not forget his spirit of patriotism." They even started a campaign to raise funds to help him fulfill his ambition of going on to university. Over the past several years, impulsive and irrational behavior like this has often taken place under the banner of patriotism. Parts of the media lacking in any sense of social justice delight in irresponsibly instigating people in this way.

The Frankfurt School analyzed the mechanisms of the mass psychology produced by fascism. One aspect they pointed to was the despotic rule of public opinion which took place under the banner of patriotism. Doing away with universal human values, indulging without restraint in offenses against and deprivation of citizens' rights, and carrying out animosity and violence against scapegoat targets as a way of venting frustration. . . Can we not discern these qualities in the behavior toward Zhao Wei that I have just described? In recent history, the farcical arson attack carried out against the British Embassy in Beijing on August 22, 1967, was also sparked by similar motives of "patriotism." In fact, I believe it is mistaken to describe such actions as patriotic. Behavior of this kind can only bring disaster and misfortune to a country. It is nothing more than irresponsible behavior on the part of the masses toward the state and the nation. What do people find in this behavior? The dividing line between civilization and barbarism has been lost.

Faced with this outpouring of popular indignation, I remembered something a friend once told me. "Government officials from China and Japan may drink toasts to each other and put on a display of friendship, but it's all fake." Perhaps his remark was exaggerated. But it deserves serious consideration all the same. As we mark the thirtieth anniversary of the restoration of diplomatic relations between China and Japan, it is well worth pausing and considering the relationship, along with some of the various issues connected with it, carefully.

2

I set off from Beijing Capital International Airport at 3:00 p.m. on January 15. It was a beautiful clear day. A little over two hours later, we entered Japanese airspace, and I looked down through a pale evening haze at the peaks of a long, thin range of mountains that stretched out along a string of islands that rose out of the surrounding expanse of ocean. My first thought was how small Japan looked. I would have occasion to revisit this first impression later.

That was on January 24, when my visit to Okinawa came to an end and I returned to the Japanese mainland. The plane left Naha airport in Okinawa at 3:00 p.m. and flew north for a little over an hour before entering airspace over Honshu via its southernmost point of Kagoshima. Looking down, I once again saw a long, thin range of deep purple mountains rising out of the surrounding sea. Later, squeezed between the mountains and the sea, a huddle of buildings like children's building blocks appeared. This was Osaka.

It is certainly true that Japan seems small when compared to China. But in comparison with European countries, Japan is rather large. Japan covers some 370,000 km^2, about 80,000 km^2 smaller than Heilongjiang Province in China. Japan has a population of 120 million, with a population density much higher than our own. This large population imposes a heavy burden on the country. Some 60 percent of Japan's landmass is mountainous, and it is extremely poor in natural resources. It is frequently beset by natural disasters such as earthquakes, typhoons, volcanic eruptions, and tsunamis. There are many examples of countries where conditions seem much more promising than this that have fallen into poverty. Japan, by contrast, has achieved a GDP of more than five trillion dollars, the second highest in the world. If we are to "seek truth from facts,"[2] we must conclude that Japan is the pride of Asia.

Over the past decade, however, the ongoing stagnation of the Japanese economy has coincided with the dramatic rise of the Chinese economy. Looking at the overall strength of the two countries and the trendlines in their development, it is now generally agreed that China will soon overtake Japan.

The February 17, 2002, *Newsweek* cover carried a photograph of a Japanese girl with tears running down her cheeks. The text next to the photo said that it was now Beijing, rather than Tokyo, that would decide the future of Asia. The magazine carried a special report on "Japan: The land of the setting sun." According to the article, Japan's unemployment rate is the worst since the war. Whereas Japan had previously looked down on countries like the Philippines, Indonesia, and Thailand that exported their women overseas as housemaids, the article said it was now Japanese engineers who had lost their jobs and were lining up to find jobs in China. Of the 1,000 biggest Japanese firms, 420 had transferred production facilities to China. Bad loans held by Japanese banks amounted to 135 billion dollars, equivalent to the foreign reserve funds of Taiwan and Hong Kong combined.

Reading a few lines of this article was enough to give the impression that Japan had collapsed already. But of course, that was not the case. Japan's enduring strengths are well known. In 2000, Japan had the highest per-capita

GDP in the world, at 35,567 dollars. Japan has some of the best manufacturing technology in the world and invests more in scientific research than any other country. Japan also has the world's largest international trade surplus, as well as the world's largest foreign currency reserve holdings at 361.6 billion dollars. And yet, according to an article in the March 2002 issue of *The 21*, a Japanese magazine, China is set to overtake Japan to become the world's second-largest economy by 2020. This seems relatively close to reality.

One day, the interpreter who was traveling with me, Matsui Miho, was wearing a beautiful cashmere sweater with a thin border pattern on a white background. Japan is famous for the fine-quality and attention-to-detail clothing. I thought I'd like one myself, and asked her where she had bought it. Her answer surprised me. "I bought this at the Beijing Yansha Youyi Shopping City," she said. "They have loads of different cashmere sweaters on the second floor." Many of the cashmere sweaters and other clothes on sale at the famous Mitsukoshi department store in Ginza are imported from China. Tokyoites joke that, just like America, their city is full of things that have been made in China. Perhaps this is another small illustration of the growth and development of the Chinese economy. In recent years, bilateral trade between China and Japan has been worth nearly 100 billion dollars. Products from China do seem to be everywhere you look in Japan.

Matsui told me that the stagnant economy was already having an impact on Japanese people's lives. Nowadays, people planned their spending carefully and were less likely to spend money on eating out or buying new clothes. The ready-made meals and precooked ingredients on sale on the basement floors of the big supermarkets were very popular.

Another friend told me of a myth that had been widely believed in earlier years: since real estate would inevitably increase in value, you couldn't possibly lose by buying land. But this approach didn't work anymore. Real estate prices had fallen, and the blow to Japanese people's confidence had been huge. Because of the stagnation and decline in the Japanese economy, many Japanese people have come to feel a vague sense of anxiety and fear about China's rise.

On the afternoon of January 16, in a light drizzle, I visited the book shops in the famous Jinbocho area of Tokyo. The most interesting part of the afternoon for me was my visit to the Uchiyama Shoten bookstore. This shop is well known among booklovers in China. The shop's ties to Lu Xun in the 1930s is a favorite episode in the history of cultural exchanges between China and Japan. The book *Chugokujin no seikatsu fukei* (*Scenes from the Daily Lives of the Chinese*), written by the shop's owner, Uchiyama Kanzo in the 1930s, was recently republished in China. The shop keeps these traditions alive today and still specializes in books related to China. They sell ancient and modern classics imported from the mainland, Hong Kong, and Taiwan, such as the *Classic of Poetry*, *Dream of the Red Chamber*, and *Evening Talks at Yanshan*, along with books by modern Chinese writers and books about China by writers from Japan and other countries. The book *Jiaofeng* (*Crossing Swords*), which Ling Zhijun and I wrote, has been published in Japanese by Chuo Koronsha, and this too was available, at the rather forbidding price of 3,600 yen (plus tax!).[3] The shop is not very big, but the shelves are crammed with books, and there is hardly room for a person to squeeze between the shelves.

Before coming to Japan, I had heard that several books had been published discussing the threat of a rising China. And indeed when I visited the Uchiyama bookshop, I noticed a number of these titles on the shelves, including *En vs jinmingen: Chugoku keizai no kyoi to Nihon no kudoka* (*Yen vs Renmenbi: The Chinese Economic Threat and the Hollowing Out of Japan*) by Miyazaki Masahiro; *Chugoku guro-barize-shon ga sekai o yurugasu: Ware-ware no unmei o nigiru Chugoku no ketsudan* (*How China's Globalization is Shaking the World: The Chinese Decisions that Hold the Key to Our Destiny*) by Kokubun Ryosei; *Chugoku wa kyoi ka: Genso no Nitchu yuko* (*Is China a Threat: The Illusion of Sino-Japanese Friendship*) by Nakajima Mineo and Komori Yoshihisa; *Chugoku wa kyoi ka* (*Is China a Threat?*), Amako Satoshi, ed.; *Iatsu no Chugoku Nihon no hikutsu: Shin-reisen jidai no makuake* (*Dominant China, Subservient Japan: The Beginning of a New Cold War Era*); and *Chugoku WTO kamei no shogeki* (*Impact of China's Joining the WTO*). I have forgotten the names of the authors of the last two books.[4] I flicked through a few of these books and felt that they all tended to exaggerate the situation. I remembered what someone had once told me: that the Japanese typically tended to be oversensitive. While this helped to drive innovation, it could also bring unnecessary tension and stress.

An *Asahi Shimbun* journalist told me: "For the past decade, the Japanese economy has been in a slump while China has continued to enjoy rapid growth. In the past, Japan felt a sense of superiority to China, but not anymore. China's development has been so fast that the Japanese people have lost their sense of superiority." Another Japanese friend told me: "Having a country with a population of 1.3 billion as a neighbor creates a massive pressure. It's as if you're living in a family with just one child and the family next door has 13 children—it's a little bit intimidating."

Since the beginning of the modern era, Japan has always walked in advance of China, with only the United States constantly ahead of Japan. For this reason, the Japanese have tended to admire the Americans and look down on the Chinese. But now, for the first time, there is the prospect that China might be about to overtake Japan in terms of overall power. We should not be surprised if Japan is finding this prospect difficult to accept psychologically.

3

Within China, however, there is a public opinion that takes a view directly opposite to the prevailing view in Japan. On February 13, after I returned to Beijing, I read on a certain website an article by someone writing under the name Gao Xingxing. Claiming that Japan already had the ability to fight a major war and was making ready to attack China first, the article stated that Japan was capable of producing a full range of nuclear weapons in the space of a month, and that within a year it could produce 20,000 mid-range ballistic missiles, 400,000 to 600,000 of the latest tanks, and 200,000 airplanes. Japan's FSX fighter had three times the capabilities of the American F-15 and F-16 fighters. Japan's reconnaissance satellites were equipped with all-weather functions that enabled them to photograph and trace targets less than one meter in size even at night. Once mobilized, Japan's army could be increased to five million, capable of sweeping through East and South Asia in just ten days.

This estimate of Japan's military capabilities is surely massively exaggerated. Many countries around the world have carried out research on Japan's military, and not a single study has ever reached a conclusion like this. The author provides surprisingly exact figures to back up his arguments, but it is unclear what the substantiation is for these figures.

Matters are not as simple as Gao Xingxing makes them out to be. In recent years, numerous books published by Chinese specialists on Japan have acknowledged that Japan today is essentially a democracy governed by the rule of law and that the government's policy and decision-making processes are subject to supervision and obstructions from many directions. Many people still seem to imagine that the "military" can simply act as it wants, but these conditions simply do not exist anymore. When I visited Japan, I paid a courtesy call on Yamaguchi Tomio, a member of the executive committee of the Central Committee of the Japanese Communist Party. He told me that one of the responsibilities of the Party is to expose the problems of the ruling Liberal Democratic Party (LDP). He told me that, "In recent years the influence of our Party has been expanding, and we have more than forty representatives in the Diet. The Communists are the largest party in 105 local regional governments around the country."

This example shows that, while Japanese politics may have a number of problems at present, including corruption, the reality is that a number of competing parties and interests within the government impose limits on one another. As is well known, various factions exist even within the LDP, and the struggles among these factions are often intense. Other political parties limit the LDP from the outside; in addition to the Communist Party, these include the Social Democratic Party (previously the Japan Socialist Party) and, even more powerful, the Democratic Party of Japan (with around 160 members in the Diet). Okada Katsuya, Democratic Party of Japan (DPJ) Policy Affairs Research Council Chairman and Chairman of the House of Representatives Committee on Security, told me: "The purpose of the DPJ is to bring down the ruling LDP."

The idea that Japan under this system could "sweep through East and South Asia in ten days" is nothing more than an idle fantasy. In addition, the international situation has changed beyond recognition since World War II. No one today would consider taking rash action against a much more powerful China.

Ni Lexiong, who is head of the research center for war and culture at the East China University of Science and Technology, published an article in *Southern Weekly* on March 28, 2002, in which he wrote:

> From the Meiji Restoration to the time of World War II, Japan followed a militaristic path. But it achieved nothing from this approach except to squander everything it had built up to that stage. After the war, Japan renounced the use of military force and sought survival through cooperation. As a result, it has achieved prosperity and success and has survived and developed without expanding its territory. The mainstream of Japanese society understands this well. At the same time, thanks to the development of its science and technology, Japan now has its population under control. The contradictions that caused Japan such anguish for so many years, between uncontrolled population growth and limited room for survival, no longer exists. In the modern era, the spirit of cooperation born of a globalizing economy is coming to occupy a dominant position in the world, and the best way to avoid military conflict is to construct and maintain strong systems of cooperation. From a historical perspective, the idea that a country that has been defeated in a war should remain forever incapable of recovering its position as a normal state was absurd. We must be psychologically prepared to face the possibility that Japan will again become a major power politically and militarily.

Ni Lexiong emphasizes the importance of distinguishing carefully between Japan's wish to recover the military standing of a normal state and any return to its prewar traditions of militarism. The two should be treated as quite separate ideas. This insight contains the essence of a new thinking that is in line with the tendencies of the times.

Even further removed from reality is the idea expressed in Gao Xingxing's comment that all Japanese people are bellicose and belligerent. "The people of Japan till a fertile soil for right-wing forces to prosper," he writes, suggesting that everyone in the country is constantly hoping for the country to revert to being "a military power." But what is the truth? I visited people in many lines of work while I was in Japan; without exception, when the conversation turned to war, they all showed a strong aversion to the idea of belligerence. In areas like Ginza and Shinjuku, the nighttime neon stretches out like a sea of light. Everything you could want is available there. The scene is even more full of life and energy than Manhattan. The streets are full of attractively dressed young men and women, walking side-by-side. Why should these young people yearn for the fires of war when they are so immersed in their comfortable modern lifestyles?

In Japanese farming villages, I saw farmers driving their Toyotas down well-paved roads, parking their cars at the side of their paddies, opening the trunk, changing into rubber boots, and going out to work in the fields. After a while they come back to their cars, put their rubber boots back in the trunk, and drive home. A look across a typical farming village reveals everything necessary for a comfortable life: modern buildings, shopping centers, clubs, and coffee shops. People can park in front of their own stand-alone houses, where single families live in comfort. Their lives are even more comfortable than those enjoyed by people in Tokyo. Why should they want to go and die a meaningless death on the battlefield? Using his own fantastic logic, Gao Xingxing criticizes the view of the Chinese government, which says that the Japanese people too were victims of World War II. He dismisses this statement as evidence that members of the government are "deceiving themselves and trying to deceive others." Even more alarmist is his claim that: "Even ordinary Japanese people use tourist travel to gather intelligence about China." With this leap of logic, the author makes clear the extent of his war hysteria. China, he says, should take careful preparations "to attack this enemy people." This is clearly irresponsible incitement.

On February 9, 2002, Jiang Zemin met former Japanese Prime Minister Kaifu Toshiki and said: "The only correct choice for both China and Japan, I believe, is to firmly maintain Sino-Japanese friendship. Friendship accelerates prosperity and will work to the benefit of both countries and their peoples." This is a wise view based on a broad and far-seeing perspective.

What does China need most at present? What would bring the greatest benefits to the country? This is an important question and we should be quite clear about the answer. The results obtained by the liberalizing policy of reform and opening up over the past twenty-four years are now attracting the attention of the world. But we also face a mountain of problems that will be difficult to solve. These include, for example, the lack of adequate rule of law, worsening corruption, bad loans in finance, income discrepancies between rich and poor, poverty in agricultural villages, the fragmentation of the markets, and a worsening environment. An even more fundamental problem that cannot be evaded much longer is the political reforms and greater democracy that are the devout wish of people at every level around the country.

When we consider China's current strength and the environment we face both at home and abroad, the danger of national subjugation and racial extermination, a real threat in the early years of the twentieth century, no longer exists. Indeed, many or most of the problems that China faces today originate within the country itself. China's leaders must use all their wisdom and exert themselves to the utmost to solve these problems.

For this reason, China's strategy should be to continue to develop stably with the diplomatic policy of *taoguang yanghui* (hide one's talents and cherish obscurity) knowing that breaking out of the current impasse within the country will be essential for this strategy. An important goal for Chinese foreign policy should be to work toward the aim of building a peaceful international environment for the next thirty or fifty years. In recent years, China has followed a diplomatic strategy of establishing good relations with neighboring countries. This policy is totally correct. Even if China continues to grow in power and stature in the years to come and has to decide how to fulfill its role as a responsible great power, this will mean only a more skillful manipulation of the international balance of power; it will certainly not be possible for China to simply do as it likes.

If we consider the situation from a wider perspective, it becomes clear that a number of choices exist in terms of Sino-Japanese relations.

1. Japan deepens its alliance with the United States and treats China with suspicion.
2. The two countries keep their distance, regard each other with suspicion, and secretly plot surprise attacks.
3. Sino-Japanese cooperation accelerates the prosperity of both countries, as well as East and Southeast Asia.

The second possibility is a temporary period of transition, and so long as we do not fall into position 1, should proceed to position 3. When we ask ourselves again which of these paths represents the most beneficial future for China, the answer goes without saying. Jiang Zemin was quite correct when he said that friendship between China and Japan was "the only correct choice," and his point dovetails with the mainstream of history. Considering this, the fighting Gao Xingxing speaks of as an impending inevitability would certainly not be good news for the Chinese people.

The idea of China as a threat has been gaining traction in many other lands as China has risen to prominence over the past few years. In Asia, many countries are watching China's movements with a sense of trepidation, and each country is preparing its own policy response. Frank-Jürgen Richter, who is responsible for Asian issues at the World Economic Forum, wrote in an article that appeared in the Chinese magazine *Caijing (Finance and Economy),* issue 21, 2002, that "China's rise is casting a dark shadow over the countries of Southeast Asia in many respects." These countries are concerned that China will suck up foreign investment like a black hole and that Chinese products will flood markets throughout Southeast Asia, hollowing out the industrial sectors in these countries. A report carried in the November 3, 2002, *Reference News* reported that in response to the demands being made by some people in Japan to change the country's constitution, a researcher at Singapore's Institute of Defense and Strategic Studies had said that: "Southeast Asia will not react to Japanese military strength in the same way as China. On the contrary, these countries are suspicious of China. I think we should encourage Japan to curb China's ambitions. From the perspective of security in the region, Japanese constitutional change is a necessary development." In addition, the head of the Japanese Studies Center at the University of Indonesia said, "Even if Japan revises its constitution, I personally don't believe it will become a major military power," while a member of the Thai government emphasized that "We welcome the active participation of the Japanese Self-Defense Forces in United Nations peacekeeping operations."

Under the circumstances, the Chinese government emphasizes the importance of peaceful unification with Taiwan and emphasizes the one-country, two-systems approach. China works to promote Sino-Japanese friendship, proactively encourages the development of ASEAN 10+3 exchanges (involving the ten ASEAN countries as well as China, Japan, and South Korea), dedicates itself to the establishment of a free trade area encompassing China and ASEAN, has started development plans for the Mekong River region, and is working to ensure the ASEAN nations also reap the advantages of Chinese economic development. Implementing these policies will ease the tensions in Asian countries and help exorcise the idea that China is a threat. During a visit to Cambodia in early November 2002, Prime Minister Zhu Rongji announced that China would write off a total of 300 million dollars in Cambodian debts and that China intends to cancel, either partially or wholly, debts that Vietnam, Myanmar, and four other Asian countries owe China. This news was received positively in Southeast Asia.

Almost immediately after a ten-year plan was launched to establish a China-ASEAN free trade area, Japan and India opened negotiations to establish free trade areas of their own with ASEAN, as if determined not to get left behind. Reflecting these developments, at a leaders' summit between China, Japan, and South Korea on November 4, 2002, Premier Zhu Rongji proposed starting research toward a free trade zone incorporating the three countries at a suitable time in the future, a proposal that was welcomed by informed figures in Japan and South Korea. Many people have been calling for a "new Asian era" moving toward greater economic integration as an Asian community, building on foundations that respect each country's distinctive cultural characteristics, and using this to spur further development. Zhu Rongji's proposal can be described as a major development that raised the curtain on a new Asian age. This is precisely the kind of bold yet deliberate attitude we need to display as a major power, always characterized by a vision that looks toward the future.

Historically there have been more inter-state wars in Europe than in Asia, and deep-seated resentments between nations ran much deeper too. Between 1814 and the fall of Paris in World War II, the French capital alone suffered at the hands of the Germans no fewer than six times. More recently, both the world wars of the twentieth century started in Europe, and Europe was the main battleground in both. Today, the peoples of Europe are seeking to transform former enemies into friends and are striving to achieve unity. In this endeavor, they are far ahead of Asian countries, as evidenced by the introduction of the single currency and the progress being made toward a common European constitution. This is one of the most impressive achievements in human history, and one of the most ambitious undertakings ever attempted in the quest for *datong* (great unity), a utopian vision of the world in which people all live peacefully as described in Chinese classic thought. Drawing upon opinion polls, the French scholar Matti Dogan paints a vivid picture of Western European countries passing through a transitory stage from traditional nationalism to union. He says that, "Many Western Europeans have a moderate pride in their nation, and though they do not place unconditional trust in the armed forces of their own country, they do trust their neighbors, and increasingly show a positive and proactive attitude toward the idea of union and greater integration as time goes by." (*Guowai Shehuixue Zuiqianxian* [*International Studies of Social Sciences*], 1997). Shanghai Academy of Social Sciences Press, April 1998.) This would certainly bring a smile to the face of Kang Youwei, the author of *Datong Sh*u (*Book of the Great Unity*), if he were alive to hear it. How long will we in Asia continue to be content with our peasants' way of thinking, happy if we can cultivate our fields and satisfied if we have clothes to wear and food to eat?

If voices such as Gao Xingxing's become more prominent, the only effect will be to cause suffering to us and happiness to our enemies, plunging China into isolation.

4

But the fact is that this piece by Gao Xingxing was not an isolated example. In fact, it represents quite a widespread phenomenon. Of the tens of thousands of posts and comments submitted to a certain website over the course of a year, most of the Japan-related content is insults to the country and its people, variously described as "the devils of the East," "*wako*" (Japanese pirates), and "dwarf Japan." Not a single post discusses the positive aspects of today's Japan. Of course, there are historical reasons for this phenomenon, but this reaction can only be described as emotional and regressive. If the winning side after a war shows a generous attitude toward the defeated enemy, this helps to create an environment of reconciliation, which in turn leads to greater safety for the victorious side. In the long run, this is surely better for the victor than taking a harsh attitude.

In the summer of 2002, the famous actor Jiang Wen visited Yasukuni Shrine, prompting a frenzy of angry reporting in the Chinese media. Some of the media cursed him as a traitor who had betrayed the nation and his people and shunned him as someone who had no right to live. Some media outlets used quotations from the famous painter Chen Yifei and other figures to argue that Jiang Wen had become degenerate and pressed famous figures to express their view of the case. The July 1 issue of the *Beijing Youth Daily* devoted a whole page to this case, in an article headlined "Emotional Patriotism is not True Patriotism." Looking back on his dealings with journalists related to this affair, Chen Yifei said, "Jiang Wen's visit to Yasukuni Shrine was a search for real-life experience as an artist and was in no way intended to pay respects to the shrine."

Film director Jia Zhangke responded: "At the time, I said that if Jian Wen had gone to Yasukuni and attended a Japanese militarist gathering, that would obviously be something that couldn't be approved. But if it was a personal act that was necessary for his work as a director, there was no room to criticize him. But when the article based on the interview they did with me appeared, what I'd said came out as something quite different."

Fellow film director Lu Chuan said that the opinion attributed to him in some parts of the media was totally lacking in facts. When approached by journalists, he had said that Jiang Wen's visit to Yasukuni had been undertaken for artistic, creative reasons and that he could fully understand it. A visit of this kind was totally different from a visit to pay respects at the shrine, and it was a mistake to confuse the two concepts. But when the article appeared, it reported the content of these comments quite differently. "I think it's wrong to force someone into such a difficult position by putting so much pressure on them like this. It goes too far. But I'm doubtful whether these attempts to paint Jiang Wen as a traitor will succeed. It makes me shudder to think that people can just deliberately fabricate the news like that," he said. The writer Zhong Ahcheng (Ah Cheng) has said that:

> Future reforms and further opening up in China will require us to have a greater understanding of international norms and what constitutes a common sense understanding of the world. Whether someone went to Yasukuni Shrine or not doesn't matter, because it's a public space in Japan. What's important is the question of what purpose, what attitude, the person went with. If a politician goes there with a certain objective in mind and demonstrates a certain political stance and says something to demonstrate that stance—that is a visit that involves showing respects to the shrine in the true sense of the term. This is just common sense. If more people had this proper understanding of matters then we wouldn't have this big commotion over a joke like this, saying Jiang Wen supposedly "visited."

In the summer of 2002, a bar in the city of Shenzhen posted a sign at the entrance forbidding entry to Japanese. The owner of the bar said this action had been taken in protest of Japanese attempts to rewrite history textbooks, among other things. There is an old Chinese saying, "Don't do to others what you don't want others to do to you." Another expression tells us to "Repay resentment with virtue." How did Chinese people feel in a previous era when they were subjected to the humiliation of signs reading "No dogs or Chinese"? Surely we should not treat other people the same way now that we have the upper hand. Until now, we have not confused politics and economics this way. The rewriting of history textbooks is something that is done by a very small number of people in Japan. Why transfer responsibility for it to ordinary Japanese? These phenomena are all reflections of the rise of nationalist feelings and how it is affecting people's attitudes to foreign relations.

Xie Mian, a professor at Peking University, wrote in an essay published in the *Xiangsheng Bao (Xiangsheng News)* on October 11, 2002, "On the night of 9.11, a certain university campus was apparently filled with voices celebrating the attacks, with people shouting out 'They've blown it up! They've done it!' This kind of twisted behavior is evidence of an extremely unhealthy character and suggests that these people have totally lost all balance in their sense of values. How else could they possibly applaud this most appalling of acts?" Professor Wu Sijing of the Capital Normal University wrote in the same issue: "Today, nationalistic feeling is on the rise and many people confuse narrow-minded nationalism with true patriotism." Several other scholars have observed that as a result of the biases of education over the long term, people often see things only in terms of the immediate interests in front of their noses. They become small-minded and lose their spirit of tolerance and forgiveness. The essayist Yan Lieshan has said that the so-called patriots who inflame people's emotions in this way in fact do serious damage to the country they claim to love.

There are two particularly important negative aspects of the patriotism that emerged in the 1990s. First, it is haughty and arrogant. It is quite right to advertise the achievements of the policy of reform and opening up and lift the morale of the people. But if that goes too far, there is a risk that people will become conceited and that passions will become inflamed. History shows us many examples of mistakes and crimes inspired by this kind of thing. In recent years, a famous scholar's words are quoted widely. He says: "Today, (Western) civilization is losing its momentum and starting to decline. History is like the Huang He (Yellow River) that flows east for thirty years and then changes direction to flow west for thirty years (suggesting that every civilization has ups and downs)." Many people are confidently proclaiming that the twenty-first century will belong to the Chinese. These people share the optimistic outlook of the book *China Can Say No,*[5] which predicts that the United States will collapse by 2010 and that "the blessings of Chinese achievements and virtues can be seen in all the progress that has ever been made in the world." Pronouncements of this kind stem from foolishness and ignorance, as well as being backward and anachronistic—they reflect a tendency to leap to arbitrary, one-sided conclusions without sufficient evidence. That such ignorant statements should be put forward by some people as "patriotism" only shows how confused their thinking must be.

The second troubling aspect is its exclusivist, xenophobic nature. In the recently published book *Quanqiuhua yinying xia de Zhongguo zhi lu. (China's Path Under the Dark Shadow of Globalization)*, there is a section espousing what the author calls "splendid isolation." Since the West is highly unified, it is not possible for China to take advantage of any differences or contradictions among the Western nations. Therefore, China should establish its own autonomous economic system and trade with itself (inter-regional trade within China), the author says. Even more alarmist is the book's claim that the true aim of the American government is the extermination of the Chinese race, and that it is developing genetic weapons for that purpose. The book even invents stories to argue that China will be unable to escape national destruction and racial elimination under pressure from the United States and other Western countries. In the book *Pengzhuang (Collision)*, globalization itself is presented as an American plot, a conspiracy by the United States to enslave the countries of the world. According to the author, the claim made by some people in China that globalization is an unavoidable trend in world history is nothing more than an ideology— one that a minority is attempting to impose on the majority. The book also claims that the difficulties facing Chinese state-owned enterprises are not caused by problems within these enterprises' systems or management but are rather the result of the introduction of foreign capital. The author of the book *Weixie zhongguo de yinbi zhanzheng (The Hidden War that Threatens China)* claims that globalization is a "soft war" started by the United States. The results of this soft war are quite sufficient to destroy China, plunge the country into a state of paralysis, and reduce it to subjugation under the control of the West.

These arguments and others like them with narrow perspectives are one-sided, lacking in facts, and unrealistic. Nevertheless, they are greeted with considerable applause in certain quarters. By the turn of the century, China was thriving and could no longer be compared to the country it had been in former years. Remarkably, however, the spirit of the Boxer Rebellion seemed to revive and we saw numerous xenophobic "close the country" melodramas played out. It has been painful to see. In an interview looking back on China's accession to the WTO, Vice Minister of Commerce Long Yongtu said that the biggest pressure on Chinese representatives during the negotiation process came not from their negotiating partners but from public opinion within China itself dismissing the country's negotiators as turncoats who had betrayed their people.

This nationalist fury is closely related to the irresponsible encouragement it gets from some sections of the media. Some of the media deliberately appeal to the emotional and lowbrow sector of the market in the hope of commercial gain. They have become depraved and have lost any sense of conscience. Without knowing the details of a story, they rush to sensationalize it with inflammatory reporting designed to attract readers. This sensationalism has damaged the environment in which public opinion is formed. The role that some of the media played during the controversies involving Zhao Wei and Jiang Wen is clear beyond any doubt. In *The Structural Transformation of the Public Sphere*, Jürgen Habermas discussed the declining function of the modern media and argued that the problem arises from consumerism, which has replaced critical consciousness. This should remind us that a healthy media environment is essential for a modern state under the rule of law. We must work to ensure a relationship between the media and the state, between society and the masses, that works to the benefit of both and strive to defend and pass on democracy and the rule of law.

5

Let us turn our thoughts to Japan again. For many years, the Japanese Cabinet Office has carried out public opinion surveys that ask people whether they feel "closeness" to China. The survey, carried out every year since 1978, asks 3,000 randomly selected people from different age groups to comment on their feelings about China. The results from more than twenty years of surveys show that public views of China were at their most positive in 1980, when 78.6 percent of the people said they felt "closeness." This fell rapidly to 51.6 percent in 1989 and just 48.8 percent as of 2000.

What is the reason for these results? One answer might be that the Japanese have formed a poor impression of China based on the behavior of a small number of Chinese, for example the large number of illegal Chinese immigrants in Japan. To give one example, on October 25 this year, the police headquarters in Nanjing brought a criminal prosecution on charges of trafficking. A group led by Chen Wenshu of Putian in Fujian Province had used nine ships over a period of slightly more than two years, traveling regularly to and from Japan from nineteen Chinese ports in ten coastal cities and had transported as many as 730 illegal immigrants to Japan as stowaways. At present, there are around 100,000 Chinese illegals in Tokyo alone. These people organize violent criminal gangs in Japan and are involved in burglaries, armed robberies, murders, the forging and use of counterfeit bills, and prostitution rings involving Chinese women. In Shinjuku, the Chinese gangs have been engaged in a battle for territory with Japanese gangs and, remarkably, have even gained the upper hand.

On March 7, 2002, the Hong Kong newspaper *Taiyang Bao* (*The Sun*) reported that the incidence of crime committed by Chinese nationals in Japan was rapidly increasing. According to reports on Japanese television, in 2001 an average of 25 Chinese nationals were arrested by the Japanese police every day. In addition, antisocial acts by Chinese people, such as riding on the subways without paying, failing to sort their trash according to the rules, monopolizing public spaces, littering, and spitting in the streets, have provoked a reaction among ordinary Japanese. Some people even warn their neighbors to move out when the Chinese start to move in. When I visited Osaka, a government official at the local city hall told me: "I don't know why, but every month about 100 Chinese women get married to Japanese men—often it's the men's second or third marriage—and then separate soon after. But they stay on in Osaka and never go back home."

These problems are reported by the media in Hong Kong and other countries; we too should not try to cover up these problems but should instead work to correct them. True confidence as a people comes only when we have the courage to look at our own weaknesses.

Of course, there are also Japanese nationalists who stir up Japanese nationalist sentiment based on unhappiness about Japan's economic decline, and discourse that goes against the currents of the times also gives rise to feelings of suspicion among ordinary people in both countries. One of the best-known figures in this sense is Ishihara Shintaro, the governor of Tokyo. As I walked through busy Shinjuku and looked up at the soaring towers of the Tokyo Metropolitan Government building, I couldn't help but remember Ishihara and his pronouncements. An article he published in the February 2002 *Bungei Shunju* with the title "The Way to Revive Japan: How to Beat China," can be taken as typical. He opens the essay by quoting from *The Shape of Things to Come* by the British author H.G. Wells in 1933.[6] Wells predicts that by the middle of the twenty-first century, the world will be united around Japan. Ishihara writes: "No doubt this English writer wanted to entrust the world 100 years into the future to Japan," but this, it must be said, is a little presumptuous. Ishihara is extremely dissatisfied with present-day Japan and believes that his country is in danger of becoming the fifty-first state of the USA or being absorbed by China. In the article, he poses the question: How should Japan face up to the United States and China, the two superpowers competing for supremacy in Asia? The prescription he offers is that facing up to the United States ("the tiger at the front gate") and keeping down China ("the wolf at the back gate") at the same time can enable the Japanese economy to recover. To resist China, Japan should establish an economic zone with the yen as key currency and link its advanced technology with the cheap labor power in other Asian countries. Naturally, China is not included in this "other Asian countries." By doing this, Japan can exert a central function in the fields of communications, finance, and distribution and become the "control tower" of a pan-Asian network. Of course, Ishihara's delusions do not represent the Japanese mainstream. It is to be hoped that the Japanese people will remain calm in the face of his provocations. Ishihara's assertions can bring nothing but harm to Japan.

During my discussions with Japanese intellectuals in Tokyo, one of them said that "Sino-centric thinking" was one of the factors that got in the way of friendship between Japan and China. When I asked him to expand on this, he said he meant the tendency for China to regard itself as the Middle Country or central power in the world and all other countries as barbarians. I told him that although that way of thinking had indeed been common in China in older times, today the reality was different. "For several decades, China has constantly espoused the five principles of peaceful coexistence, something the whole world knows." But he went on to say: "If China becomes powerful, it will stand over Japan telling us what to do." I told him that it was normal for there to be some degree of friction between the two countries and that it was possible to resolve this friction by equal discussion. "After all, doesn't Japan have friction with other countries too? China has no wish to lord it over Japan—that is just a misunderstanding held by some Japanese people who are unnecessarily nervous."

Aside from these somewhat disconcerting comments, the other thing I felt during my sojourn in Japan was that, perhaps unsurprisingly, the general tendency was for people to speak strongly in support of friendship between China and Japan. Among the figures I met personally were Machimura Nobutaka, Acting Secretary-General of the Liberal Democratic Party; Tomon Mitsuko, deputy chief of the Social Democratic Party; Okada Katsuya, Policy Affairs Research Council Chairman of the Democratic Party of Japan; Yamaguchi Tomio, member of the Central Committee of the Japanese Communist Party, as well as scholars from Waseda University, Rikkyo University, and the National Graduate Institute for Policy Studies. All these people had very positive views about Sino-Japanese friendship. All of them were positive about pushing forward relations between China and Japan and hoped for stronger cooperation and understanding between the two sides. For example, Machimura Nobutaka told me, "People in both countries have their opinions, so we must work hard to provide leadership to young people in particular in the years to come." Tomon Mitsuko said, "The Social Democratic Party has always felt close to China," while Okada Katsuya has been involved in the signing of a friendship agreement between his home prefecture of Mie and Henan Province in China and has donated five million yen to a Hope School[7] in Luoshan County, Henan Province. Yamaguchi Tomio expressed support for the content of Jiang Zemin's speech of July 1, 2001, in which he announced that owners of private companies that fulfilled certain conditions would be accepted into the party.[8] This shows clearly that Jiang Zemin's conclusion that maintaining friendly ties is the only correct choice for both China and Japan is a view shared by informed parties and intellectuals in both countries.

At the sixteenth National Congress that has just closed, one of the main themes that was stressed was the idea of *chuangxin* (innovation). I believe that this is true of Sino-Japanese relations as well. We need to discard our old ideas and start to move forward with a new way of thinking. China should demonstrate the boldness and mettle of a major power that was victorious in the war and does not need to be excessively harsh on Japan. In any case, nearly sixty years have passed since the war ended. The November 4 issue of the Hong Kong magazine *Asia Weekly* carried an article titled "The Need for Reform in Extremely Optimistic China." The article said: "In the future, historians will look back on 2002 as the year that China achieved an important shift. The important events that took place this year show that China has already become a moderate member of the international community." This shift is a sign of maturity and shows that in the field of international relations we have already started to apply the lessons learned from the radical course of the 1960s. Former Prime Minister Murayama Tomiichi and current Prime Minister Koizumi Jun'ichiro have visited places like the Marco Polo Bridge and Shenyang to express their condolences and have expressed remorse for Japan's war of invasion. The question of a Japanese apology has already been resolved, and there is no need to insist on a particular format or wording for such an apology. Between 1979 and 2001, Japan repeatedly provided low-interest yen loans to China worth a total of around 2,667,909 million yen. Japan has also supported some 150 infrastructure building projects, including the second phase construction work on the Beijing subway, expansion work on the Beijing Capital airport, the Beijing sewage treatment plant, Wuhan Tianhe airport, Wuqiangxi Hydroelectric Power Project, the second Chongqing Yangtze River Bridge Construction Project, Qinhuangdao Port, the Shuohuang Railway, and the Nanning-Kunming Railway. These ODA loans had an interest rate of between just 0.79 and 3.5 percent, and a repayment time of between thirty and forty years. This too indicates sincerity on the Japanese side. For many years, we have not done enough to educate people about these facts, which are not adequately appreciated today.

Nor do we need to make an undue fuss about Japan's desire to act as a major economic and military power, for example by sending its troops overseas to participate in United Nations peacekeeping operations. More importantly, we must be forward-looking. The new stage for competition will be economic systems and markets. China and Japan are crucial hubs in Asia, and the people of both countries must look more introspectively at their own nationalism and work to overcome their narrow-mindedness in the cause of greater unity and community. For China, our mission must be to move toward the early ratification of a free-trade area between China and ASEAN and to make progress toward signing a three-country free-trade agreement involving China, Japan, and South Korea. This is the direction in which the hearts of people in Asia are tending and the unmistakable tendency of the times.

NOTES

1. All data and personal job titles etc. given in the text are as of the time of original publication. The current text differs in some small respects of notation from that published in 2002;

2. *Shi shi qiu shi* in Chinese.

3. Ma Licheng and Ling Zhijun, trans. Shigeru Fushimi, *Koho: Kaikaku, kaiho o meguru tonai toso nouchimaku* [Crossing Swords: Records of the Three Thought Revolutions of Contemporary China], Chuo Koron-sha, 1999.

4. The first of these was co-written by Keitaro Hasegawa and Mineo Nakajima. The second was edited by Samejima Keiji and the Japan Center for Economic Research.

5. The original title was *Zhongguo keyi shuo bu*. By Song Qiang, Tang Zhengyu, Qiao Bian, Zhang Cangcang, Gu Qingzheng, trans. Mo Bangfu, Suzuki Kaori as *No to ieru Chugoku*, Nihon Keizai Shimbun-sha (*Nikkei Inc.*), 1996.

6. Japanese translation by Yoshioka Yoshiji, *Sekai wa ko naru: Saigo no kakumei*, in two volumes (new edition), Meitoku Shuppansha, 1995.

7. Elementary schools established to assist children in poor areas who are unable to attend school for economic reasons. The Project Hope promoted by the China Youth Development Foundation supports the improvement of education conditions in poverty-affected areas and helps the education of children who would otherwise not attend school. Many Japanese individuals, organizations, and companies support this scheme.

8. A reference to the speech given by General Secretary Jiang Zemin at a meeting to mark the 80th anniversary of the founding of the Chinese Communist Party. As well as speaking in general terms about the party's achievements and experiences, he reemphasized the importance of the "Three Represents" that he had put forward the previous year. This important theory claims that the Party should always represent: 1. The requirements for developing China's advanced productive forces, 2. The orientation of China's advanced culture, and 3. The fundamental interests of the overwhelming majority of the Chinese people. These ideas were later incorporated into Party regulations and the preamble to the Constitution.

CHAPTER THREE

The Inspiration behind the "New Thinking": Deng Xiaoping, Hu Yaobang, and Their Views on Japan

Why did Deng Xiaoping, a leader who threw himself into the war against the Japanese, and Hu Yaobang, who was an important officer in that war, have such praise for Japan and work so hard to build a framework of friendship between China and Japan that would last for generations? Surely no one could claim that people like Deng Xiaoping and Hu Yaobang, who had previously given all their strength to resist and fight against the Japanese aggressors, were somehow "traitors" to their country in their attempts to build friendship with Japan.

Deng Xiaoping was a major figure in the war against Japan. When the war of resistance against Japan broke out in earnest, the most important divisions of the Red Army[1] were reorganized to form the Eighth Route Army of the National Revolutionary Army in August 1937. Deng Xiaoping was appointed deputy director of the Eighth Route Army political department. At the time, Zhu De was commander-in-chief, Peng Dehuai his deputy, Ye Jianying chief of staff, and Ren Bishi director of the political department. In 1938, Deng Xiaoping became political commissar of the 129th division, one of the three major components of the Eighth Route Army, as well as director of the political department.

The 129th division was blessed with some of the finest talent available. Liu Bocheng was the commander and Xu Xiangqian his deputy. Other figures who held important positions in the 129th division were Zhang Hao, director of the political training department, his deputy Song Renqiong, and Liu Zhijian and Huang Zhen, both deputy directors of the political department. The chief commander of the 385th brigade under the jurisdiction of the 129th division was Wang Hongkun, and the chief commander of the 386th brigade was Chen Geng, with Chen Zaidao his deputy. The commander of the 769th regiment was Chen Xilian, with Qin Jiwei in command of a separate detachment. In addition, Bo Yibo was political commissar of the Taiyue military area command under the jurisdiction of the 129th division and deputy political commissar for the Jin-Ji-Lu-Yu[2] military area.

The 129th division achieved great military feats in the war against Japan. Shortly after the outbreak of the war, in October 1937, at the age of just 24, the 769th regiment's commander Chen Xilian led his troops in a surprise attack on the Yangmingbao airfield, where they destroyed 24 Japanese planes. Later, the 129th division developed a base area of resistance to the Japanese in the southeastern part of Shanxi Province, and in the Hundred Regiments Offensive of 1940 they achieved victory in the campaign against the Zhengding-Taiyuan railway. In 1943, the 129th division carried out mopping up and totally destroyed Japanese army observer groups. During the war, the 129th division wiped out 420,000 Japanese troops and established a liberated area encompassing Shanxi, Hebei, Shandong, and Henan

Provinces, a total of 180,000 km^2 and a population of some 24 million, and the number of troops increased to about 300,000. There can be no doubt whatsoever that Deng Xiaoping was a great patriot.

The war of resistance against Japan ended with victory in Japan's unconditional surrender in August 1945. To deal with the war crimes committed by Japan's militarists, the International Military Tribunal for the Far East was convened in early 1946 and Japan's Class A war criminals were put on trial. At the same time, a total of forty-nine other trials were held in countries that had been victim to Japanese crimes or had been at war with Japan (not including the Soviet Union) to try Class B and Class C war criminals. Ten such trials were held in the Chinese sector. The trials lasted a total of ten years, 991 defendants being sentenced to death, 491 to life imprisonment, and 2,946 to lesser sentences. These figures include more than 2,200 cases tried in the ten war crimes trials relating to the Chinese front from 1946 to 1949. Death sentences were handed down to the notorious perpetrators of killings during the Nanking Massacre, including Tani Hisao, Mukai Toshiaki, and Noda Tsuyoshi.

During the American occupation of Japan after the war, a major campaign was undertaken to remove and eradicate the militaristic-authoritarian system which had caused the war. Democratic reforms were carried out systematically, and the occupation helped Japan build a democratic political system. Human rights were guaranteed within Japan, and democracy was introduced. The path of peace and development became the mainstream within Japanese society. These huge changes in Japan were among the conditions underlying CCP policy toward Japan after the founding of the People's Republic of China.

In 1955, the CCP Central Committee showed lenience to more than 1,000 war criminals held on the mainland. The instructions of the Central Committee were to show mercy to the Japanese war criminals who would not be sentenced to death or life imprisonment. A few would receive jail sentences, but the instructions indicated that their sentences could be reduced or commuted if they showed a good attitude. On instructions from Mao Zedong, Zhou Enlai outlined these instructions to the Standing Committee of the National Political Consultative Conference in March 1956.

On April 25, 1956, the Standing Committee of the National People's Congress passed a "decision of the Standing Committee of the National People's Congress on the handling of the war criminals in custody following the Japanese war of aggression against China." The decision decreed: "Considering the changes in conditions and circumstances that have occurred over the ten years or so since Japan surrendered, the current status, the development of friendly relations in recent years between the peoples of China and Japan, and the fact that most of the war criminals have demonstrated some degree of remorse for their crimes, it has been decided to deal with these war criminals on an individual basis with a policy of leniency."

Following this, the Supreme People's Procuratorate three times released decision papers granting exemption from prosecution for Japanese war crimes, and leniently granted release in cases brought against 1,017 Japanese war criminals. In addition, although prosecutions were brought against another forty-five Japanese war criminals, the sentences handed down were for limited periods of imprisonment ranging from twelve to eighteen years, with time already served taken into consideration. Some of them had their sentences reduced or were released early for good behavior. Many of these war criminals worked to contribute to Sino-Japanese friendship after their return to Japan. Thus it was that the trials to settle accounts and bring charges against Japan for its war crimes came to an end.

The 1956 Japan tour by Mei Lanfang and his Peking opera group was a great success. That same year, a festival of Japanese films was held in ten major Chinese cities and an exhibition of Japanese paintings was held in Beijing, as was a major event to commemorate 450 years since the death of the Japanese painter Sesshu. In 1957, there were successful visits to China by a leading group of *shingeki* (new drama) actors, an educational study tour mission, and a group of Japanese doctors, among others. The Chinese media at the time reported that cultural exchanges between the two nations were brilliant and colorful. Is it conceivable that the Party would have given permission for such "brilliant and colorful" cultural exchanges if Japan had not undergone major changes after the war and had still been under the same militaristic rule? After this, the scale of political, economic, and cultural exchanges between China and Japan continued to grow even more.

Building on these foundations, the two nations ratified the September 1972 Sino-Japanese Joint Communique in Beijing and normalized their diplomatic relations. This "normalization" or restoration of diplomatic ties refers to a situation in which normal relations previously existed between two countries but were interrupted for some reason or another or fell into a state of abnormality or conflict and are now restored to normality.

To recount the background to the normalization of relations between China and Japan: Diplomatic relations between China and Japan were severed as a result of Japan's invasion and war of aggression. After the war, in the context of the Cold War, the Japanese government concluded a Sino-Japanese Peace Treaty (commonly known as the Treaty of Taipei) with the government in Taiwan. Because this treaty was never recognized by the

Chinese government, relations between the two countries continued to be abnormal until this aspect of the situation came to an end in 1972. In 1972, Japanese Prime Minister Tanaka Kakuei visited China, signed the Sino-Japanese Joint Communique with the Chinese government, and announced that the abnormal state of affairs between China and Japan would come to an end. The Japanese government acknowledged that the People's Republic of China was the sole legal government of China and diplomatic relations formally began between the two governments.

The Joint Communique contained the following line: "The Japanese side is keenly conscious of the responsibility for the serious damage that Japan caused in the past to the Chinese people through war, and deeply reproaches itself." This was followed by agreements on trade, navigation and shipping, aviation, and fishing. In August 1978, the two countries signed a Treaty of Peace and Friendship in Beijing. With this treaty, the governments of the two nations made a joint declaration that they "shall develop relations of perpetual peace and friendship between the two countries" on the basis of the principles of peaceful coexistence, "hoping to contribute to peace and stability in Asia and in the world."

On October 22, 1978, at the invitation of the Japanese government, Deng Xiaoping visited Japan to attend a ceremony to exchange the instruments of ratification of the Treaty of Peace and Friendship between China and Japan. This was significant as Deng Xiaoping's first trip overseas following his third rehabilitation. The Chinese newspapers followed his itinerary and speeches and reported on them in detail for several days running. A little after 10:00 the following morning, Deng Xiaoping gave a speech at the Prime Minister's Official Residence. He said: "The peoples of China and Japan need friendship, and they need solidarity. The relationship between China and Japan must be one of close and friendly cooperation. This is the common wish of the one billion people of our two countries and represents the direction in which the tide of history is moving."

Early that afternoon, Deng Xiaoping paid a courtesy call on Emperor Hirohito. Deng Xiaoping told the emperor: "Let's let bygones be bygones and look forward positively from now on." What was Deng Xiaoping referring to when he spoke of past events in this way? Naturally enough, he was referring to the previous war between the two countries. But what he said does not in any way diminish the fact that he was a great patriot. It merely demonstrates that he understood the trends of the times and was a great historical figure who could stand on the heights and look ahead into the future. The "New Thinking on Relations with Japan" article I published in 2002 was based on this verdict of Deng Xiaoping's, offering a new interpretation of it in line with the changing times.

From today's perspective, the period when Deng Xiaoping was active was still relatively soon after the war. Normally, common sense would suggest that hatreds are more pronounced the clearer the memory of war is. As we move further away and memories become less clear, hatred also naturally fades. For example, during the Yuan dynasty, China invaded Japan twice during the Mongol invasions. Chinese troops landed near Fukuoka and penetrated aggressively into various parts of Japan. The fighting was extremely fierce and brutal. Today, people have more or less forgotten about these incidents. This is because so much time has passed.

But something strange is happening. Deng Xiaoping could say to the emperor "let's let bygones be bygones" in 1978. Why is it that memories of the war refuse to slip into the past today, more than thirty years later? Some people claim that this is because of the outrageous statements made by the Japanese right wing. But wasn't the Japanese right wing just as vociferous in Deng Xiaoping's time? If the right wing stirs up commotion, it is enough to expose them and criticize them and fight back against them. We must not confuse this with the major issue of reconciliation between China and Japan.

The difficulty lies not in the statements made by the Japanese right wing but in the gulf that exists between our understanding and Deng Xiaoping's understanding of Sino-Japanese relations. The biggest issue of all is whether we can consider the problem from the strategic framework of China's modernization and whether we are able to consider the problem from the perspective of the strategic structure of the world as a whole. For example, since 2008, the United States, Japan, South Korea, Australia, Singapore, India, and more have frequently discussed the practical possibility of establishing some kind of Asian version of NATO—but should we recommend Japan for a military alliance of this kind?

In the October 23 afternoon meeting with Prime Minister Fukuda Takeo, Deng Xiaoping said: "Friendly and cooperative relations between our two countries and between the peoples of our two countries will develop and grow from generation to generation. Nothing could make us happier." During his visit to Japan, Deng also paid inspection visits to Nissan and Nippon Steel and rode the Japanese bullet train. "I now understand what modernization means," he said. He also said: "The first thing we must do is recognize that we have fallen behind. To honestly acknowledge that we have fallen behind marks the beginning of hope. Next, we must be good learners. One reason why I have made this visit to Japan is to ask for Japan's guidance and teaching." It was after Deng Xiaoping's return to China that the policy of reform and opening up, which would have such an impact on China's destiny, began.

During that visit, Deng proposed the two countries "shelve" their dispute over the Diaoyu/Senkaku Islands. According to the *People's Daily* of October 26, in response to a question from a journalist at the Japan National Press Club on the afternoon of October 25, Deng Xiaoping said: "As for the Diaoyu/Senkaku Islands, we call them the Diaoyu Islands. The two sides have differing views and see the matter quite differently. We even call them by different names. When normalizing relations, both sides promised not to touch on this issue. And during the negotiations that led to the Treaty of Peace and Friendship, both sides agreed not to address the subject." He also said: "Some people want to use the problem of the Diaoyu/Senkaku Islands to stifle the development of good Sino-Japanese relations, but we believe that the best thing is for the two governments to avoid the issue for now." This flexible and practical attitude impressed and won over the Japanese, and his spirit of humility and decisiveness attracted them even more. This proposal by Deng Xiaoping is supported by historical evidence. In 1972, as Mao Zedong decided on normalization of relations with Japan and had Zhou Enlai implement that decision, China clearly demonstrated its intention to shelve the debate with Japan over the Diaoyu/Senkaku Islands.

Hu Yaobang was also an important officer during the war of resistance against Japan. By early 1934, at the age of eighteen he was already general secretary of the central committee of the Communist Youth League in the Central Revolutionary Base.[3] That October, he took part in the Long March and was wounded in the campaign in which the Communist troops "crossed the Chishui River four times." In 1935 he entered the Counter-Japanese Military and Political University in Yan'an. After graduation, he took up a position as deputy head of the political department at the university on instructions from Mao Zedong. In 1937, he was instructed by Mao to found the university newspaper, *Sixiang zhanxian* (*Battlelines of Thought*). The realistic and colorful pages were highly praised by Mao. According to an account in Tang Fei's *Hu Yaobang zhuan* (*A Biography of Hu Yaobang*) (co-published by the People's Publishing House and the CCP History Publishing House, November 2005), orders were issued in 1938 for the students of the first battalion of the fourth term cadre regiment of the Counter-Japanese Military and Political University to move from Yan'an to Mt. Miliang in Wayaobu. Mao accompanied Luo Ruiqing to see off the students. At the time Su Zhenhua was the platoon leader and Hu Yaobang the political commissar. In a short speech, Mao singled out Hu Yaobang for special praise, saying: "I have watched his growth with my own eyes. He has a keen appetite for learning and is an exemplar of the revolution with high spirits. Now he is writing with indefatigable energy for the newspaper, and his writings are welcomed and esteemed by readers."

In 1939, Mao appointed Hu deputy head of the organizational division of the general political department of the CCP Central Military Commission, and subsequently head of the division. In 1940, Hu took up a position as head of the political department under the jurisdiction of the Central Military Commission, and he later became a member of the rectification and guidance group under the jurisdiction of the Central Military Commission. Throughout the war of resistance against Japan, Hu Yaobang was constantly in important leadership positions within the heart of the Central Military Commission, and he served for six years as head of the organizational division of the general political department. Under Mao Zedong's leadership, Hu Yaobang cooperated with Wang Jiaxiang, head of the general political department, to carry out observations of the leadership cadres of the army and shouldered important responsibilities coordinating personnel assignments and dispatches within the Eighth Route Army, the New Fourth Army,[4] and the anti-Japanese base areas, tasks that he completed with great aplomb. These prominent achievements saw him receive a number of appointments from Mao Zedong during the war of liberation; he served as director of the political department in the Ji-Re-Liao[5] military area, political commissar attached to the fourth column of the field army in the Jin-Cha-Ji[6] region, director of the political department of the first corps under the jurisdiction of the Central Military Commission, and director of the political department of the eighteenth corps, establishing great military feats as part of the leadership at important campaigns such as the Qingfengdian campaign, the Shijiazhuang campaign, the Taiyuan campaign, the battle of Xianyang, and the Chengdu campaign.

After the establishment of the People's Republic of China, Hu Yaobang served as party committee secretary for the Chuanbei region and director of the administrative branch office. After this, he served as first secretary of the Central Committee of the Communist Youth League, director of the Hunan provincial party committee secretariat, party secretary for the Xiangtan region, second secretary of the CCP Central Committee Northwest Bureau, first secretary of the CCP Shaanxi Provincial Committee, first deputy group leader of the leadership group (which served as the "core" of the party) at the Chinese Academy of Sciences, vice principal of the Central Party School, chief of the Central Organizational Department, party secretary general, head of the Central Propaganda Department, and CCP Central Committee General Secretary. He selflessly devoted himself to the interests of the people and strove diligently to carry out reforms, working to encourage whatever was beneficial and to exclude whatever was harmful. The people of the nation had heard of his shining deeds and noble character from an early stage and could tell of these things in detail. All the party and the people of the nation could affirm that Hu Yaobang was a great patriot who suffered long trials for the good of his party and nation.

The period from 1982 to 1983 was the beginning of the period of reform and opening up, and many things that had fallen into disrepair were expected to be revived. Hu Yaobang repeatedly recommended former Japanese Prime Minister Yoshida Shigeru's book *Nihon wo kettei shita hyakunen (Japan's Decisive Century 1867–1967)*[7] to the senior management of the party and the cadres of the Communist Youth League. I was working as deputy head of the editorial department at the *China Youth Daily* at the time and personally overheard him recommending the book to fellow attendees when I attended a senior leadership meeting of the Central Committee of the Communist Youth League. Yu Guangyuan has also recalled having seen Hu Yaobang reading the book. Shen Baoxiang, former editor of *Lilun dongtai (Theoretical Trends)*, the journal of the Central Party School, also says that he read the book at Hu Yaobang's recommendation. The book looks back on the tumultuous century from the Meiji Restoration to the period of postwar development in Japan. Hu Yaobang said that he had received considerable enlightenment and instruction from the book.

According to Chapter 12 (which is about the hardships of the Cultural Revolution) of Tang Fei's *A Biography of Hu Yaobang*, when the Lin Biao Incident[8] took place in 1971, Zhou Enlai took the opportunity to release a group of leaders who had fallen from grace, one of whom was Hu Yaobang. Zhou Enlai called Hu back to Beijing from the cadre school in Henan Province, sent him for a physical exam, and had him start recuperation and medical treatment. During his convalescence, Hu read a number of books relating to Japan, including those relating to Tanaka Kakuei's thinking and his book *Nihon retto kaizoron (Building a New Japan)*. Hu's thinking at the time was as follows. For many years, China's economy had been stagnant, and its science too was lagging. Japan presented a contrast. Despite the hardships of the immediate postwar years, Japan had concentrated its strengths and devoted its efforts to science and education. As a result, its economy had developed quickly and it had risen to become a major industrial power. The Japanese experience offered lessons that we could learn from.

Hu Yaobang recommended Yoshida Shigeru's book *Japan's Decisive Century 1867–1967* because he wanted people to learn from the spirit of reform, the priority given to education, and the innovativeness of the science and technology in Japan, and to accelerate the Communist Party's modernization. In October 2005, when Shaanxi Normal University Publishing House reissued a new edition of the book, the afterword noted that the book had "created a storm in China in the 1980s." This was undoubtedly because of Hu Yaobang's strenuous efforts to recommend and promote the book.

On September 28, 1982, just after being selected as General Secretary at the 12th National People's Congress, Hu Yaobang met Japanese Prime Minister Suzuki Zenko in Beijing. Hu said: "China and Japan are two of the great nations of the world. The relationship between the two countries is one in which they will benefit together if they are at peace but will both suffer injury if they drift apart." In saying this, he was thinking of benefits in terms of world peace and happiness for our descendants in future generations, he explained.

On February 20, 1983, Hu Yaobang met with Nikaido Susumu, who had come to China as a special envoy of the Japanese prime minister, in Wuhan. He said: "In relations between the two countries, we emphasize the importance of thinking in a forward-looking manner."

On September 29, Hu Yaobang had a meeting in Beijing with Ishibashi Masashi, the chair of the Socialist Party of Japan, and told him: "The history of China and Japan has proven that the relationship between the two countries is one in which both sides suffer if we fight and we prosper together if we are at peace. We must educate our children and grandchildren so they maintain and develop friendly relations between our countries forever."

On October 3, Hu Yaobang had a meeting with a delegation of Japanese journalists headed by Mizukami Kenya, chief of the editorial bureau at the *Yomiuri Shimbun*, and said: "Our two countries must never again be enemies."

On November 23, 1983, Hu Yaobang set out for Japan. He gave a speech in the House of Representatives in which he said: "We must take up a vantage point on the heights so that we can observe and deal with Sino-Japanese relations from a comprehensive and long-term perspective; we must turn our eyes forward to the future. We need the kind of vision and determination held by people of good sense and reason with the ability to see all aspects of the relationship." At a Tokyo reception organized by Japanese business figures to welcome him to Japan, he said: "Both China and Japan have their own strengths, and this will no doubt continue to be the case several decades into the future. We should deepen our cooperation and use our strengths to help each other compensate for our weaknesses."

On the 26th, at a gathering of young people held to welcome him to Japan, he said: "The pressing problem for the immediate future will be to pass down the relationship of friendship that our generation has built and pass this relationship on to the next generation and then the generation after that, to continually develop friendly relations without pause for the next thirty or sixty years into the future." Based on the framework decided by Deng Xiaoping of continually developing friendly relations from generation to generation and an agenda fixed by Hu Yaobang following discussions within the party's Central Committee just before leaving for Japan, in this speech Hu Yaobang extended an invitation to 3,000 Japanese youth to spend a week in China in 1984, the following year. This was the best-known high tide of the surge in friendly relations between China and Japan during the 1980s.

On the 28th, during a visit to a factory in Osaka, Hu wrote words of encouragement: "I express my admiration and respect for the industrialists, scientists and engineers, and the many workers of Japan, who have created one of the finest modernization efforts and the highest levels of industry in the world." The next day, on the 29th, during a visit to the Mitsubishi Heavy Industries Nagasaki shipyard, he wrote a message in the guestbook wishing that "Sino-Japanese friendship will endure forever."

During this visit to Japan, Hu Yaobang and the Japanese side agreed on the four principles of friendly ties between China and Japan: peace and friendship, equality and mutual benefit, reciprocal trust, and long-term stability. High-level representatives from both countries reached a consensus on establishing a China-Japan Friendship Committee for the twenty-first Century in 1984 to help strengthen the relationship between the two countries in the lead-up to the twenty-first century. This committee was duly established in 1984; the chair representing the Chinese side was Wang Zhaoguo, then a member of the Secretariat of the party's Central Committee. The committee was proactive and engaged in carrying out its duties. One result, for example, was the famous Sino-Japanese Youth Exchange Center in Beijing, which was built with Japanese ODA funding.

Ni Jian published a piece in issue 24, 2005, of the Beijing magazine *World Affairs* titled "Recollections of the 3,000 Japanese Youths' visit to China," in which he wrote as follows. In order to implement the Visit to China of the 3,000 Japanese youths invited by Hu Yaobang, the Party Central Committee established a preparatory committee at the end of 1983 that would be responsible for accepting them and making the necessary arrangements. The members of the committee were: Wang Zhen, then honorary president of the China-Japan Friendship Association, as chairman; Wang Zhaoguo, first secretary of the Central Committee of the Communist Youth League, as deputy; Hu Jintao, then director of the All-China Youth Federation, as chief secretary; and, Liu Yandong, deputy director of the All-China Youth Federation, as deputy chief secretary.

In 1984, 220 organizations and departments in Japan sent 3,017 individuals to visit China. By coincidence, 1984 also happened to be the 35th anniversary of the foundation of the People's Republic of China. On the night before National Day, 3,000 Japanese young people came from the various places they were visiting around China and gathered in Beijing. On September 29, the Chinese side held a reception in the Great Hall of the People; this was the largest number of people at any event held at the National People's Congress. At the military procession on National Day, special seats were set up for the Japanese visitors on the observation dais in Tiananmen Square. One member of the Japanese delegation, Hozumi Kazunari, was suddenly taken ill during a visit to Nanjing, bleeding from his stomach and losing consciousness. It was an emergency, but Hu Jintao himself took charge of the response and the man's life was saved. Later, when Hu Jintao visited Japan for the first time as Vice President of China in 1998, he met Hozumi again. Hozumi shook his hand firmly and told him that China had given him a second life.

When the Japanese visitors came to Beijing, Hu Yaobang met with senior members of the delegation. Later, many of them assumed important roles in a variety of fields and became important pillars within Japan promoting reconciliation between the two countries. After the Japanese visitors returned home, an invitation was extended for a return visit to Japan by a group of young people from China. In 1985, a group of 504 young people led by Liu Yandong, director of the All-China Youth Federation, visited Japan, where they met many Japanese people and were treated with great kindness and hospitality.

The Chinese scholar Xia Gang, who teaches at Ritsumeikan University in Japan, submitted an article about the Japanese people's visit to China to issue 24, 2005, of the magazine *World Affairs*. Once a general framework for citizen diplomacy is created, he wrote, it achieves an effect akin to rainwater steadily dripping on a stone, gradually extending from "points and lines" and widening its effect. The *Guanzi* says: "When planning for a year, plant corn. When planning for a decade, plant trees. When planning for life, train and educate people." This saying is useful for appraising the accomplishments achieved through hard work and struggle by Hu Yaobang for the sake of bringing about reconciliation between China and Japan, and also in understanding the significance of the Century Committee for China-Japan Friendship for the 21st Century established by Hu and Prime Minister Nakasone Yasuhiro of Japan. The long-term efforts that Hu put into diplomacy with Japan are like a fine wine whose bouquet becomes richer the longer it matures, and have brought profound effects and benefits for many years.

Why did Deng Xiaoping, a leader who threw himself into the war against the Japanese, and Hu Yaobang, who was an important officer in that war, have such praise and work so hard to build a framework of friendship between China and Japan that would last for generations? Surely no one could claim that people like Deng Xiaoping and Hu Yaobang, who had previously given all their strength to resist and fight against the Japanese aggressors, were somehow "traitors" to their country in their attempts to build friendship with Japan.

In *Jiqi yu jingshen* (*Machines and Spirit*), Lin Yutang wrote very reasonably and very sensibly that there are different approaches to patriotism, but the most important thing is to ensure that one's thinking is clear. If this love of country is something based on emotion alone and does not incorporate logic, and if one does not understand the difference between right and wrong, between profit and loss, and does not have a clear understanding of the civilizations both of one's own country and of other countries, then this love of country becomes something conservative and reform becomes tantamount to submission to a foreign country. This will not bring happiness to the future of our country.

The commotion that arose between China and Japan in 2012 in connection with the Diaoyu/Senkaku Islands was caused by Japanese right-winger Ishihara Shintaro and others like him. For China to issue a protest was only natural. It is also important not to relax our vigilance with regard to people who are scheming to bring about a military confrontation between the two countries. From China's point of view, if another major war broke out with Japan, it would destroy all the hard work China has put into its modernization and would lead to the worst possible result—like the snipe and the clam who fought, only to both be captured to the fisherman's profit. This is why Hu Yaobang emphasized that China and Japan will benefit together if they are at peace but both will suffer if they drift apart. An armed conflict between the second and third biggest economies in the world, both located in Asia, would be a tragedy for the whole of Asia. Even if things don't come to that, squabbles and disagreements between those "younger sons" would surely only serve to help the "big brother" solidify his position as the global hegemon. Hu Yaobang and Hu Jintao have spent thirty years passionately arguing that China and Japan will both benefit if they are at peace but will both suffer if they drift apart. Even so, there are still people who stir up the embers of conflict between the two countries. This has led to an excess of emotion in society and has given people a mistaken understanding of the situation. At the moment, the tendency to use "patriotism" to enflame the passions of the people is damaging China's long-term fundamental interests. This is a development that we need to watch carefully. In the

August 2012 issue of the magazine *Tongzhou Gongjin* (*Advance in the Same Boat*), major general Xu Yan of the National Defense University published an article titled "Assessing the Economic and Military Power Disparity between China and the US" In it, he strongly criticized people who talk casually of war. He writes: "Mao Zedong and Deng Xiaoping emphasized that the dispute could be shelved for the long term, but some people still bang the drum and say that we should resolve the issue as quickly as possible using military force. If we ever did such a thing, peaceful development would become quite impossible."

What about Japan? A military conflict with China would inevitably cause huge damage to and suffering for Japan, and there is no way that the Japanese government or the vast majority of its people would approve opening hostilities. Therefore, people from all walks of life in Japan must work to expose, stop, and criticize the extremely small number of right-wing agitators who foment commotion and stir up nationalist feelings. They must arouse a spirit of vigilance in Japanese society.

China has disputes with many neighboring countries over territorial rights and maritime rights, and in some cases the territories or islands in dispute are much larger than the Diaoyu/Senkaku Islands. At a speech to the opening ceremony of the 9th China-ASEAN Business and Investment Summit on September 21, 2012, Xi Jinping said: "We are firm in safeguarding China's sovereignty, security, and territorial integrity and are committed to resolving differences with neighbors concerning territorial land, territorial sea, and maritime rights and interests peacefully through friendly negotiations."

The Diaoyu/Senkaku Islands problem is neither the main issue nor the central concern of Sino-Japanese relations. The most important aspect of the relationship is the duty to continue the process of reconciliation and to push ahead with developing a mutually beneficial relationship based on common strategic interests. In the absence of a better solution, the best thing to do with regard to the Diaoyu/Senkaku Islands issue is to continue to shelve the dispute and to carry forward discussions based on the principle of joint development.

On August 29, 2012, which was when the uproar over the Diaoyu/Senkaku Islands was reaching its peak, Tang Jiaxuan, who had previously served as State Councillor and Minister of Foreign Affairs and who now serves as president of the Sino-Japanese Friendship Association, gave a very fine speech. According to a report in the online version of the *People's Daily*, he attended an international academic symposium that day to mark forty years since the normalization of diplomatic relations between China and Japan and spoke as follows.

On the 27th of this month, the official car of the Japanese ambassador had its progress blocked and the flag on the front of the car was torn off. This incident does not represent reasonable love of country; it is the kind of "patriotism" that damages the country. Behavior of this kind does not represent the wishes and thinking of the majority of the Chinese people. Most Chinese people are reasonable and rational. I want the relationship between China and Japan to be a healthy and friendly one. At present, the relevant departments in China are investigating the event, and I am sure that a thorough-going investigation will be carried out. The relationship between China and Japan is currently undergoing a tumultuous period of difficulty, but the future of the relationship is filled with confidence. That the relationship develop as a healthy and stable one in the long term is, I firmly believe, the shared wish of both governments and peoples, and represents the fundamental interest of both sides. It is also the universal hope of the international community.

Based on China's premise of defending state sovereignty, working to promote reconciliation between China and Japan using logic, interests, and moderation and overcoming difficulties to develop a mutually beneficial relationship based on common strategic interests between the two countries is the intelligent choice for anyone who loves the nation. Love of country that does not incorporate rationality only brings harm to the country. This is the lesson given to us by Deng Xiaoping and Hu Yaobang and their view of Japan. This perspective of theirs was also the source of my thinking when I proposed my New Thinking on Relations with Japan.

NOTES

1. The armed forces led by the CCP had different names in different times. During the period between 1927 and 1937, they were called the Chinese Workers' and Peasants' Red Army (Red Army).

2. Jin-Ji-Lu-Yu encompasses Shanxi, Hebei, Shandong, and Henan Provinces.

3. The main revolutionary base area led by the Communist Party of China from 1927 to 1937, also known as the Central Soviet.

4. The New Fourth Army of the National Revolutionary Army was formed with the Red Army as its chief strength as a national army to fight a united front against Japan following the second alliance between the Kuomintang and the Communist Party of China (KMT-CPC Alliance) of 1937.

5. Ji-Re-Liao refers to the then Hebei, Rehe, and Liaoning Provinces.

6. Jin-Cha-Ji encompasses modern Shanxi, Hebei, and Liaoning Provinces and the Inner Mongolia autonomous region.

7. Yoshida Shigeru, *Nihon wo kettei shita hyakunen: Fu omoidasu mama* (Chuokoron-Shinsha, 1999).

8. Also known as the "9.13 event," since it took place on September 13, 1971. Lin Biao helped develop the movement to study Mao thought during the Cultural Revolution and was regarded as a potential successor to Mao. However, relations between the two men deteriorated and Lin Biao plotted an assassination against Mao. When this failed, he attempted to go into exile in the Soviet Union but was killed when his plane went down in Mongolia. This attempted coup d'état by the number-two power (vice chairman of the CCP Central Committee) caused a massive shock in China and around the world and the true details of what happened are still the subject of lively debate.

CHAPTER FOUR

I am Not Alone on My Journey:
He Fang, My Mentor

The mainstream fundamentals of the relationship between China and Japan continue to be strong. Although outstanding issues continue to exist and disputes sometimes arise in the relationship, this is nothing unusual. If both sides adhere strictly to the joint statement they made when they normalized relations, the Treaty of Peace and Friendship, and the four basic principles, it should not be too difficult to resolve any problems that may arise, or at least ensure that they do not adversely impact the development of friendly and cooperative relations. Friendship between China and Japan is in the basic interests of the Chinese people and is an important guarantee of peace in Asia and the wider world.

On the morning of October 19, 2011, I visited He Fang at home to celebrate his 89th birthday. Also in attendance at the celebration were Zi
Zhongyun, Qian Liqun, Ding Dong, Xing Xiaoqun, Lei Yi, Yang Jisheng,
Wu Si, Cui Weiping, and a number of other friends from academia. We
gathered around He Fang at his house and took turns expressing our best
wishes and respects. In my remarks, I recalled that I did not yet know He
Fang personally and had not yet read any of his writings when I wrote my
New Thinking on Relations with Japan essay. When I did eventually read
them, I realized that he had been expressing ideas very similar to my own
from a much earlier stage. Even though I never studied under him directly,
I said, I regarded myself as his pupil and wanted to take this opportunity
to acknowledge him as a mentor. With a laugh, He Fang kindly agreed to
recognize me as his protégé.

My New Thinking on Relations with Japan article was published in Beijing in December 2002, appearing in issue 6 of the bimonthly *Strategy and
Management*. One day not long after the article appeared, I was walking in
the grounds of the residential compound of the *People's Daily* when I happened to bump into Hu Xijin, editor-in-chief of the *Huanqiu Shibao (Global
Times)*. It was he who first told me that He Fang had previously outlined
ideas and analyses close to my own. Perhaps because of the pressure I was
under at the time, this news filled me with an immediate sense of respect
and affinity for He Fang and I became quite interested in him. A little later a
friend told me a little more about him: Now old, he had been responsible for
founding the CASS Institute of Japanese Studies and had been its first head.
Learning this made me more eager than ever to meet him.

Soon afterward, thanks to arrangements made by Ding Dong, Xing Xiaoqun, and other friends, I was able to visit He Fang at his home in the eastern
suburbs of Beijing. From this very first meeting I received such wise advice
and insights from him that it was like a breath of fresh air. I couldn't help
wishing I had had the opportunity to meet him earlier.

He presented me with a copy of his magnum opus, *Lun heping yu fazhan
shidai (On the Epoch of Peace and Development)*. This collection of essays
written over many years outlines his thinking on some of the leading issues of

our times in the context of international relations and was published in May 2000 by the World Affairs Press under Ministry of Foreign Affairs auspices. On the front page, he wrote: "To Comrade Ma Licheng: I look forward to your valuable criticisms." But how could I possibly criticize the work of such an esteemed senior figure? At that first meeting, I also met his wife, Song Yimin, who worked at the Ministry of Foreign Affairs as a high-level researcher until her retirement and who has many valuable opinions of her own on international relations and other subjects. After this first meeting, I visited He Fang at home several times and saw him at various other meetings. We gradually became close, and I used to ask him for his advice whenever I had an opportunity. And once I had his *On the Epoch of Peace and Development*, I read through the essays and learned much from him that way.

Now an elderly man with white hair and a beard, He Fang was born on October 18, 1922, in Lintong, Shanxi Province, and still speaks with a strong Shanxi accent. In 1938, when he was just sixteen, he joined the struggle against the Japanese invaders and studied at the Counter-Japanese Military and Political University in Yan'an, staying on at the school after graduation to assume a teaching position. After this he studied Russian at the Yan'an School of Foreign Languages, from which he graduated in 1945. In Yan'an, He Fang became acquainted with Zhang Wentian, a senior figure in the Communist Party leadership. Zhang became general secretary of the Party after the Zunyi Conference in January 1935, and at the beginning of 1938 concurrently took up a position as head of the propaganda department. In 1945, he was elected to the Central Committee at the 1st Plenary Session of the 7th Central Committee. Zhang was well known in the party as a brilliant leader, and people expected great things of him. He was well known for his intelligence and learning.

After the war against Japan was won, He Fang was sent to the northeast. In 1948, he became head of the propaganda department of the party committee in Liaoyang County, and in 1949 became deputy secretary of the Liaodong provincial committee youth work committee. At this time, Zhang Wentian was Liaodong provincial committee secretary, and when he learned of He Fang's talents as a writer he had him reassigned to come under his direct command and appointed him division head of the propaganda department of the regional party committee, where he was responsible for speeches and other writing tasks. In Liaodong, Zhang Wentian argued that individual capitalism was an organic component of the economy and suggested using foreign capital in exchanges with the developed capitalist economies. While carrying out his duties, he remained devoted to the idea of developing high standards of democracy and revealed plans to energize literature and the arts. Liaodong accordingly made great progress in all areas under Zhang's leadership. Zhang Wentian's approach had a profound influence on He Fang, who was then in his twenties. He believed that if this kind of thinking had been accepted from an early stage, China might subsequently have seen even more thorough efforts for liberalization than the reforms and opening up currently in force.

In 1950, Zhang Wentian left his position as provincial party secretary and entered the world of diplomacy. He Fang followed him to Beijing and began to devote himself to diplomatic work. In 1951, Zhang was appointed China's ambassador to the Soviet Union, and he hired He Fang to head the research department at the embassy. In this environment, He Fang received challenging training and valuable experience in the study of international issues, and several of the reports he wrote had a major impact in China. In 1954, He Fang followed Zhang from Moscow to Geneva to attend the Geneva Conference as a member of the Chinese delegation, which was headed by Zhou Enlai.

He Fang helped draft several speeches for Zhou Enlai, with whom he was often in contact during the conference, and Zhou Enlai was full of praise for his ability. When Zhang Wentian discovered this, he immediately sent He Fang back to the embassy in Moscow during a break in the conference proceedings and reported to Zhou Enlai that he would be unable to return to Geneva due to his work. Why did he do this? Zhang told He Fang, "The premier seems very interested in you and has great faith in your abilities. I'm worried that he might try to take you away from me." His fears seem to have been quite well founded. Gong Peng, who worked as an assistant to Zhou Enlai and was one of his foreign affairs secretaries, later told Song Yimin that Zhou Enlai had intended to hire He Fang for his own office staff. He Fang says today that if he had been transferred to work under Zhou Enlai at the time, his life would probably have taken a quite different course.

In 1955, Zhang Wentian returned to China to take up a position as deputy minister for foreign affairs and appointed He Fang as the deputy head of his office, with responsibility for writing articles and editing publications. Zhang also made He part of a "brain trust" that wrote articles and other pieces on international issues within the Central Committee. At the Lushan Conference[1] in 1959, Zhang Wentian made remarks critical of Mao's left-wing mistakes and the policy of the Great Leap Forward, which led to his being labeled a member of an anti-Party clique including Peng Dehuai, Huang Kecheng, Zhang Wentian, and Zhou Xiaozhou[2] and purged from his positions after being subjected to a barrage of criticism. He Fang also got caught up in the criticism that followed and was accused of belonging to a group of "rightist, opportunist elements." He was excluded from positions of political power for some twenty years. Zhang Wentian died in July 1976. In 1979, He Fang was rehabilitated. He left the Ministry of Foreign Affairs and joined an international affairs writing group within the Central Committee. In 1980, he was instructed to establish the CASS Institute of Japanese Studies, where he served as first head until 1988. After this, he was deputy chair of the international affairs issues research center at the State Council and was invited to teach at Peking University and Nankai University. He also served on the National Committee of the Chinese People's Political Consultative Conference for the party's 7th and 8th conferences and was elected an honorary member of CASS in 2006.

Since his retirement in 1999, he has continued to research international issues. He has made regular contributions to contemporary debates and has published widely on the question of what kind of age we are living in. Based on wide-ranging arguments, he has contended that the present age is ultimately one of peace and development and has had a major influence by encouraging people to reflect on the older understanding still adhered to by many on the left who argue that we are still in an age of revolution and war. Later, He Fang pulled his thoughts on these subjects together and compiled them into a lengthy piece titled *Ten Lectures on Issues Relating to an Age of Peace and Development*, which has been called his definitive work.

In addition to this, He Fang also opened up a new field of study—research and writing about Party history. He was from Yan'an and served as assistant to Zhang Wentian for many years, and his own life was full of vicissitudes due to conflicts within the Party, which meant that he naturally wished to set the record straight on a number of questions. In 2005, he published *A Historical Record of the Party* in two volumes; in 2007 came *Cong Yan'an yilu zoulai de fansi; He Fang zishu* (*Reflections on the Road from Yan'an: An Autobiography of He Fang*), again in two volumes, which received high praise from many quarters. In 2010, he published *He Fang tanshi yiren* (*He Fang Talks about History and Looks Back on the People He Has Known*), published by World Affairs Press, in which he wrote about his relationships with important politicians and scholars including Zhang Wentian, Liu Ying, Li Yimang, Meng Yongqian, Huan Xiang, Ji Chongwei, Li Shenzhi, and Chen Lemin.

These books by He Fang set down important historical facts about the history of the Party and represent important progress in restoring a true historical picture of the life and career of Zhang Wentian in particular. Most previous histories of the Party, for example, had tended to give only vague sketches on the leadership positions Zhang Wentian held from the beginning of 1935 to the end of the 1937, generally describing him in ambiguous terms simply as having "been in a position of overall responsibility." He Fang drew on voluminous research and personal knowledge to demonstrate clearly that Zhang Wentian was chosen as party secretary at the Zunyi Conference. He also analyzed the important role Zhang played at a number of crucial turning points in Party history and modern history generally, and thereby helped plug important gaps in our understanding. He Fang's important contributions to the research are widely recognized among scholars of Party history.

Over the course of a long and illustrious career, this CASS Institute of Japanese Studies founder has made many important contributions through his ideas and achievements in the field of Sino-Japanese relations. It is to be hoped that these major ideas will help open people's minds and play an important role in promoting the development of Sino-Japanese relations.

I have already mentioned He Fang's book *On the Epoch of Peace and Development*, a collection of twenty-two essays published in May 2000. Of the essays contained in this collection, five dealt with Sino-Japanese relations: "Great Power Relations in the Asian Region after the Cold War: On the New Triangular Relationship between the United States, China, and Japan," "Sino-Japanese Relations in the New Context," "Japan Faces Its Third Major Historical Choice," "Some Observations and Opinions on Sino-Japanese Relations," and "The Approaching Arrival of a New Stage in the Development of Sino-Japanese Relations."

In what follows, I would like to quote excerpts from these articles to illustrate his views. Let me first look at his evaluation of the current situation in Japan today. "Sino-Japanese Relations in the New Context" was originally a speech given before a findings committee on the international situation in 1988. In it, he asked:

> Is a revival of militarism likely in Japan? This must surely be described as unlikely, at least if we mean the kind of militarism that existed before the surrender. There are two reasons for this. First, the general situation does not allow it; and second, the development of Japan itself does not require it. Important changes took place in Japan in the years after the war, and pacifism and democracy have put down deep roots. Going back on these changes would not be easy. . . It is indeed true that the right-wing groups are making advances, but these groups are not in a position to realistically hope to achieve large numbers. From what I hear, there are around 200 such groups in Japan as a whole, but the number of people in each group is very small.

Japan, he wrote,

will need to lean on China's strengths diplomatically, while the two countries complement each other economically. Putting effort into Sino-Japanese friendship will also be useful in terms of stabilizing political conditions there. In Japan, relations with China are not only a foreign policy issue but are also closely linked with domestic politics. . . . This is the main reason and mainstream. Another aspect is that some people fear the rise of China to a position of prominence and power because of the differences in social systems and ideologies between the two countries. Additionally, the history of the prolonged resistance against Japan in the past means that Japan still tends to see China as a potential rival, and in some cases as an enemy state.

"Japan Faces Its Third Major Historical Choice" was a keynote address given at an international symposium in 1996. In it, he remarked that the Japanese economy had entered a slump in the 1990s and that numerous problems had become apparent.

For example, Japan has a large budget deficit, and the government does not have much leeway or wiggle room on the economy. Its savings rates are on a downward trend, and the society is aging . . . It is unlikely that the average growth rates of ten percent we once saw in the period of rapid economic growth will ever return. From the transitional situation it is in today, the economy can only hope to achieve medium growth, and Japan must be content to occupy a position as just a moderate economy in the context of global economic development.

"Some Observations and Opinions on Sino-Japanese Relations" was an article published in 1997. In it, he wrote:

After World War II, pacifism and democracy set down deep roots among the Japanese people, and it has become all but inconceivable that the country might return to despotism and embark on military invasions of foreign countries again. . . . At the end of the Cold War, Japan faced its third historic choice, following the Meiji Restoration and the changes of the immediate postwar years. The past several years have indicated clearly the path that Japan is following. As the recent past has shown, the greatest potential lies in adapting to the dominant world trends and becoming an important pole within the global structure—a major economic and political power exercising a degree of influence and strength at the center of the world economy and technological development.

Similarly, he wrote in "Sino-Japanese Relations in the New Context:"

> Democracy and pacifism have become deeply accepted in the hearts of the people, and this is one of the chief reasons why conservative factions have not been able to achieve their aim of changing the constitution, despite their best efforts over a period of more than 40 years. Of course, constitutional change may well take place if the appropriate conditions arise in the future, but the possibility of any revival of fascist rule in Japan has essentially been ruled out. Additionally, it goes without saying that following the path of peaceful development also contributes to improving the lives of the people and stabilizing the social order, as well as improving Japan's position in the international community.

He also writes that, "The important aim of Japan's state strategy must be to become a major political power."

Next, let us look at He Fang's discussion of the fundamental issues affecting political relations between China and Japan. In "Sino-Japanese Relations in the New Context," he suggests that there are three main problems relevant to political relations between China and Japan. The first is historical issues, the second is the Taiwan question, and the third is the disagreement regarding sovereignty over the Diaoyu/Senkaku Islands and the continental shelf.

How should the two countries deal with these three issues and eventually resolve them? Let us consider historical issues first. In our conversations, He Fang has always stressed that we must not make history the foundation or precondition for our future relationship. If history were inevitably the foundation for relations between two countries, he says, the United States and Great Britain would never have been able to build a positive relationship, and the same would have been true of the relationships between Britain and France, France and Germany, or Germany and Russia. All these countries fought brutal, destructive wars in the past. England and France once fought for 100 years—much longer than the wars between China and Japan. This wise approach represents a major insight that can help us to break through a shallow and short-sighted understanding of the issues and see the situation from a broader perspective. These ideas were formally compiled and published with the title "Breaking Through the Impasse between China and

Japan" in issue 29 of *Liaowang Dongfang Zhoukan* (Oriental Outlook) on July 15, 2004. The article consisted of He Fang answering questions about Sino-Japanese relations from Lin Chufang, a journalist with the magazine. He made the following points.

To handle the problems confronting the relationship between China and Japan skillfully, it will be crucial to reduce the importance attached to historical issues. It is impossible to build a positive relationship between any two countries while constantly harping on a reckoning of historical wrongs. For example, Russia once invaded and occupied 1.5 million km^2 of Chinese territory, but if China had insisted on recording this fact forever in the historical ledger—even if China had said that we didn't want the territory back but simply demanded that Russia admit the historical fact—there would have been no hope of ever building a positive relationship with either the Soviet Union or Russia. It was precisely because we did not insist on a black-and-white reckoning of the rights and wrongs of the issue that it eventually became possible for friendship to develop between China and the Soviet Union at a certain stage in history, and this in turn made possible the stronger relationship of friendship we enjoy with Russia today. Why should that kind of lingering bad blood exist between us and Japan today? Japan launched a sudden surprise attack on Pearl Harbor, after which Japan and the United States both devoted themselves to a bitter total war in the Pacific. But today? Americans certainly do not retain the same feelings about Japan that many people in China still have.

In "Some Observations and Opinions on Sino-Japanese Relations," He Fang argues that we need to face up to history with a forward-looking attitude. He continues:

> Following the long opposition, a basic understanding of the war is now shared by the mainstream factions in Japan and is accepted by most of the country's people. This view accepts that Japan invaded and colonized China and Korea and acknowledges the violence committed by the Japanese armed forces. (There is somewhat less acceptance of the idea that the Pacific War was also a war of aggression, however.) . . . Overall, it seems highly unlikely that this basic understanding of the war will undergo any major changes in the future.
>
> Internationally, the reactions against past Japanese invasions are growing milder all the time, and it is now difficult to see these reactions to history becoming a major factor in the future. The United States and the United Kingdom can hardly be called calculating in their attitudes to Japan. In ASEAN, India, and Burma, most peo-

ple already feel no resentment about the Japanese invasion (the situation albeit a little different in Singapore, where there is a large Chinese population and where massacres took place). In Malaysia, the Philippines, and Indonesia, many people, Mahathir in particular, have repeatedly said they are opposed to the idea of further Japanese apologies. Even in Vietnam, no commemoration was held to mark the fiftieth anniversary of victory against Japan. China alone, along with North and South Korea, continues to cling to this part of history, alternating in its attitude between criticism and engaging in negotiations.

Regarding Japan itself, he writes: "Among the government, the mass media, and most ordinary people, there is already widespread displeasure at the continued focus on historical issues, and many people feel resistance and aversion to criticism from foreign countries. In private sector exchanges, even some Goodwill Ambassadors have these feelings.

In this essay, He Fang recalls the attitude of Zhou Enlai and Chen Yi to historical issues and writes:

China's leaders have consistently stressed that the country's relationship with Japan must be forward-looking. For example, as early as 1961, Zhou Enlai noted that: "As many as 10,000 Japanese friends apologized when they met Chairman Mao, Chairman Liu, and myself. We said that these events already lay in the past. We must look forward and work to build friendly relations between China and Japan." In 1964, Vice Premier Chen Yi said: "The attitude of the Chinese government and the Chinese people to our relationship with Japan has always been to look forward rather than backward. Fixating excessively on the mistakes and criminal actions of the other side only serves to cause unhappiness and offense. . . . The dispute over the border between China and the Soviet Union was also prolonged because the Soviet side refused to accept that Czarist Russia had invaded Chinese territory and forced China to sign unequal treaties, but the problem was later quickly resolved once China decided to relax its insistence on the matter.

He continues:

Publicity and propaganda should respect both sides equally, taking care not to provoke or wound, and must take care not to provoke aversion among ordinary people on the other side or damage bilateral relations in any other way. . . . Even when carrying out patriotic education or criticizing the Japanese right wing or other anti-Chinese discourse, care must be taken to consider the overall situation and to ensure that the criticism is moderate and proportionate. Failure to do this will stir up nationalistic feelings in our own country, which can adversely affect political decision-making and lead to a kind of vicious circle.

Second is the issue of Taiwan. He Fang notes that the relatively long and close relationship between Taiwan and Japan means that the relationship with Japan has a significant influence in Taiwan but says that this does not cause serious problems because the Japanese government places a high priority on China's response.

The third issue is that of sovereignty over the Diaoyu/Senkaku Islands and the dispute over the continental shelf. Here He Fang agrees with Deng Xiaoping's proposal that the two sides shelve the issue and conduct joint development. The two sides should decide how to resolve it in the future depending on the circumstances at the time. He has also been critical of Japan. In conversations with me, he has suggested that some Japanese people are excessively devious and fond of tricks.

Finally, I want to introduce his overall strategy for resolving the issues pertaining to Sino-Japanese relations, as put forward in his "Sino-Japanese Relations in the New Context."

> The fundamentals of the relationship between China and Japan continue to be strong. Issues exist and disputes sometimes arise in the relationship, but this is nothing unusual. If both sides adhere strictly to the joint statement they made when relations were normalized, the Treaty of Peace and Friendship, and the four basic principles, it should not be too difficult to resolve any problems that may arise, or at least to ensure they do not adversely impact the development of a friendly and cooperative relationship. Friendship between China and Japan accords with the basic interests of the Chinese people and is an important guarantee of peace in Asia and the wider world.
>
> We should bear the banner of friendship that exists across generations of the Chinese people and work to ensure that, even when problems occur, they do not affect the relationship adversely. . . . The problem at present is that excessive emotion is causing people to question the diplomatic policy of developing Sino-Japanese friendship. Instead, some people argue that China needs to take a strong stance with regard to Japan, and some extremists argue that China should

demand war reparations from Japan again. But if China were to take a severe attitude against Japan politically and persistently fight in this way, the situation between the two countries would only get worse. This would not only directly affect the economic relationship but would also lead to heightened tensions in the region and would harm our attempts to develop the national economy and develop greater openness to the rest of the world. Another problem is that demanding reparations is simply unrealistic. We have already publicly renounced any right to further reparations, and we must keep our word to ensure we do not lose the trust of the international community. If China ever did make such a proposal, Japan would certainly not only refuse but would not even take the idea seriously. And where would that leave us? In effect, the only result would be to harm the relationship and damage our international standing for no practical benefit at all. We must deal with this kind of emotional thinking very carefully, arguing against it and providing leadership and explanations. As Lenin said, we must not allow the temporary sentiment of the times to influence our policy.

NOTES

1. Refers to the expanded session of the Politburo held in Lushan, Jiangxi Province, in the summer of 1959, and the 8th Plenum of the CCP Central Committee that followed. The most important event at Lushan was the public disclosure of a letter written by Defense Minister Peng Dehuai to Mao Zedong in which he criticized the Great Leap Forward, resulting in the purging and harsh criticism of Peng and his supporters as a "military clique" and members of a "rightist opportunistic anti-Party faction." After this meeting, it became dangerous to criticize Mao in public, leading to a personality cult around the leader that saw the Great Leap Forward carried forward uncritically, leading to the Cultural Revolution.

2. Peng Dehuai (defense minister), Huang Kecheng (chief of staff and member of the Secretariat of the party's Central Committee), Zhang Wentian (first vice minister of foreign affairs), and Zhou Xiaozhou (first party committee secretary for Hunan Province) all opposed the policy of the Great Leap Forward and were labeled the "Peng-Huang-Zhang-Zhou anti-party clique." They were purged from their positions at the Lushan Conference and stripped of power.

CHAPTER FIVE

Emotions Must Not Be Allowed to Dictate Policy:
Two Great Supporters of the New Thinking

The fundamental idea behind the new thinking is that our relation-ship with Japan should be dealt with from a position grounded sol-idly in the strategic interests of the state and that emotions should not be allowed to dictate policy.

After the controversy caused by my article "New Thinking on Relations with Japan," published in issue 6, 2002, of the magazine *Strategy and Management*, two well-known scholars in Beijing published articles of their own supporting my ideas for a new approach to our relationship with Japan and developing the argument from their own perspectives. Both articles attracted widespread attention. The two men in question were Professor Shi Yinhong of Renmin University of China and Feng Zhaokui, formerly deputy chair at the CASS Institute of Japanese Studies. Wang Zhongyi, editor of the Japanese edition of *People's China*, a magazine published by the China International Publishing Group, jokingly called us "the Big Three of the New Thinking." Each of us had his own points of approach and perspectives, and our arguments were not the same in all respects, but we certainly shared something in common insofar as all three of us were writing on behalf of a new approach to relations with Japan.

In addition to being a professor at the Renmin University of China School of International Studies and head of the university's Center for American Studies, Shi Yinhong also serves as chairman of the Chinese Society of American History. Since February 2011 he has served as a Counselor of the State Council. In April 2003, he published an article titled "Sino-Japanese Rapprochement and 'Diplomatic Revolution'" in issue 2 of the bimonthly *Strategy and Management*. This was followed by further essays outlining the new thinking on the relationship with Japan in more detail, among them "Strategic New Thinking Needed to Improve Relations with Japan" and "Japan's Quest for a Position as a 'Normal Country' and Sino-Japanese Relations." These articles continue to provoke a major response.

The essay "Sino-Japanese Rapprochement and 'Diplomatic Revolution'" consisted of four parts. The essay opens with a summary full of alarm and warning:

> For the past few years, prolonged and serious tensions in China's relations with Japan have been a source of particular concern in China's relations with the outside world. Although relatively few in number, these represent areas that are already causing or threaten to cause

problems; all of them require urgent consideration. Of particular concern as a prominent tension that presents the most serious dangers is the atmosphere of animosity and mutual dislike that has been growing rapidly in recent years between large parts of the populations of China and Japan—what we might with some exaggeration almost call a national or ethnic antagonism between the two countries. Truly, as one commentator recently wrote in the subtitle to an important essay on the subject, we are confronted once again by "the malaise that exists between the peoples of China and Japan."

(This is a reference to my "New Thinking on Relations with Japan: The malaise that exists between the peoples of China and Japan.")

The second part of the essay argues that if this mutual dislike and animosity between the two countries continues unchecked, it could lead to serious dangers for China. "The Chinese mainland, which is frequently at odds with the United States and Taiwan and could easily find itself at odds with India too, would find it unbearable if it were forced into a relationship of antagonism with Japan." China, he argued, needs to base its approach on the principle of a concentrated strategy. In other words, China should distinguish between problems and priorities in international affairs and prioritize its dealings with important countries. To this end, China should make rapprochement with Japan a reality and concentrate its energy on responding to pressure from the United States. The basic policy of the United States is to thwart China's rise to prominence. For the past few years, China has been putting up with humiliation in its relationship with the United States while shouldering great responsibilities and has paid two major prices for this. First, its freedom of maneuverability in its relationship with the United States is limited. Second, the public regards the government's American policy as weak, resulting in a lack of public support for the government's foreign policy.

Under the circumstances, China needs to adjust the framework of its diplomacy based on strategic flexibility, freeing itself from its passive position in its relationship with the United States and strengthening the "levers" of its American policies. What needs to be emphasized here is that rapprochement with Japan is an important choice—one that can be described as a "diplomatic revolution" for China. Although Japan is allied with the United States, China and Japan are nevertheless neighbors and Japan is surely desirous of better ties with China in consideration of economic cooperation and improved relations with other Asian countries. Bringing about rapprochement between China and Japan would almost certainly enable China to put itself in a less passive position in its relationship with the United States. As

I have already said, being closer to Japan would bring China major benefits. In reality, China needs improved Sino-Japanese relations more than Japan does. This requires the Chinese government to work positively and proactively to achieve rapprochement with Japan based on the idea of developing a new cornerstone for its foreign policy based on strategic decisions, thereby improving China's diplomatic position and security environment.

The third part of the essay proposes five things that China should do to bring about rapprochement. First, on the official expressions of remorse and apology that the Japanese government has already made over quite a long period with regard to Japan's past invasion of China and the criminal acts it committed at that time, China should probably be satisfied with the current extent of these apologies, unless the Japanese government makes dramatic retractions or backslides on this issue. This means that the disputes over Sino-Japanese history should be struck from the foreign policy agenda with Japan for now, which at the same time means setting aside any propaganda or special pleading on this subject by the government or other entities.

Second, China should work to massively increase Japan's exports to and investment in China to stem the decline of Japan's economy. At the same time, based on its strategic needs, China should make appropriate concessions in its trade relations with Japan. The Chinese government should ensure that top leaders speak frequently in public to express proper thanks for the vast amounts of money that Japan has offered in assistance since the start of China's reform and opening up policy.

Third, China should take a tolerant policy regarding Japan's wish to increase its military strength. The center of China's strategy is preparation for a possible war with Taiwan, which means working to achieve speedy modernization of our military. China should take care not to get carried away in its pronouncements about Japanese military power. Saying too much can bring harm but can bring no advantage. There is a need to construct a mechanism as quickly as possible for mutual trust between the two countries on the military side. On this question, China should have no illusions; simply doing nothing is not an option. We must explain repeatedly to Japan that China has no expansionist aims in strengthening its military capability.

Fourth, China should encourage and invite Japan to get involved in important international issues. China should regard Japan as a great power—both in the sense of the major economic power it is today and as the major political power force it will be in Asia in the future. Based on the principle that great powers should prioritize coordination and cooperation and avoid conflict, the two sides must handle their relationship within an international context. Recently, there have been two important issues in particular. The first involves strengthening cooperation with Japan to promote peace in connection with the North Korea situation. The second is to coordinate with Japan to avoid clashes in the process of economic integration with ASEAN.

Fifth, in relation to reforming the United Nations Security Council, China should take an unbiased view of requests from countries like Japan and India to become permanent members of the Security Council and should not make special demands of Japan. Perhaps China should even go one step further and positively support Japan's efforts to become a permanent member of the Security Council.

In the fourth part of the article, Shi Yinhong writes that rapprochement between China and Japan—the five points I have just summarized—would represent a diplomatic revolution that would come at no great price and would neither damage China's fundamental interests nor require us to give up protecting our own security. The five cither serve to achieve a strategic aim and avoid impediments while creating a win-win relationship or represent the avoidance of negatives. Some things may be impossible to prevent entirely, but in those cases, we should not try desperately to prevent the unavoidable. Rather, we should allow matters to take their course and look to turn the development into a positive resource. Certainly, a number of points raised in this article differ substantially from the policies that China has followed with regard to Japan in the past, and in this sense his proposals would certainly represent a diplomatic revolution.

I should perhaps say a few words here about the concept of diplomatic revolution as used in Shi Yinhong's article. This concept has particular implications and is a specialist term used by academics in the field of international relations. The term dates back to the period of the War of Austrian Succession, which lasted from 1740 to 1748, when a dramatic change took place in the relationships among the various European powers as a result of a sudden and dramatic alignment of interests. The term is often used to refer to a sudden shift in the relationship between two or more powers from one of animosity to one of alliance and friendship. Shi Yinhong uses the expression to refer to a dramatic change in the relationship between two countries that have opposed each other until a dramatic rapprochement occurs. For example, the visit of US President Nixon to China in 1972 would represent a diplomatic revolution. Gorbachev's visit to China in 1989 would be another example.

On July 15, 2003, *Liuxuesheng Xinwen* (*Ryugakusei Shimbun*), a newspaper published in Tokyo for Chinese students living in Japan, carried an article by Shi Yinhong with the title "Strategic New Thinking Needed to Improve Relations with Japan." In this article, Shi Yinhong argues that it is vital to speak clearly about two major points and address the impasse between China and Japan on historical issues. The first is to organize a set of strategic principles. (I have already considered this.) The second is to ensure that while we do not forget history, nor do we become obsessed with history. The article argues that the most important aspect of our policy is not history but rather taking a clear and realistic view of the interests of the state and its development. To avoid impediments to our policy and implement China's great state strategy more effectively, we should probably put historical issues aside for now and accept that it is all right to leave these issues until such time as they can be truly resolved. We must not take the view that an enemy in the past must be an enemy for all eternity. Major changes have happened in China, in Japan, and in the wider world as well. We must not allow our memories of the past to impose themselves on the way we observe the present or our visions for the future. The most important lesson to be gained from our relationship with Japan during the period from the Sino-Japanese War to the end of the War of Resistance is that we must stimulate the development of the state, pursue our own priorities with determination, and become a strong nation adapted to the historical currents of the times.

A structural change is underway in the relationship between China and Japan. China is aiming to become a strong and powerful state while Japan is aiming to become a "normal country." The question of how to guarantee eternal peace between the two countries is the most central problem in the relationship. One aspect that is particularly difficult to handle at present is the influence of historical issues on public opinion in China. The government and academics must take the lead in guiding public opinion to become more forward-looking and must not drown in the emotions and feelings of the masses. As Hu Jintao once rightly said, we need to "take a long-term perspective and focus on the big picture."

The two countries should deal with their relationship from a big-picture perspective, promoting stability in Asia and fostering world peace. China today does not need emotional thinking. The focal points of strategic relations with Japan are as follows. First, preventing any conflict between the two nations in the long term. Second, working to build strategic mutual trust at the appropriate levels. And third, strategic cooperation that will benefit stability, peace, and prosperity in Asia (for example, dealing with the North Korea issue). This means both sides working together for peace and shared prosperity and both achieving appropriate international positions. In Sino-Japanese relations, the remorse and apology that the Japanese government has already expressed on historical issues is the minimum base line from which it must not seriously retreat. If the Japanese government does retreat in a major way from its position on this issue, it will be necessary to rethink our relations with Japan.

On September 5, 2003, Shi Yinhong published an essay in the Hong Kong newspaper *Ta Kung Pao* with the title "Japan's Pursuit of a Position as a Normal Country and Sino-Japanese Relations." Shi Yinhong's analysis suggested that there are several characteristics a country must possess in order to be considered a "normal country." First, it must have an independent foreign policy. Second, it must have a normal relationship with its local surroundings. (In Japan's case, several outstanding historical issues still cloud its relations with its neighbors.) Third, it must have an accurate understanding of its own past, present, and future—but here again, several problems exist with Japan's understanding of itself. Fourth, it must have its own healthy characteristics that are particular to that country. Fifth, it must bear an appropriate level of responsibility in global and regional politics. Sixth, it must have a normal position appropriate to that country. On several of these points, Japan can still not be said to be wholly satisfactory.

On the question of historical issues between China and Japan, Shi Yinhong wrote:

> Resolving the problems of history requires confidence and tolerance. Resolving the problems of history ultimately means the Japanese people having a correct understanding and awareness of Japan's history and of the path the Japanese people as a whole have followed in the past. In this sense, it is perhaps fair to say that, in the end, it is the Japanese people who must resolve the problem. On historical issues, as well as continuing to fight where necessary in line with our interests and with moderation, we should also look further ahead and work proactively and determinedly to contribute to achieving the historical conditions that will make a positive solution to the problem of historical issues possible. Particularly important is the need to be a more positive influence among the Japanese population than at present.

On this subject, Zhao Quansheng, a professor at the American University School of International Service who has made several important contributions to the study of Japanese foreign policy, recently published a perceptive piece that is worth quoting.

> Historical issues are just one of several issues that exist and cannot be said to occupy a position of chief importance among those important

factors. We need to think clearly about our priorities. If we (China) are to carry out economic cooperation with Japan, for example, and work with Japan on security issues, we need to demand that Japan support the "one China" principle. These issues are just as important as resolving the historical issues. Of course, all of these issues are related in various ways to other issues. Any approach that leads to these other issues being neglected because of the history problem is likely to prove invalid and inadequate.

China is a genuine great power. If our attitude, from the government down to the regular people, is in accord with logic and we have relatively good policies, it should be possible to have a substantial influence on Japan's future.

The publication in short succession of my "New Thinking on Relations with Japan" followed by Shi Yinhong's "Sino-Japanese Rapprochement and the 'Diplomatic Revolution'" caused widespread debate and controversy. In June 2003, the recognized authority Feng Zhaokui entered the debate in support of the new thinking, offering insightful commentary on the new thinking from a variety of angles. Shi Yinhong and I are not specialists in Japanese studies, but Feng Zhaokui, born in 1940, has a long career as a Japan specialist behind him. For many years, he was the deputy chair of the CASS Institute of Japanese Studies. After retiring from that position, he served as an advisor to the Chinese Association for Japanese Economic Studies and as deputy head of the Society of Sino-Japanese Relations History. He is also an honorary member of the CASS.

During the year from August 2003 to June 2004, Feng Zhaokui wrote a succession of articles, all of them clear, thorough, and packed full of insight. He published nine articles in this time commenting on the new thinking. The longest of these were major studies some 30,000 characters long. Some of them were reorganized versions based on his lectures, but these nine essays helped carry the debate forward in new directions and helped make the implications of the new thinking much richer.

The most important of the nine pieces were the first four. Let's look at the first one first. "A Consideration of the New Thinking on Relations with Japan," some 30,000 characters long, appeared in issue 4, 2003, of the bimonthly *Strategy and Management*. He opens by asking "Does the Sino-Japanese relationship need a new thinking?" Then he writes:

> The answer to that question is Yes. New thinking is certainly needed if China and Japan are to break out of the current stalemate that has

arisen as a result of the almost unending political tensions that cloud the relationship. New thinking is certainly needed if they are to emerge from the current deadlock and push ahead with dialogue and achieve further development in the political, economic, cultural, and security fields.

He points out that the new thinking is an idea that had been incubating for some time in Chinese academic circles. Since 1999, a lively debate has been underway regarding relations with Japan in international relations research institutions and among academics studying Japan. The fact that the new thinking on Japan was publicized after the 16th National Congress in 2002 demonstrated that China had thoroughly freed up thinking in the field of foreign policy and was a concrete manifestation of a new school of thought that would seek the truth based on the facts, develop in accordance with the times, and open up a new fulcrum for China's foreign policy. It was a concrete manifestation of the constantly increasing democratization of Chinese politics and its scientific policy-making and showed how this now extends to the field of foreign policy. The constructive new idea extolled at the 16th National Congress, which declared that China would seek to build positive relations with its neighbors and make them partners, had now become a concrete reality.

The article consists of three parts. In the first, he writes on the five principles of the new thinking as follows. First, the most important principle is state interests; emotions must never substitute for policy. China has cause for historic resentment with all the major Western powers, but if we are going to squabble about the injustices of the past, how can we justify describing our policy as one of openness to the world? In designing our international strategy, we should follow the words of Deng Xiaoping, who said: "When considering relations between two countries, it is important to build the relationship on the strategic interests of the state . . . and not indulge in arguments about the rights and wrongs of this or that historical injustice."

Second, boosting productivity and ensuring the economic interests of the state should be the very core of our most important principles. We should enhance our productivity through the development of our relationship with Japan in pursuit of the economic interests of the state. This is in pursuit of the "three represents"[1] and is the core principle for dealing with China's relationship with Japan.

Third, China should regard protecting the peaceful development of the region and the wider world as its noble mission. The relationship between China and Japan benefits both sides and peace is in the interest of Asia.

A conflict situation would not only damage both sides but would also harm the rest of Asia. Both countries have a responsible to Asia and the world for developing the Sino-Japanese relationship. China and Japan must not betray the hopes of Asia again.

Fourth, the new thinking represents the inheritance and development of what has always been CCP policy on Japan. From the time of Mao Zedong and Zhou Enlai to the present, China has always placed great importance on relations with Japan. The Joint Communique of 1972, the Treaty of Peace and Friendship of 1978, and the Joint Declaration of 1998—all three of these documents embodied the constant principle of the development of the bilateral relationship. The new thinking is therefore built on the foundations of our policy to date and represents a new development of this in accordance with the changing times.

Fifth, the Sino-Japanese relationship represents the process by which the two sides influence each other. Just as it is impossible to clap with just one hand, Japan too needs a similar kind of new thinking on its relationship with China. Since China has modified its policy on Japan and taken the first step, it appears to be more proactive. But in this context, there is no need for calculations about who made the first move and who followed, or for any concern about potential disadvantages that might accrue from taking too proactive a lead. As a major power, we should look at the situation from a broad perspective, hold a clear image of the big picture in our hearts, and continue to maintain a proactive attitude.

In the second part of the essay, Feng Zhaokui offers nine characteristics of the new thinking on relations with Japan. First, it is adapted to the latest changes in the international situation and looks for a new point of agreement between China and Japan on their strategic interests. The relationship between the two countries now stands on new foundations to respond to the post–Cold War world and the rise of terrorism and other new threats. These issues include, for example, financial stability, environmental protection, drug smuggling, international crime, and pandemic disease. On the security front, there is no need to continue to view Japan's wish to become a military power or a normal country as tantamount to a revival of militarism, as has sometimes been the case in the past. Whether addressing a new threat or an old one, everything should be done in the pursuit of peace and development. "If these two great neighbors allow a war to break out between them again, they will both surely be ruined. And this would be a pitiful defeat. It is fair to say that avoiding a war between China and Japan represents the largest point of agreement between China and Japan in terms of the strategic interests of the Sino-Japanese relationship."

Second, it accurately grasps the position of the Sino-Japanese relationship within the trilateral relations between China, Japan, and the United States. For Japan to side with the United States in a situation in which there is no confrontation between China and the United States is not something that China need be antagonistic about, and the Japan-US alliance is not something that obstructs the pursuit of shared interests in Sino-Japanese relations. There is nothing contradictory about working to develop China's relations with Japan and with the United States at the same time.

Third, Japan's wish to become a major political power is something made possible by the growing multipolarity of international relations. During the controversy over China's application to join the WTO, Japan gave strong support to China's position. When the Western powers were imposing sanctions on China after the protests of 1989,[2] Japan took the lead in lifting sanctions and resuming its loans to China. At the time, China's leaders praised Japan for its boldness.

Fourth, it continues to press ahead with the development of economic and trade relations between China and Japan and with increasing the number of large-scale cooperation projects.

Fifth, it sets out to resolve historical issues while developing the important aspects of the relationship. Deng Xiaoping said, "We must develop the relationship and continue in eternal friendship, and this is more important than all the other issues that exist between us." We must not make finding a solution to the history issues a precondition for developing the relationship between our two countries. When numerous issues exist between China and Japan, it would be wrong to make resolving this one problem a precondition for resolving the others and making progress with dialogue. It is only by continuing constantly to develop Sino-Japanese relations that it will be possible to find a solution to the problem of historical issues, and not the other way around. We should not make historical issues the key to developing our wider relationship. Finding solutions to the issues affecting Sino-Japanese relations requires a process; we must deal with people with generosity and tolerance and earn the other side's heartfelt respect and admiration.

Sixth, it realizes that we must work to evaluate the current state of Japan accurately and objectively. Japan leads the world on many indices—the competitiveness of its science and technology, manufacturing industries, the education of its people, environmental protection, public hygiene, the quality of its products, and more. We also need to stick to the facts in evaluating the development of the relationship since the normalization of diplomatic ties. Although it is important to recognize that many areas of tension remain, we should not ignore the fact that there have also been many close exchanges. The prospect of boundless development for the Sino-Japanese relationship exists, and with effort we should be able to avoid the kind of tragedy that tensions could cause.

Seventh, the new thinking realizes that Japan is the leading example of a country that has succeeded in industrializing and catching up with the West. As two states both in the process of reform and change, China and Japan should learn from each other's experiences. Even if other countries praise our burgeoning economy and other achievements, we must not become conceited and proud. We must maintain an attitude of humility in the international community and learn from the strengths of other countries.

Eighth, China and Japan should be tolerant and forgiving of each other and must avoid becoming oversensitive to criticism from the other side, or harboring suspicions that everything the other side says has some malicious intent. When someone, having considered the benefits of the state, is bold enough to make proposals with regard to diplomatic foreign policy issues, the most sensitive area of policy, that person must not be accused of being a "traitor," "betrayer of the nation," "Japanese shill," or "sucking up to Japan." This is unhealthy and unhelpful ideology.

Ninth, we should promote the development of private-sector exchanges. Cultural, media, educational, and athletic exchanges can be effective ways of strengthening the development of the relationship between the two countries.

The third part of the essay discusses how economic benefit is the foundation and core where Chinese and Japanese interests intersect. In this section, he discusses the importance of economic cooperation between China and Japan in seven areas, including trade and investment, China's exports to Japan, Japan's ODA to China, regional cooperation, cooperation in the energy conservation and environmental protection fields, and intangible exchanges in fields such as scientific research and cultural exchanges, arguing that economic cooperation between the two countries has given rise to a win-win relationship that benefits both sides and forms a truly strong and robust foundation for the bilateral relationship.

Feng Zhaokui's second essay was "Reconsidering the New Thinking on Relations with Japan," which appeared in issue 5, 2003, of *Strategy and Management*. Whereas the essay I have summarized above discussed the content of the new thinking on a comprehensive level, this second essay responded to five issues that have arisen in the course of the controversy and debate.

The first of these issues is the relationship between the new thinking and history issues. Feng Zhaokui notes that Japanese still do not have a satisfactory understanding on the history issues and that finding a solution to the problem is extremely complicated and difficult as a result. It will be necessary to proceed from two directions at once—to work to find a true resolution to the problem of history issues while also moving ahead pro-actively to advance the relationship. Solving the problem of history issues and developing the bilateral relationship reinforce each other and can be pursued at the same time. Progress on history issues may have stalled, but the historical awareness problem will ultimately be resolved by the Japanese themselves through education.

The second issue addressed is the relationship between the new thinking and more traditional thinking on the subject. Feng writes that Mao Zedong and Zhou Enlai's Japan policy was based on keeping the big picture always in mind and looking toward the future, and that it united principles and flex-ibility. This involved "making enemies into friends, and changing passive factors into active factors," and great results were achieved thereby. Today, the new thinking on relations with Japan has achieved a new development in line with the times, both inheriting these old traditions and adapting them to the changing times.

The third issue concerns the connection between relations with Japan and total overall national power. On this subject, Feng Zhaokui reminds us that the history of Sino-Japanese relations over the past 2,000 years has not been so much that of a strong China and a weak Japan as it has been that of a strong Japan and a weak China. Today, as China's overall national strength increases, the Sino-Japanese relationship is confronted by an unprecedented situation in which both sides are strong at the same time. How will the two sides deal with this situation? A process of adaptation is needed on both sides. The proposal of this new thinking on relations with Japan therefore represents a situation in which both sides are looking for a way to deal with this new balance in the relationship. Central to this is thinking that gives greater priority to the influence and impact of soft power. Today's China does not need to gain retribution over its enemies from the past, and there would be no reason for such a thing. Seeking to respond to power with power will only cause mutual damage and destroy both sides.

The fourth issue is that of the relationship between the new thinking on Japan and new thinking on Asia. Feng Zhaokui hopes that the new thinking on relations in Japan might be developed into a new thinking on relations with Asia as a whole. This new thinking on Asia would actively promote a new regionalism with Asian characteristics and build a mechanism for regional cooperation with Asian characteristics in such fields as economics, environmental protection, information, and security. This would help bring about the emergence of Asia as a superpower in the twenty-first century.

The fifth issue concerns the relationship between academic research and government policy. Feng Zhaokui says that although the arguments of academics do not represent government policy, they can nevertheless have an influence and deserve to be treated as reference points for the government to consult in drawing up policies. The debate and controversy stirred up by the publication of the articles about the new thinking on relations with Japan drew major attention in both China and Japan, and in other countries as well. There can be little doubt that this debate will stimulate academic research in international relations, helping the field develop and leading to positive results. The debate was therefore very significant.

Feng Zhaokui's third essay, "Considering the New Thinking on Relations with Japan for a Third Time," appeared in issue 6, 2003, of *Strategy and Management*. Feng clearly believes that the Sino-Japanese relationship has entered an era of new development, and this essay discusses the significance of this fact from five different angles.

First, this new era in Sino-Japanese relations is one that is adapted to the trend toward an era of peace and development. In this essay, he argues that peace and development are the main issues of concern. China and Japan have a shared interest in defending peace and development in Asia. But at the same time, the prevailing heightened feelings of nationalist identification are pressuring the government to be tough on Japan, leading to a vicious circle. If nationalism is allowed to grow unchecked, it may reignite smoldering embers and cause another outbreak of war. If China and Japan were to go to war, the United States would reap all the benefits without having to do anything but sit and watch. The government must therefore ensure that it does not allow national policy to be swayed by the emotions of the people, and informed opinion must not allow emotion to take the place of considered thought. Of course, Japan needs to resolve the issue of integrating itself into Asia. Feng raises a good question in his essay. If we oppose the US-Japan alliance, and also oppose the idea of Japan's becoming an independent, autonomous nation, then in what direction is Japan supposed to turn?

Second, this new era in Sino-Japanese relations is adapted to the trend toward economic globalization. The Chinese and Japanese economies are both massive, and the level of trade between them has increased dramatically, putting the two countries in a relationship of mutual and inseparable interdependence. The two economies now work to reinforce and support each other. However, this economic closeness has not been matched in politics, where the relationship remains chilly. Japanese investment in large-scale projects in China has suffered from the impact of the political relationship. For example, in 2003, the question of whether Japanese invest-ment should be allowed in the building of a high-speed rail link between Beijing and Shanghai caused a major controversy. This demonstrates how nationalistic feeling can easily damage economic cooperation between the two nations if it is allowed to get out of hand. Feng Zhaokui's essay criti-cizes the calls to boycott Japanese goods—calls that were a popular rallying cry during the anti-Japanese demonstrations that swept through several cit-ies in 2003—saying that in practice they amounted to calling for a boycott of Chinese goods.

Third, the new era in Sino-Japanese relations is in accord with the global trend toward greater unification of regional economies. There is a global trend toward greater economic cooperation within regions. Of the world's leading nations by GDP, only China, Japan, and South Korea were not part of any regional free-trade agreement in 2003. In this sense, progress in East Asia is lagging that in Europe, the Americas, and Africa. Premier Wen Jia-bao suggested the three countries look into establishing a free-trade area, but this would require a decision among all three countries involved. In order to adapt to global trends, China, Japan, and South Korea should cast aside their old resentments and not allow differences among them to interfere with regional economic cooperation.

Fourth, the new era in Sino-Japanese relations is in accord with the global trend toward a revolution in science and technology. Japan is the big-gest supplier of technology to China's industrialization. Japan has provided China with technology, investment, markets, and official development assistance, as well as offering its advanced management experience, and has played a major role in China's industrialization. China has a continuing need for advanced technology. Developing economic and trade cooperation with Japan is an effective way of accelerating the development of China's productivity, as well as speeding up the development of Chinese culture and helping to improve the standard of living of the people.

Fifth, Sino-Japanese relations: New Age and New Thinking. Feng Zhaokui says that the new thinking on relations with Japan was born out of the theory and practice of Chinese diplomacy and foreign policy. The fun-damental idea behind the new thinking is that our relationship with Japan should be dealt with from a position grounded solidly in the strategic inter-ests of the state and that emotions should not be allowed to dictate policy. In Marxism, productivity is held to have a decisive impact on relations of pro-duction; developing production is therefore fundamental to the interests of the country. Recently, some people have been brandishing various theories to make the import of Japanese technology a political issue, and others have caused problems by arguing about whether this or that policy or person is patriotic or traitorous to the nation. This is outdated ideology-first thinking that runs counter to the interests of the state. It is unworthy of consideration.

On December 25, 2003, Feng Zhaokui gave a speech on the New Thinking on Relations with Japan at a conference held at Waseda University in Tokyo. His fourth essay on the new thinking brought together the contents of this speech in printed form. The speech opened with a joke. He said:

> This spring, I read two essays about China's relationship with Japan that appeared in the Chinese magazine *Strategy and Management*— one by Ma Licheng and the other by Shi Yinhong. Their essays caused quite a stir in Japan. By a happy accident, their names when read in the Japanese style become Ba-san and Ji-san, making them sound almost exactly like the Japanese words for grandma and grandpa. Given this, it was perhaps inevitable they would rise to fame in Japan. Of course, these two articles also caused tremendous controversy and debate in China. The response was especially strong online, and in extreme cases they were cursed as traitors to their people and the nation. While I was taken aback by the ferocity of this reaction, this also caused me to reflect on all the many background problems in Sino-Japanese relations that this reaction highlighted. The articles by Ma Licheng and Shi Yinhong had a big impact on me, and after thinking about them for a while I came to feel that both sides need a new thinking.

Feng Zhaokui said that developing a new thinking on relations with Japan was a process. It was a process of repeated thinking about relations with Japan by scholars, diplomats, and other informed intellectuals in China, a process that was still underway, and that the road was a winding path full of difficulties.

Feng Zhaokui's idea is that the economy is the central issue in the new thinking on relations with Japan and that economic issues should be at the center of our approach. The economic relationship forms the foundation for the wider relationship. If China and Japan make economic development the central issue, the economies of the two countries will become mutually dependent. By contrast, historical and political issues are extremely complex. On top of this, the two countries' values differ, which means that at least for some time it is difficult to see a solution to these issues. But the cooling of political relations is having an impact on the economic relationship, and heated nationalistic feelings are likely to have a particularly damaging impact on economic cooperation. Both countries must continue to address the need to find a solution to the historical and political problems causing the current chill in relations. Prime Minister Koizumi's visits to Yasukuni Shrine while in office are unhelpful to the development of the bilateral relationship. China's new thinking on Japan is one structural component of China's new thinking on its overall diplomacy. China's new thinking on Japan should work in concord with Japanese new thinking on China, for only then will even bigger effects become possible.

Feng Zhaokui made the following proposals.

1. Both countries should discuss measures to prevent the phenomenon whereby some people in both countries feel resentment and antagonism toward the other side, and both must work to prevent the continuing deterioration of public opinion.
2. Both countries must deal correctly with the relationship between economics and politics, and between the private sector and the government, and must not allow the economy to be turned into a political issue. At the same time, both sides should develop small and medium-sized human channels or contacts and enable them to perform a role in helping to improve the bilateral relationship.
3. The two countries should establish a contact and coordination mechanism for dealing with any abrupt outbreak of an incident.
4. Steps should be taken to strengthen media and educational exchanges between the two countries, and work should be done to make better use of students studying abroad.
5. Steps should be taken to harness the boosting effect between Sino-Japanese relations and multilateral international relations. For example, China and Japan are both strengthening their cooperative relationships with ASEAN, and this should be used to accelerate the development of Sino-Japanese relations.

At the end of his lecture, Feng Zhaokui quoted from a talk given by former prime minister Nakasone Yasuhiro in 2003. Nakasone said: "In Asia, Japan must build a mechanism for cooperation with China and ASEAN. If Japan and China clash over ASEAN issues, Japan will not be able to achieve a single thing." Feng said that this represented constructive thinking for Japanese diplomacy and accorded with one type of new thinking as he saw it.

Following the publication of essays by Shi Yinhong and Feng Zhaokui, and the appearance of essays by other academics expressing their support, the New Thinking on Relations with Japan began to establish itself as a relatively well-ordered system of thought.

NOTES

1. This idea, unveiled by Jiang Zemin in 2000, holds that the CCP should represent "the requirements for developing China's advanced productive forces, the orientation of China's advanced culture, and the fundamental interests of the overwhelming majority of the Chinese people." Following this, private business entrepreneurs were allowed to join the Party. The Three Represents are included in the preamble to the national Constitution and the constitution of the Communist Party and are considered an important part of Party ideology, alongside Marxism-Leninism, Mao Zedong Thought, and Deng Xiaoping Theory.

2. This refers to the Tiananmen Square troubles of 1989. Because reporting and research on the events is subject to strict controls in China, phrases such as "the disturbances" or "political unrest" are often used. At the time, the Western countries imposed economic sanctions on China in response to its use of military force to suppress pro-democracy demonstrations by students and other civilians. The visit to China by Japanese Prime Minister Kaifu Toshiki in 1991 drew attention as the first visit by a "Western" leader since the demonstrations.

Don't Hide behind Patriotism:
Was I Really Beaten Up in Hong Kong?

Since publishing my essay "New Thinking on Relations with Japan,"
I have been beset by false rumors that have achieved wide distribution online. This chapter mentions just a few typical examples.
I want to make it clear that I retain the right to take legal action
against people who start such false rumors and the platforms that
help them proliferate.

At the beginning of 2004, I was working as a commentator for Phoenix Television in Hong Kong. During a business trip to Beijing, I met Luo Rongxing, a former colleague from the *People's Daily*. Almost immediately his first words to me were: "Have you been to the hospital to have your injuries looked after?" At first, I wasn't sure what he meant. "What injuries do you mean?" I asked. "I heard you were beaten up in Hong Kong?" he said. I laughed it off. "That's just a false rumor," I said. "Hong Kong is an open, civilized place. Why would I get beaten up there?"

Luo was referring to a photograph that had appeared on a certain website on December 16, 2003. The image, which had been doctored by a group of people with an ax to grind, purported to show a screenshot from the late-night news on Phoenix Television. On screen was newscaster Li Hui, who presented Phoenix Television's late-night news at the time. The time on the screen showed 01:04—four minutes past one in the morning. Across the bottom of the screen ran a banner headline announcing the breaking news. "Ma Licheng, a news commentator for this station, was assaulted and badly beaten last night by a group of patriotic youths in Central." The photograph was posted online with a comment by someone with the username "Yita Hutu" (meaning something like "All Messed Up"). The comment ran as follows.

> I don't know much about Ma Licheng's talents. All I know is that he has run off all the way to Hong Kong in the face of harsh criticism from patriots in mainland China and managed to obtain a position as a news commentator. No doubt he will continue to come in for further barrages of criticism, but for him this is like water off a duck's back. And now, as he was sleeping with his pillows propped high about him, came news that he had been beaten up by patriotic youths in Hong Kong's Central. News reports in Hong Kong and Taiwan to the effect that he has been beaten up are likely to upset Ma Licheng. Phoenix Television news has reported that "Ma Licheng, a news commentator for this station, was badly assaulted yesterday by a group of patriotic youths in Central."

Luo had seen the photograph and related reports online. He said he had been worried for my safety since my essay "New Thinking on Relations with Japan" was published. I told him that Hong Kong is a place that guarantees freedom of speech and that I had never heard of incidents of violence caused by a mere difference of opinion. My commentary on the television news had been well received since I arrived in Hong Kong. People sometimes recognized me and came up to say hello when I was out shopping, often asking for a photograph together. People from all walks of life in Hong Kong invited me to restaurants and I was enjoying my time there very much. I was in good health and no one had so much as laid a finger on me. So where did this story come from? Besides, even if the story had been true, why would Phoenix Television want to broadcast details of an internal affair like this to the world by putting it on the news? Surely the station would want to avoid anything that might damage its reputation. The whole thing, I said, was a fabrication cooked up by people who weren't worth thinking about to cause trouble. The Hong Kong media normally chase any promising news story aggressively, and some media outlets are quite fond of gossip, I said, but not one media outlet in Hong Kong had reported this piece of "news."

Let me take the story back a little. I accepted a position at Phoenix Television after Phoenix Television CEO Liu Changle came to see me personally in Beijing in February 2003 and invited me to join his company. At first, I was hesitant. Although I had occasionally appeared on programs as a guest, I had never worked in television as a specialist. While it was true I had eventually accepted Liu's offer, it could hardly be said that I had "run off" to Hong Kong.

Another, even stranger, piece of false information appeared later. On April 28, 2007, an Internet user operating under the handle "Yuyuantan Yinghua" (the cherry blossom of Yuyuantan Park) spread another groundless rumor in a blog post on Sina. The blog claimed:

> According to unofficial sources at Phoenix Television, the decision to invite Ma Licheng to appear as a special commentator was made at the request of several Japanese companies that are among the channel's most important advertisers. It is likely that the companies would have severed their connections with the channel if their request had been refused. The advertisers said they were prepared to increase their advertising budgets if Ma Licheng were invited to appear on the channel as a commentator.

The claim was totally without foundation. My position with Phoenix Television was due entirely to an independent initiative at the highest level in the company and to my personal consent to the offer. No Japanese company was involved in any way, and Phoenix Television did not carry any advertising for any Japanese products during the time I worked at the station.

Another example of a defamatory rumor is the so-called "Baidu Encyclopedia Entry on Ma Licheng" carried on the search engine Baidu. This claims that "in the first half of 2004, Ma Licheng's new books *Thoughts and Lessons on the Sino-Japanese War* and *New Ways Forward for China and Taiwan* were republished in Japan. These books rapidly became unexpected hits with the Japanese right wing, and Ma Licheng became a close friend and partner for the Japanese right wing."

I have never written so much as a single word on these subjects, let alone two books with these titles. People who spread baseless rumors like this on Baidu should have to provide evidence backing up their claims. The Baidu website contains a disclaimer explaining that keywords, topics, articles, and other content in the encyclopedia are provided by users and do not represent the views of Baidu itself. But the administrators also bear some responsibility, since they are the ones providing a platform for this kind of slander and baseless rumor.

Since I published my essay "New Thinking on Relations with Japan," rumors like these have swarmed like locusts and have been distributed far and wide. The examples mentioned in this chapter are just a few typical examples. I want to make it clear that I retain the right to take legal action against the people who start these false rumors and the platforms that help them proliferate.

Another thing that I would like to make clear is that, before starting my job with Phoenix Television, I completed a book in early July 2003 which I titled *Beyond Apologies*.[1] The book suggested that China and Japan should move beyond history issues and look forward, building a new relationship on the foundation of Japan's expressions of acknowledgement and regret for the enormous damage it had caused China by its war of invasion and should work to promote reconciliation and development together. I mentioned that the Japanese government had apologized twenty-one times for the war and criticized calls by Ishihara Shintaro and other Japanese right-wingers for Japanese politicians to visit Yasukuni Shrine. I proposed that both sides try to restrain nationalist feelings and work to establish a free trade zone in East Asia. The title was inspired by a remark made by Huang Zhong, editor-in-chief of *Yanhuang Chunqiu* (*China through the Ages*) when he took part in a discussion about the arguments in my book. I liked his remark so much I decided to use it as the title. I finished my manuscript and handed it to my publisher in Beijing, telling them to publish it as quickly as possible.

Toward the end of July, after arriving in Hong Kong, I sent the manuscript to the Bungei Shunju publishing company in Japan, with a view to having a Japanese version published. Later, it became impossible for my Beijing publisher to put the book out, for various reasons. But Bungei Shunju arranged a translator and a Japanese edition of the book was published in late February 2004. Although the translation itself could be described as faithful to the original, the publisher decided to change the title of the book for the Japanese edition.

On the afternoon of April 19, 2004, as I was working in my office at the editorial department at Phoenix Television, I received an unexpected call from a journalist at the *Sing Tao Daily*, a Hong Kong newspaper. The journalist said: "I understand your latest book has just been published in Japan. Is it true that the title is *Japan No Longer Needs to Apologize to China*?" Taken aback, I replied that I had written no such book. "In that case," the journalist suggested, "you should go to the bookstore and see for yourself."

I immediately left the office and went to JUSCO, a Japanese supermarket where I knew they often had new Japanese books for sale. And there was a newly published book with the title, *Japan No Longer Needs to Apologize to China*. And sure enough, the book was published by Bungei Shunju and I was listed as the author. I bought a copy and went back to the office. Back at the office, I called the journalist from the *Sing Tao Daily* back and tried to explain. "The book I wrote did not have this title. This is some kind of foul-up by Bungei Shunju." When the journalist said this only made the story even more newsworthy, I said I would dictate a letter of protest over the phone and suggested it be published in the paper the following day. The journalist agreed.

The following day, April 20, 2004, the *Sing Tao Daily* carried a story on page A24 headlined, "Commentator criticized for his proposals on new thinking." The article read:

> Ma Licheng, a former *People's Daily* editorial writer, came in for considerable criticism from scholars and net users on the mainland a little over a year ago when he published an article called "New Thinking on Relations with Japan." Recently, he has come in for renewed criticism online following the publication of his latest book *Japan No Longer Needs to Apologize to China*, which criticizes people with anti-Japanese views on the mainland as narrow-minded nationalists. Internet users in mainland China have been outraged by the book and have subjected the author to a barrage of abuse and criticism since the book came out.

However, Ma Licheng says that the book was originally titled *Beyond Apologies*. He says his aim in writing the book was to express his hope that China and Japan would not become mired in the apology issue and to urge the two countries to work to build a new relationship that would enable joint development by the two countries. As well as criticizing Chinese nationalists, he also singles out more than 100 right-wing individuals and organizations in Japan for criticism. Ma Licheng is negotiating with his Japanese publisher about the problem and working to address the problems caused by the publisher's decision to change the title of the book to *Japan No Longer Needs to Apologize to China*.

At the end of 2002, Ma Licheng published "New Thinking on Relations with Japan" in *Strategy and Management* arguing that China should not obsess over history issues relating to Japan's war of aggression against China but should regard Japan as a normal country and cooperate with Japan on that basis. After the article was published, the author came in for considerable criticism from scholars and Internet users in mainland China. Not long after, Ma Licheng left the *People's Daily*, where he had worked for many years, and took up a new position as news commentator at Phoenix Television.

After the *Sing Tao Daily* carried this report, I felt I needed to make my position clear in the mainland media as well. I copied the article from the *Sing Tao Daily* and added the title "The Japanese Should Apologize to Ma Licheng for Changing the Title of His Book Without Permission." This was published on May 5, 2004, in several important online media outlets, including *People's Daily Online*'s "Strong Nation Forum," *Xinhuanet* "Development Forum," and *China Youth Online* "China Youth Forum," as well as "Sohu Community," "Society Wide-Angle," and "Discussion Focus" all operated by Sohu. On May 8, the article was carried in several places on Sina web network, including "Books and Debate" and "Books Salon," and on NetEase's "Virtual Community Discussion forum." Later, the article was also carried on the Capital Online Network's "Haiyuntian Luntan", Xici Online's "Journalists' Home," and other websites.[2]

In late May, I met *Asia Weekly* journalist Jiang Xun at a party in Hong Kong and told him the story of how Bungei Shunju had tampered with the title of my book. Jiang Xun's analysis was that Bungei Shunju had probably changed the title for commercial reasons, hoping that it would attract attention and sell more copies. At the time, the Japanese publishing industry was in a slump and publishing companies were losing money. "That is probably the case," I replied, adding.

Several friends have told me the same thing, and publishers in mainland China often change the titles of books too. But in this case, Bungei Shunju distorted the title of the book without even asking me. The company has gone too far and has caused me serious damage. The truth needs to come out. The meaning of my original title was that we should move forward on the basis of Japan's apologies and expressions of remorse and work to develop a future-oriented relationship between the two countries. To say Japan doesn't need to apologize would mean ignoring the criminal acts of history. How could that be?

Jiang Xun agreed and suggested writing an article in *Asia Weekly* to explain the situation. *Asia Weekly* is an extremely influential publication in Asia, and it was obviously a great plus for me to have the magazine be so proactive in supporting me this way. Soon after, *Asia Weekly* arranged an interview with me. The June 6, 2004, edition of the magazine carried a long article by Jiang Xun headlined "How *Beyond Apologies* Was Sabotaged by its Publishers." The article read:

> *Beyond Apologies*, published in Japan by the critic Ma Licheng, proposes new thinking on Sino-Japanese relations. But the Japanese publisher Bungei Shunju-sha changed the title to *Japan No Longer Needs to Apologize to China*, bringing a barrage of fierce online criticism down on the author. The author has responded to this twisting of his intention and is in negotiations with the publisher to resolve the issue. Recently, Ma Licheng spoke to *Asia Weekly* about what happened. He says his book was originally titled *Beyond Apologies* but that the Japanese publishers deliberately distorted his sense and changed the title to *Japan No Longer Needs to Apologize to China*. Moving beyond apologies is quite different from saying that apologies are not necessary. "For example," says the author, "if I'd written 'mama' and they'd translated that as 'mother,' obviously that would be no problem— but if the translation had rendered my original as 'grandmother,' that would be unacceptable."
>
> The Japanese edition was published by Bungei Shunju-sha in mid-February with the title *Nihon wa mo Chugoku ni shazai shinakute ii* (*Japan No Longer Needs to Apologize to China*). The translator was Yako Kimie. A white *obi* was wrapped around the lower part of the book's cover, declaring the book "A brave statement by a senior critic and columnist on the *People's Daily* who has been castigated by Chinese nationalists for his views." After the book came out, many

Internet users were outraged by the title and the author came in for aggressive barrages of criticism from many people.

Ma Licheng previously published "New Thinking on Relations with Japan," and last year his book *Han-Nichi kara no dakkyaku* (*Breaking Away from Anti-Japanese Rhetoric*) was published in Japan. In his writings, he argues that China should not allow its relations with Japan to become bogged down in the historical issue of Japan's wartime invasion of China. Instead, he argues, China should regard Japan as a normal country, take a fresh look at Sino-Japanese relations, and cooperate with Japan. History issues, he says, should be put to one side as a matter of secondary importance. In his article on the new thinking, he wrote that the growing mistrust between ordinary people in the two countries since the 1990s is a problem that needs to be urgently resolved and proposed new ideas for achieving a fundamental solution to the tensions between the two countries. Many scholars in both China and Japan have said that the new thinking offered a way to break through the barriers standing in the way of better relations between the two countries.

The initial controversy became even more one-sided after these articles were published. Since last year, public support for Ma Licheng has fallen silent, particularly online. Many people assume that the new book *Japan No Longer Needs to Apologize to China* also summarizes the content of the other articles he has written over the past several years, and see him as essentially "a spokesman on behalf of Japan."

Online critics say that Ma Licheng should be made to study the history of Japan's invasion of China. They say he should be punished by being banned from eating rice for a year, or sent to Erdao Hezi[3] for five years of hard labor. Others claim that he is one of a number of traitors preaching treasonous views under the banner of "reflection." Other commentators vented their frustration at Japan. "Japan: narrow-minded and arrogant race of people," "Who needs to be afraid of whom now? If it comes to a fight with the Japanese bastards, what do we have to worry about?" "Japan should be blown away with atomic bombs." "I'll be the first to boycott Japanese products."

Looking at the mainstream trends in Japanese society, Ma Licheng believes that people in general have a clear understanding of history. He quotes the novelist Jin Yong: When does the back-and-forth of reprisals end? A generous and forgiving attitude is the sign of strength. Ma Licheng says: "Japan is a country with freedom of speech. Because of this, there will always be some outrageous views and bizarre arguments. We can refute these any time. But we mustn't look on the mass of the Japanese people as if they are devils. Basically no young people in Japan today want to fight a war. The idea that Japan might revive its former militarism is highly unrealistic. Democratic systems are in place, and various forces obstruct one another and limit the power any one faction can have. Japan is a long, thin island nation, with fifty-odd nuclear power stations around the country, making it vulnerable to attack. If you consider modern missile warfare, Japan has no strategic depth. Even if a small number of crazy people try to revive militarism in Japan, they simply won't be able to achieve it."

Ma Licheng has always believed that, as China rises to great power status, it should aim to become a rational, responsible, and well-balanced power and must not become filled with hatred and lusting for retribution. This approach will help to minimize clashes and collisions, and this will also be to China's advantage in helping the country achieve its aims.

After writing and making statements in the media in Hong Kong and mainland China, I obviously felt I wanted to make a similar statement in the Japanese media. In June 2004, the Japanese writer Suzuki Joji, an old friend of mine, visited Hong Kong to interview me and I took the opportunity to discuss the matter with him. Suzuki has written for many years for the influential journal of opinion *Chuo Koron* and I thought there could be no better way of achieving my purpose than getting a statement published in *Chuo Koron*. Suzuki agreed. We arranged for him to interview me about Sino-Japanese relations and agreed that he would bring up the problems caused by Bungei Shunju's decision to distort the title of my book to expose the issue and castigate Bungei Shunju for what they had done. The article by Suzuki appeared in the August 2004 *Chuo Koron*[4] and he spent quite a lot of space in his article clarifying the incident and criticizing the irresponsible behavior of the people at Bungei Shunju. Many of my friends in Japan read this article and felt extremely upset by the way Bungei Shunju had behaved, and many people got in touch with me to express their sympathy.

In the face of domestic and international pressure, Bungei Shunju republished the book in February 2006 with a new Japanese title that accurately reflected the one I had originally given it: *Shazai o koete* (Beyond Apologies).[5]

1. The Japanese translation by Yako Kimie was published as written by Ma Licheng but retitled *Nihon wa mo Chugoku ni shazai shinakute ii*, (Bungei Shunju-sha, February 2004). A paperback edition was published in February 2006 by Bunshun Bunko with the title *Shazai wo koete: Atarashii Chunichi kankei ni mukete* [Beyond Apologies: Toward a New Sino-Japanese Relationship].

2. These are all influential websites and online content sites in China. People's Daily Online is operated by *People's Daily*, Xinhuanet by Xinhua News Agency, China Youth Online by China *Youth Daily*. Sohu, Sina, and NetEase all have their portal sites, and are popular with their blog and microblog services, such as "Weibo."

3. Erdao Hezi is a place name. Places with the same name exist in the provinces of Heilongjiang, Jilin, and Liaoning, and the Inner Mongolia Autonomous Region, so it is impossible to be certain which is intended here. The name is being used to refer to an isolated place in the middle of nowhere.

4. Ma Licheng, Suzuki Joji, "Sanpi ryoron sameyaranu tai-Nichi shinshiko-ron no sono-go: Nashonarizumu no chokoku ga saidai no kadai da" ("The Latest on the Ongoing Debate about the 'New Thinking on Relations with Japan': Overcoming Nationalism is the Biggest Challenge.") *Chuo Koron*, August 2004 (issue 1443), Special Edition: The True Picture of China's Peaceful Rise.

5. A note on the final page of the paperback edition says the title was changed for its publication in paperback.

CHAPTER
SEVEN

Is it Treason to Forgive Japan?
The Ge Hongbing Controversy

Only when there is Chinese forgiveness toward Japan will it be possible to build true reconciliation between the two countries. Whatever attitude Japan might take should not be a precondition for reconciliation. This is my basic view. But this is certainly not to say that we should forget the crimes the Japanese have been guilty of. The crimes Japan committed were so serious that Japan cannot escape from them alone, and that is why our forgiveness is necessary.

Born in 1968, Ge Hongbing is an accomplished author and literary critic, as well as being a talented calligrapher and painter. He received his doctorate at the age of thirty and became a professor at thirty-two. This made him the youngest professor in the humanities at any institution of higher education in the country.

Today, in addition to his work as a professor and doctoral supervisor in the Shanghai University Department of Chinese Language and Literature, Ge Hongbing serves as the head of the university's Research Center for Creative Enterprise. He has also been a visiting professor at Guizhou Normal University and the University of Macau, a researcher at Nanyang Technological University in Singapore, a visiting researcher at the University of Cambridge, and director at the Chinese Association of Contemporary Literature director and the Chinese Association of Literary and Art Theory.

He is a prolific and hard-working author. Among his novels are *Taikong shiming* (*Outer Space Mission*), *Dixia wangguo* (*Underground Kingdom*), *Wo de N zhong shenghuo* (*My N-Type Life*), *Sha chuang* (*Sand Bed*), *Cai dao* (*Path to Wealth*), *Weilai juntuan* (*Future Army*), and *Shanghai diwang* (*Shanghai Real Estate King*). His novels have been highly praised for their "penetrating analysis and critical sensibility" while his good looks have endeared him to his fans as "the heartthrob author."

As a professor of literature, Ge Hongbing has also published academic studies on literature, language, and artistic criticism. These include *Wusi wenxue shenmei jingshen yu xiandai Zhongguo wenxue* (*The Aesthetics of the May 4 Movement and Modern Chinese Literature*), *Wenxueshi xingtaixue* (*Morphology of Literary History*), *Tuifeizhe ji qi duiliwu* (*Decadents and Their Antagonists*), *Renwei yu renyan* (*Human Acts and Human Speech*), *Wenxue gailun tongyong jiaocheng* (*General Practical Instruction in Literature*), *Zhongguo wenxue de qinggan zhuangtai* (*The Emotional Conditions of Chinese Literature*), *Wenxue shixue* (*Studies in Literary History*), *Zhengwu de shixue* (*Poetics at Noon*), *Weinasi de chouti* (*The Drawer of Venus*), and *Zhenshi de huangdan* (*The Absurdity of Truth*). He is widely recognized by his fellow scholars as one of the foremost literary critics and theorists among the current generation.

In addition to his literary writing, Ge Hongbing has a keen interest in current affairs and the state of contemporary Chinese society and thought and has published several books on these subjects, including *Shenti zhengzhi* (*Politics of the Body*), *Zhang'ai yu rentong: Dangdai Zhongguo wenhua wenti* (*Obstacles and Identity: Contemporary Chinese Cultural Problems*), and *Zhongguo sixiang de dixian* (*Bottom Line in Chinese Thought*). The core values in all these books are a rational approach, independence of character, and a free spirit. With this background and early career, everything seemed to be set fair for Ge Hongbing, and he must have looked forward to a successful future. He could not have predicted the chaos that would disrupt his life after an article on his private blog caused a major controversy.

On June 12, 2007, Ge posted on his Sina blog about appropriate ways to memorialize World War II. Ge himself has said that his original title was "China, What Is the Best Way for You to Commemorate World War II?" But in the process of being reproduced on the Internet, the title was changed and the article was eventually posted under the heading: "China Should Stop its Anti-Japanese Propaganda that Spreads Hatred." A translation of the blog entry follows.

I understand a cross-party alliance in Japan's National Diet was recently formed to demand the removal of anti-Japanese photographs on display at museums commemorating the War of Resistance to Japanese Aggression in many places around China. I don't know what these people's true objective is.

Of course, if their aim is to conceal the facts about Japan's invasion of China, then naturally we must remonstrate and fight back against what they are doing. But if they are doing it out of consideration for building a friendly future between the two countries, then I am not sure that their excuses can be dismissed out-of-hand as being entirely without rationale.

The information on display in many places in China about World War II uses audio and video technology and photographs to provide vivid and realistic representations of the brutal and barbaric acts carried out by the Japanese during the war, including mass murders and rapes. It is possible to take the view that this vivid and impressive propaganda is intended to "propagate feelings of hatred" against the Japanese. Memorials that aim to spread hatred have no positive meaning for those who visit them; this is particularly true for children and other young visitors. Indeed, they are more likely to have a bigger negative impact. It is likely that museums and memorials of this kind will fill the children's minds with hatred. Instead of teaching them that war is a tragedy for all humankind, these displays will impart the lesson that we must become strong and ensure that we destroy our enemies in any future war.

Propaganda like this fails to make children aware of the cruelty and inhumanity of war and teaches them to thirst after a righteous war of retribution. They become belligerent and cruel because they have been shown the cruelty of the enemy repeatedly and in graphic detail. They come to believe that only by becoming crueler than the enemy and by physically destroying the enemy can "we" achieve true victory.

This tendency to memorialize World War II in a way that spreads hatred has transformed Chinese memorials to the war into something quite different. It has turned them into anti-Japanese propaganda that encourages hatred of Japan. This approach prevents us from seeing that Japanese people too were victims of World War II and stops us from seeing that war brings disaster to the whole of humanity. It blinds people to the fact that today's Japan is already a democratic country. The fundamental idea of a democratic state is to gain the necessary living space through markets, not through war. The objective is not to destroy the other side by military force but to make a profit through discussion and cooperation.

Spreading a message of love and peace should be the purpose of all memorials and propaganda about World War II. Remembering the wars of the past by spreading hatred goes against humanitarian values. The result of this approach to remembering the past is already apparent among young people today, who are increasingly narrow-minded and aggressive, and tend to regard hate as something glorious. This state of mind is the direct result of this approach to remembering the past. These devil children have been spawned by the propaganda and the hatred of Japan that have dominated discussions of the war over the past half-century.

Museum displays around the country are filled with graphic and gory photographs and illustrations. These will not contribute to an education that helps to instill a sense of humanity. They are particularly unhelpful in instilling a correct view of humanity and a correct understanding of war in the minds of elementary and junior high school students. Being exposed to horrific photographs and illustrations like this can easily cause them trauma and hinder their intellectual development. I have visited many memorials to World War II in countries around the world. All these countries suffered profoundly in the war. It cannot be claimed that these countries suffered less than we did. But it is rare to see graphic photographs showing blood and gore in their museums. The children who visit these places are still young. At the same time as learning about the war, they should be taught about the essential goodness of human beings, that humanity is a wonderful thing, that tomorrow's world will be a world of peace, and that we must work together to cherish, respect, and protect peace. I once wrote a piece with the title "How does Britain remember World War II?" I think we can learn from the British example.

It is now more than fifty years since the war ended. We should learn from the way the countries of South East Asia and countries like Singapore and Thailand remember the war. In those countries, there is no sense of lingering hatred for Japan. These countries have success-fully built positive relations with Japan. We should also learn from the example of countries like France and Britain. They do not continue to hate Germany but cooperate with their former enemy. Now that half a century has passed, we should not continue to grumble that we still lag behind because of the effects of the Japanese invasion or complain that the wounds from the violence of that time have still not healed.

Hatred is a poison. It is a toxin that dims people's intelligence and weakens the brainpower of the state. Germany, having lost World War I, was so damaged by the resentment and hatred that followed that it waged a second war. We must learn the following lessons from this. Punishment and retribution against an aggressor country must be held to within certain limits. If they exceed these limits, there is the risk that they will have an effect opposite to that intended. We must not treat the guilty the way they treated us. Demanding repeated apologies from the guilty party, seeking to humiliate them and make them kneel, or working to "educate" them about their guilt—this is the wrong approach. We run the risk of one day finding that, unintending, we have committed the same wrong as that carried out by the original guilty party.

Magnanimity and generosity are an effective medicine for healing the wounds and restoring a sense of shared humanity. This medicine is effective between states as well as between individuals. When we remember the war, we should do so with the aim of spreading peace and love, not hatred and resentment. The aim of war memorials should be to express opposition to war and to express remorse for the suf-fering and loss that human beings have suffered as a result of war. They should not put unnecessary emphasis on the perspective of one country with the aim of spreading hatred or animosity toward another country.

Ge Hongbing's piece considers the issues rationally. Anyone who disagreed had only to publish another article expressing their own opinion. The more debate and discussion there is, the clearer the facts become.

What happened instead was that Ge Hongbing was subjected to a remarkable torrent of online abuse after the essay appeared. He was called a treasonous dog, the dregs of his race, an animal lower than a pig or a dog, a trash-talker, a shameless idiot, human trash, and worse. The people who wrote these things did not engage in any serious discussion about what he had written but merely enjoyed rushing to write foul-mouthed insults. In the space of a week, he received 700 emails filled with this kind of content. Some people even insulted his ancestors by name. One made public his home address and phone number and wrote: "Anyone who reads this should feel free to go to where he works and denounce him, to phone him, or send him emails. Let's bring this piece of trash down and curse him to death for the shame he's brought on his nation! The traitorous dog!" It was a terrible situation that he was facing.

On the evening of January 9, 2010, a publisher in Beijing invited several writers and other figures to a dinner to discuss the publication of books. I was there, along with Ge Hongbing, who had come up to the capital from Shanghai. I was seated next to him at the dinner, the first time we had met. He was very restrained and hardly said a word.

I asked him about what had happened in June 2007. He spoke slowly in a low, sunken voice. He told me that after he published his essay, outside calls had been placed to senior management at the university and the heads of various departments demanding he be dismissed on the grounds that he was "a traitor to the people." A group of twenty-some people had pushed their way into Shanghai University to conduct a sit-in demonstration, protesting his "traitorous discourse" and demanding "discussion" with him. The head of the university had protected him, had sent a staff member, and had arranged for him to meet with the demonstrators for five minutes, during which time Ge had expressed remorse and apologized for what he had written. This failed to satisfy them and for a while they continued to kick up a fuss around the campus. Even more seriously, someone put a photograph of the entrance to his house online and encouraged people to hold a demonstration there. He had been forced to evacuate to a hotel with his wife and their eleven-year-old son for half a month. Some people had gone to the Shanghai city courthouse and called for him to be prosecuted for "treason against the state," but the court had refused to take their charges seriously. Such was the situation he had faced.

In the middle of this tense situation, an anonymous blogger published a piece online titled: "How to show lenience and forgive Japan: On Ge Hongbing's right to free speech and the question of how to commemorate the War of Resistance to Japanese Aggression." The article argued:

> On the question of Sino-Japanese relations and how China ought to commemorate the Anti-Japanese War, my own views overlap those of Ge Hongbing in several areas and are somewhat different in others. In the face of the recent violent online expressions of popular nationalist sentiment, however, I want to stand alongside Ge Hongbing. I want to stand with him against the overwhelming barrage of insults and attacks to which he has been subjected. As the French philosopher Voltaire said: I may not agree with what you say, but I will defend to the death your right to say it. Ge Hongbing's right to free speech must not be stolen from him by the majority, however correct their views may seem to be. When "patriotism" is regarded as the highest value and is used as an excuse for oppressing people, I do not want to be among the crowd persecuting them.

The writer then expressed his support, quoting the views that Ge had expressed in a different blog article:

> Germany's crimes cannot be redeemed simply by an act of kneeling. The true reason Germany was forgiven was the compassion and understanding of the people who suffered from their crimes. Whether the problems of Sino-Japanese relations can be solved or not is ultimately up to China. Only when there is Chinese forgiveness toward Japan will it be possible to build true reconciliation between the two countries. Whatever attitude Japan might take should not be a precondition for reconciliation. This is my basic view. But this is certainly not to say that we should forget the crimes the Japanese have been guilty of. The crimes Japan committed were so serious that Japan cannot escape from them alone, and that is why our forgiveness is necessary.

To this the anonymous online writer added, "To love those we ought by rights to love represents no challenge to our humanity. It is by loving those whom by rights we should not love that we raise ourselves to a higher level."

Such is not to say the anonymous commentator agreed with everything that Ge Hongbing had written.

> I cannot agree with Ge Hongbing that children should be kept from historical documents that show the blood-stained truth about the past. He believes that the photographs and illustrations on display at World War II memorial museums around the country do not instill a correct view of humanity and war in the many elementary and junior high school students who visit them. He believes that such images can traumatize children and have an adverse effect on their developing intelligence. This belief probably stems from a desire to protect children's innocence. But in fact, this approach would deprive them of the right to know the truth about the world. Children should grow up in a healthy manner, but this should be achieved not by trying to expose them to sunlight alone but by allowing them to confront the dark side of this world as well. In the American capital of Washington, DC, is a museum to commemorate the Jewish Holocaust that contains reproductions of rooms in the Nazi concentration camps and the punishments inflicted there. The darkness and ugly, excruciating brutality on display are hard to bear. But many parents, guardians, and teachers take children to visit the displays and give them detailed explanations about this unbearable episode in history. This represents a page in human history. These things truly happened, and children need to understand all aspects of life and the world. Attempting to cosset children in a beautiful, sun-filled world without darkness is not in their best interests and will not help them grow up in a healthy manner.

This piece represents a rational response to Ge Hongbing's blog. It is debate and discussion like this that increases understanding and leads to enlightenment. Since Ge Hongbing published his blog, however, reasonable responses of this kind have been few and far between. Instead, he has been tormented by a flood of insults and abuse. As one anonymous commentator wrote online:

> Nationalism is a dangerous, double-edged sword. Nationalism sucks in many young people (and I too was once a victim of my education and was filled with a hatred of Japan that seeped into my bones, something that can be seen in my earlier writings), but nationalism cannot deal a true blow to one's opponents and will not make you strong and mighty. In previous times, the Yihetuan Movement brought serious

harm to China during the Boxer Rebellion with its blind, anti-foreign activities. It seems that many people have yet to awake from the blood-thirsty chaos of those years. The thinking and beliefs of the Yihetuan, as well as its words and deeds, live on inside many Chinese people today.

As a result of the enormous pressure put on Ge Hongbing and a demand from university administrators that he take steps to resolve the confusion that followed the publication of his views, ten days after posting "China Should Stop Its Anti-Japanese Propaganda That Spreads Hatred," Ge Hongbing published an online "Apology and Explanation" apologizing and withdrawing what he had written. He wrote:

> Recently, a personal blog entry in which I wrote about how we remember World War II was widely referred to, reported, and quoted in the online media, sparking a massive debate whose impact went far beyond anything I could have predicted. Several days ago, I instructed all websites other than Sina Blogs to delete all copies and summaries of my text, complete and partial, and to delete all quotations of what I had written. Now, I hereby retract what I wrote, which will be deleted from Sina Blogs as well. I am not a researcher on Sino-Japanese relations, and this piece of writing was not an academically mature view written as the result of deep academic research. My blog injured the nationalistic feelings of many readers, for which I apologize. I apologize too for the impact that what I wrote had on the host website. I would like to thank my colleagues for their criticism, and all my readers for their concern.

For a scholar to release this kind of statement about his own writing is a kind of tragedy. The incident attracted wide interest around Asia, and detailed reports appeared in the media in Japan, Singapore, Taiwan, and Hong Kong. Following this event, Ge Hongbing threw himself into his teaching, research, and writing. In 2008, he was invited by the Shanghai city government to become one of the chief members of the planning team for the China Pavilion at the Shanghai Expo. At Shanghai University, he was commissioned to put in place a cutting-edge platform for the new field of Chinese literature and creative writing. Creativity is the nucleus and engine of the cultural industries. Creative writing exists as a subject in Western countries, Japan, and South Korea, but until now there had been no such subject taught in China. This platform that Ge Hongbing played a leading role in creating was the first of its kind anywhere in China. His previously mentioned novel *Shanghai diwang* was published in Beijing in 2010. The novel vividly depicted human emotions and living conditions in the coastal metropolis in the years since the policy of reform and opening up through the complex and sudden changes in the real estate conditions in the city. At the same time, it also touched on the sensitive topic of changes in the land system and was well received. He has apparently already finished work on another novel, *Qinhuai shusheng* (*The Student of Qinhuai*).

CHAPTER EIGHT

Curbing Hot-Headedness with Reason:
A Letter from Zhu Liang
and an Article by Yuan Weishi

The only way to avoid extreme actions that obstruct progress toward modernization in China is to enhance openness, understand all the broader facets, and not allow our world to be confined to the limits of what we can see with our own eyes. If we can preserve freedom of speech at the same time, then more of the public will surely become calmer and more reasonable in their opinions through the process of debating freely and coming into contact with various points of view. This is surely the path the state will have to travel to achieve long-term stability.

Zhu Liang, former director of the CCP International Liaison Department, sent me a handwritten letter on July 9, 2007. I have cherished that letter ever since, and it has been a source of great encouragement and motivation to me in my thinking and writing about Sino-Japanese relations.

For the past ten years, I have been attending dinner meetings with senior members of the Party leadership almost every month. Du Runsheng[1] organized them while he was still in good health until a few years ago. Hu Deping[2] used to attend from time to time, and he would invite senior Party members, and I was able to take part from time to time. Zhu Liang also occasionally attended these meetings, and it was there that I first made his acquaintance. Zhu Liang was born in 1924 but looks at least ten years younger than his age. Even as an old man, he is tall and dignified, with an educated look. Although a man of relatively few words, he is a very warm person who never displays a hint of arrogance or haughtiness in his dealings with others.

I have long been interested in international relations and foreign policy. Zhu Liang has been involved in foreign policy since 1951 and can fairly be called one of the pioneers of Chinese diplomacy. I look up to him as a teacher and have learned much from him. Zhu Liang was originally from Chaoyang in Guangdong Province but he moved with his family at a young age to Shanghai, where he studied at Shanghai High School. In 1939, at the age of fifteen, he joined the Kang-Ri Jiuwang Xiehui (Anti-Japanese National Salvation Association) organized by Shanghai students. In 1943, he entered the chemistry department at St. John's University (now the East China University of Political Science and Law) in Shanghai, where he also took part in the student movement.

In June 1945, he joined the Party, becoming a party organization leader at St. John's University and commissioner for the local chapter and party chapters' headquarters. In 1947, he was put in charge of the Shanghai Regional Students' Federation. Around this time, he had to escape temporarily to Hong Kong when his identity as a member of the Party was revealed.

When Shanghai was liberated in 1949, Zhu Liang became the Shanghai Youth Federation secretary-general. In 1951, he served as the China Central

Committee Communist Youth League[3] delegate to the headquarters of the World Federation of Democratic Youth in Hungary. His performance in this role saw him appointed division leader in the China Central Committee's Communist Youth League International Liaison Division following his return to China in 1954. In 1960, he was sent to Hungary as a delegate again. On his return to China in 1962, he served as deputy director and then director of the Communist Youth League Central Committee International Liaison Division, then secretary-general of the All-China Youth Federation. During the Cultural Revolution, he came under attack and was sent to a May Seventh Cadre School.[4] In 1972, following a recommendation from Zhou Enlai, Zhu Liang and several other senior figures were transferred to the Party's International Liaison Department. Around this time, he served as deputy bureau chief and bureau chief of eight bureaus responsible for liaison work with Western Europe. In December 1982, he was appointed deputy director of the International Liaison Department. He served as director there from 1985 to 1993, working on exchanges with more than 400 political parties, politicians, and international organizations around the world. He was elected to the Central Committee at the 13th National Congress. He also served three terms on the Chinese People's Political Consultative Conference. When he retired from his position as division head in March 1993, he was appointed to a term on the Standing Committee of the National People's Congress and made head of the National People's Congress Foreign Affairs Committee.

When I met Zhu Liang at a dinner in the early summer of 2007, I spoke to him about the controversy that had been stirred up by the publication of my essay "New Thinking on Relations with Japan" in 2002. He said he had heard a little about what had happened but was already retired and at home at the time of the controversy. He told me he would like to read my pieces again and asked me to send him copies.

At the time, my essay "New Thinking on Relations with Japan" and another essay "Ma Licheng Returns to the New Thinking on Japan," which had been published in the March 1, 2004, *South Reviews*, had subsequently been collected in the *Undercurrents* book published by East China Normal University Press in 2004. Another essay of mine on "Deng Xiaoping and Hu Yaobang's Views on Japan" had been published in the March 2007 issue of a small-circulation journal from Shanxi Province called *Zhongguo Fangyu* (*China Region*). I sent Zhu Liang a copy of *Undercurrents* and *China Region* with a request for criticism from this senior figure (Zhu was then 83 years old) in the world of foreign affairs and veteran of the resistance movement against Japan.

On July 9 that year, Zhu Liang sent me a handwritten letter. With his kind permission, I quote the letter in its entirety.

Comrade Licheng:

I received the copies of *China Region* and *Undercurrents* you were so kind as to send. I have read all three essays and am impressed by how well written they are. In particular, I am impressed that you were proposing a "new thinking" in your essay in *Undercurrents* as early as 2002. I quite agree with your views. (With the exception, however, of the question of China's "peaceful rise.") It is important to lead the thinking of the people, particularly the young people, in the correct direction.

I addressed this issue directly in an essay titled "Major Events in Sixty Years of Sino-Japanese Relations," which was published in issue 2 of the magazine *Yanhuang Chunqiu* (*China through the Ages*). People without an understanding of history will probably not be able to discern the problems that these essays focus on. I submitted my essay to *China through the Ages* because I did not feel that the main-stream media would agree to publish a piece of this kind.

I leave Beijing tomorrow for a month's rest in Beidaihe. In closing, let me wish you all the best for the summer. I hope that your excellent writing will reach a wider audience.

Zhu Liang, July 9, 2007

Zhu Liang's essay "Major Events in Sixty Years of Sino-Japanese Relations" was a major piece more than 10,000 characters long. The essay looks back in detail over the winding course of Sino-Japanese relations from Japan's defeat in the war in 1945 up to 2006. As most readers will be aware, anti-Japanese demonstrations broke out in many cities around China in 2005 and Sino-Japanese relations fell once again into a difficult trough. There was an upsurge of hatred and resentment toward Japan and it became harder to feel confident that relations with Japan would continue to develop in a positive direction. Zhu Liang's essay focused precisely on these conditions, writing rationally and without illusions, laying out a vision of the future from a lofty perspective, and insisting on an optimistic view that encouraged reconciliation between the two countries.

In particular, Zhu looked back on a talk Mao Zedong gave to a delegation of Japanese Diet members during their visit to China in December 1955. In his remarks, Mao said: "Over the course of our long relationship, China and Japan have sometimes had disputes and gone to war, but we can forget these incidents from the past. We must use every means at our disposal to remove American hands from Japan. China and Japan must build a relationship in which each country helps the other, flexibly making up for each other's deficiencies, moving forward in peace and friendship, and using cultural exchanges to build a normal relationship." Zhu Liang also recalled that, when the border dispute with the Soviet Union was approaching climax in 1973 and 1974, "Mao Zedong repeatedly recommended the United States improve its relations with Japan and ensure that Japan not be pulled toward the Soviet Union."

Essentially, whether China's chief adversary was the United States or the Soviet Union, Mao believed that China could afford to make allowances with regard to Japan and should use all available means to keep Japan close. Zhu's essay devoted considerable space to the time and effort that Zhou Enlai invested in his work with Japan and his efforts to promote friendship between China and Japan. Starting in 1959, important Japanese figures from various sectors visited China, including, for example, former prime minister Ishibashi Tanzan and Matsumura Kenzo, an important Liberal Democratic Party politician.

"Zhou Enlai held long meetings with friends from Japan that would often last four or five hours. When he took Matsumura to visit the Miyun Reservoir they sat opposite each other in the train in close discussion." While maintaining principles, Zhou Enlai's strategy on Japan was flexible and based on human feelings and reason. In particular, he endeavored to "keep the focus on the people," and worked to obtain the greatest possible understanding from the masses of ordinary people in Japan.

Zhu's essay praised Deng Xiaoping and Hu Yaobang's efforts to promote reconciliation between China and Japan. Zhu looked back on the shifts of history, recalling that when Mao Zedong, Zhou Enlai, and Deng Xiaoping held power, they had adopted a policy of shelving the question of sovereignty over the Diaoyu/Senkaku Islands. Zhu writes that when Deng Xiaoping visited Japan to attend the ceremony to ratify the Treaty of Peace and Friendship in 1978, a promise was made with the Japanese side not to touch on the question of the Diaoyu/Senkaku Islands. In October 1984, Deng Xiaoping proposed shelving the issue of sovereignty and working toward joint development. Zhu also recalled the tremendous success achieved in 1984, when Hu Yaobang invited 3,000 youth from Japan to visit China. Many of the Japanese youths spontaneously signed a vow swearing that Japan and China would never go to war again and declared that they felt very much at home in China. Marshal Nie Rongzhen invited the daughter of a Japanese woman he had saved during the war, to share a meal at his home.

Zhu Liang wrote that the Japanese government loans to China between 1979 and June 2006 amounted to a total of more than 3.2 trillion yen, equivalent to around 30 billion dollars. Zhu wrote: "In a sense, this was Japan's response to China's decision to renounce its demands for war reparations."

Zhu criticized right-wingers like Ishihara Shintaro who foment nationalism in Japan, Nakasone Yasuhiro for visiting Yasukuni Shrine while he was prime minister in 1985, and Prime Minister Koizumi Jun'ichiro for continuing to visit Yasukuini during his time in office. He also criticized the overwrought passions of nationalist feeling within China itself, writing, "There is a good deal of emotional reporting in the various media and on the Internet. In 2004 and 2005, we saw violent demonstrations by large crowds at a China-Japan soccer game, leading to incidents that should never be allowed to take place.[5] In addition, some Chinese people visiting Japan fail to behave themselves in a fitting matter, and these actions too have been detrimental to Japanese feelings of affection for China."

At the end of his essay, Zhu Liang summarized his long years of working on diplomatic strategies for dealing with Japan as follows.

1. Use the public sector to encourage the bureaucracy and the bureaucracy to encourage the public sector, and work toward lasting friendship and cooperation between the two countries.
2. Strengthen exchanges between young people and develop the people who will carry on the work of friendship between China and Japan in the next generation.
3. Adopt a flexible strategy and be ready to break though blockages when an opportune moment presents itself.
4. Sino-Japanese relations will not always be smooth sailing, but China should analyze the hawkish elements in Japan, gauge the situation, carry forward the work, and endeavor to change the situation.
5. Maintain a stable strategic work team on relations with Japan, develop Japanese studies to build an understanding of Japan, and work to develop deep personal relationships with people in various areas of life in Japan.

Zhu Liang's encouragement for me was the embodiment of his rational arguments in favor of reconciliation with Japan over the years. The lessons imparted by this important senior figure in the diplomatic world made my faith even more unshakeable. In his letter, Zhu had expressed doubts over the phrase *heping jueqi* "peaceful rise." This slogan, put forward by the government some time earlier, had sparked debate and controversy, with many people feeling that the concept of a "rise" to power was a little alarming. Subsequently, the phrase was amended in government writing and changed to "peaceful development."

The vast majority of the people I have encountered since the publication of my "New Thinking on Relations with Japan," be they from the world of politics or academia, from Heilongjiang to Yunnan, from Shanghai to Xinjiang, have shown understanding and sympathy for the new thinking. After circulating my article among their membership, a leadership group of Standing Committee members in one major city even expressed their support as a group. However, in recent years, nationalism has been increasing dramatically, so that government officials often receive emotional threats comparable to the language used by the Yihetuan during the Boxer Rebellion, and this makes them reluctant to make their own attitudes clear. This makes Zhu Liang a courageous high-level government official. György Lukács, currently the most prominent Marxist thinker in Europe, has written a book with the title *The Destruction of Reason*. In it, Lukács writes that irrational thinking and careless movements led to the rise of German fascism and triggered the outbreak of World War II. He argues that there is thus a need to assume a "philosophical responsibility" for the rise of fascism and the outbreak of the war. Reasonable, rational thinking among the political elite as represented by Zhu Liang is without doubt a blessing for China.

By comparison, scholars seem to be a little less concerned than government bureaucrats. In Chapter One of this book "An Earth-Shaking Controversy," I showed how a number of scholars supported the views I had expressed regarding a new thinking on China's relations with Japan. Of these, the most prominent was an essay by Professor Yuan Weishi of Sun Yat-sen University in Guangdong entitled "Views on the Recent Nationalist Countercurrents," published in the May and July 2007 issues of the bimonthly *Yangtze*. The article expressed praise and support for the new thinking.

Born in 1931, Yuan Weishi is an influential professor in the philosophy department at Sun Yat-sen University. His publications include *A History of Modern Chinese Philosophy*, *Essays on Modern Chinese Thought*, *Philosophical Currents and Individuals during the State of Emergency in the Late Qing Dynasty*, and *Signposts and Torture of the Soul*. He has also edited the *Modernity and the Classics* series and a *Collection of Academic Sources on the Wasteland*. He is an extremely influential figure in academic circles. His arguments lamenting the condition of the country and people have always been honest, straightforward, and clear. His "Views on the Recent Nationalist Countercurrents" is made up of two parts.

The first part lays out six concrete conditions in which extreme nationalism manifests itself at present. These are:

1. In politics, calls for the establishment of a Confucian socialist republic,
2. In economics, attempts to treat international economic activities across the board as political issues,
3. On the military side, calls for extreme military expansion,
4. In education, blind calls for children to be taught the classics,
5. In academia, jingoistic espousal of the idea of ethno-national subjectivity, and
6. In thought and culture, the creation of ideological fear.

The second part analyzes why extreme nationalism is produced:

1. Excessive narrow-mindedness on morality,
2. An obsession with the idea of China as a humiliated ancient power,
3. A lack of cool-headed objectivity with regard to China's traditional culture, and
4. A tendency to undervalue the ability of Chinese people to take in progressive culture from the outside.

Yuan Weishi writes:

What is cultural subjectivity? In an age when the world is moving toward unity, the core values of contemporary civilization are individual freedom and human rights. The gradual move toward rule of law and constitutional government to guarantee civic rights represents subjectivity within contemporary culture. In simple terms, the rights of people—the rights of citizens—are supreme. Departing from this to argue for the cultural subjectivity of a state or nation is a self-absorbed and inward-looking excuse for obstructing social change and represents a trap by which the rulers usurp the rights of the people—a veil by which to maintain despotic rule. Whether we look at different societies around the world or look at societies throughout history, the results are the same no matter how many times the experiment is repeated. The Chinese people have already had enough bitter experiences, and there is no need to walk down the same path again.

In his essay, Yuan Weishi cites the example of my "New Thinking on Relations with Japan," which he says made it clear that some people were trying to create an atmosphere of ideological fear in the areas of philosophy and culture. He writes:

> Ma Licheng has written an essay with the title "New Thinking on Relations with Japan." Any fair-minded person who reads this essay, which was published in Beijing in December 2002, would surely be impressed by the author's vision for the future and his wisdom and perception. It is true his discourse differs from the views of many hot-headed people at the time, but as I will show in what follows, in many points his views are either the same as or similar to those expressed by Premier Wen Jiabao in his speech to the Japanese House of Representatives on April 12, 2007.[6]

1. Ma Licheng writes: "In recent years, numerous books published by Chinese specialists on Japan have acknowledged that Japan today is essentially a democracy governed by the rule of law and that the government's policy and decision-making processes are subject to supervision and obstructions from many directions. Many people still seem to imagine that the "military" can simply act as it wants, but these conditions simply do not exist anymore. . . . When we consider China's current strength and the environment we face both at home and abroad, the danger of national subjugation and racial extermination, a real threat in the early years of the twentieth century, no longer exists. Indeed, many or most of the problems that China faces today come from within the country itself."

   In his speech before the Diet, Wen Jiabao said: "After the war, Japan embarked on the path of peaceful development and became a leading economic power and influential member of the international community."

2. Ma Licheng argues: "The question of a Japanese apology has already been resolved, and there is no need to insist on a particular format or wording for such an apology."

   In his speech, Wen Jiabao said: "The Chinese Government and people, have all along taken a forward-looking approach. We believe that we need to take history as a mirror to guide the growth of our ties in the future. By stressing the importance of drawing lessons from history, we do not mean to perpetuate hatred. Rather, we want to secure a better future for our relations. Since the normalization of diplomatic ties between China and Japan, the Japanese Government and leaders have on many occasions stated their position on the historical issue, admitted that Japan committed aggression, and expressed deep remorse and apology to the victimized countries. The Chinese Government and people appreciate the position they have taken."

3. Ma Licheng goes on to say that: "Between 1979 and 2001, Japan repeatedly provided low-interest yen loans to China worth a total of around 2,667,909 million yen. Japan has also supported some 150 infrastructure building projects, including the second phase construction work on the Beijing subway, expansion work on the Beijing Capital airport, the Beijing sewage treatment plant, Wuhan Tianhe airport, Wuqiangxi Hydroelectric Power Project, the second Chongqing Yangtze River Bridge Construction Project, Qinhuangdao Port, the Shuohuang Railway, and the Nanning-Kunming Railway. These ODA loans had an interest rate of between just 0.79 and 3.5 percent, and a repayment time of between thirty and forty years. This too indicates sincerity on the Japanese side. For many years, we have not done enough to educate people about these facts, which are not adequately appreciated today."

Wen Jiabao said: "China has received support and assistance from the Japanese Government and people in its reform, opening up, and modernization drives. This is something the Chinese people will never forget."

4. Further, Ma Licheng says: "More importantly, we must be forward-looking. The new stage for competition will be economic systems and markets. China and Japan are crucial hubs in Asia, and the people of both countries must look more introspectively at their own nationalism and work to overcome their narrow-mindedness in the cause of greater unity and community. For China, our mission must be to move toward the early ratification of a free-trade area between China and ASEAN and to make progress toward signing a three-country free-trade agreement involving China, Japan, and South Korea. This is the direction in which the hearts of people in Asia are tending and the unmistakable tendency of the times."

Wen Jiabao said: "Peace will benefit China and Japan, while confrontation can only do harm to them. China and Japan both share increasing common interests and face major challenges. With this in mind, we the leaders of the two countries have reached agreement on building a strategic relationship of mutual benefit. Thanks to years of mutual efforts, our two economies have become increasingly interdependent. China-Japan economic cooperation is a relationship of mutual benefit and win-win progress. The economic development of both countries presents opportunities for rather than poses threats to each another. During my meeting with Prime Minister Abe Shinzo yesterday, we agreed to upgrade bilateral economic cooperation by launching China-Japan high level economic dialogue mechanism."

Revolutionary new arguments are unlikely to be immediately understood by the ordinary masses of the people, but they are extremely important for the development of the state and society. Ma Licheng's views, published in 2002, whether they were correct or not, are perfectly ordinary accusation made by an individual member of the public and should not be restricted. Five years later, however, Yu Quanyu, a member of the Chinese People's Political Consultative Conference, said that this discourse constituted "traitorous" or "seditious" speech. This accusation represents cultural absolutism and is a classic example of an attempt to quash freedom of speech. In a modern state, freedom of speech is regarded as a fundamental human right of citizens that must not be infringed and an important driver of social progress. Ma Licheng was just one member of the editorial team at the *People's Daily* and held no state authority or power. He was not guilty of selling any state secrets, so how could he be described as a "traitor"?

Fortunately, Ma Licheng is a mature and magnanimous person who understands that the greatest contempt is silence. He sensibly scorned to argue with someone who had previously been his direct superior. (Yu Quanyu had previously worked as a member of the editorial committee and head of the office of the editor-in-charge of the *People's Daily*). Otherwise, Yu Quanyu would have found it difficult to escape censure for the crime of defamation.

This was no accidental mistake by Yu Quanyu. He argues that some scholars of modern Chinese history are guilty of spreading a traitorous discourse that denies the facts about the invasions of China by Japan and other imperialist powers, and has said that a law should be enacted to prohibit such seditious speech and punish offenders severely. He even proposed a draft for such a piece of legislation to the Chinese People's Political Consultative Conference. In this case, we witnessed an abject attempt to create a literary inquisition. Anyone with any understanding of the state of historical studies in China today knows that not a single historian in mainland China today fails to censure the imperialist invasions of China. Having sniffed out seditious speech in pieces written by others, he then accused Ma Licheng of the same crime, claiming that his arguments were the same as those of the "traitors." In fact, this was nothing but complete fabrication on his part.

People sometimes start to commit acts that go beyond their authority in hope of acquiring a minor bureaucratic position. We often see people who make self-serving judgements based on their own limited understanding and judgment and who declare that all discourse that does not accord with their own views is dangerous heresy that must be purged. Even worse are people who falsify materials and put the blame on innocent people, and in extreme cases plot to put people they don't like in jail. In all cases, they aim to present themselves as defenders of loyal thinking, pander to leaders, treat the people with derision, insult the weak, and maneuver for personal gain. Is it not ridiculous that such people should then claim to be the very model of patriotism?

We should note that Yu Quanyu, who submitted the draft for the legislation, is a member of the CASS advisory board and that several of the people who approved his proposal were members of the Academy faculty committee. They colluded to submit this proposal that earned the laughter of popular opinion, clearly not caring at all for the damage they did to the honor of the Academy. I was reminded of what happened in 1947 when the central research committee of the academy chose its first members. At the time the Academy was under the control of the KMT, but as is well known, the "non–party Bolshevist" Guo Moruo was elected without difficulty, despite his close ties to the Communist Party. The reason was that the only criterion that counted for the electors was the level of a candidate's scholarship.

The only way to avoid extreme actions that obstruct progress toward modernization in China is to enhance openness, understand all the broader facets, and not allow our world to be confined to the limits of what we can see with our own eyes. If we can preserve freedom of speech at the same time, then more of the public will surely become calmer and more reasonable in their opinions through the process of debating freely and coming into contact with various points of view. This is surely the path the state will have to travel to achieve long-term stability.

A China governed by rule of law, a free China, a China that practices democratic and constitutional law in which pluralistic cultures coexist and compete with one another in resplendence—this is what the Chinese people wish for and dream of: a bright future in which the people are prosperous and the country is rich and flourishing. It is also the systemic foundation that will allow the Chinese people to live well-balanced harmonious lives. We must not allow currents of extreme thought to once again lead China down a mistaken path.

Professor Yuan Weishi is a virtuous and respected person who is regarded as a leading figure and the conscience of academia, both inside and outside China. I hope his essay will encourage some people to be a little more circumspect and calm-headed in their views and the way they express them.

NOTES

1. Du Runsheng (born 1913) was a specialist in rural reform, served as director of Rural Development Research Center of the State Council and director of the Central Committee Rural Policy Research Office, and promoted rural reforms as part of the reform and openness policy. At present he works as an advisor to the reformist journal *China through the Ages*.

2. Hu Deping (born 1942) is the eldest son of Hu Yaobang and served as vice-director of the Central Committee United Front Work Department and as a member of the standing committee of the National Committee of the Chinese People's Political Consultative Conference. He is the author of *Why China Must Reform: In Memory of My Father Hu Yaobang* (People's Publishing House; 2011) and other books. In recent years he has attracted attention as a central member of a reformist group supporting constitutional law and democratization.

3. The Communist Youth League of China is a youth group that cultivates young leaders under the leadership of the Communist Party of China. Previous first secretaries include Hu Yaobang and Hu Jintao. The All-China Youth Federation brings together youth groups centered on the Communist Youth League and is regarded as the patriotic united front organization for Chinese youth. In fact, the cores of the Communist Youth League and the All-China Youth Federation are one and the same organization, and in international exchanges the name All-China Youth Federation is used.

4. During the Cultural Revolution, "reeducation" schools called May Seventh Cadre Schools were established throughout China. The name refers to the date on which Mao Zedong issued orders that government workers should go to rural villages and reform their thought.

5. In the summer of 2004 the soccer Asia Cup was held in China, with Japan beating China in the final. There was loud booing from some Chinese fans during the performance of the Japanese national anthem and during the game, and after the game an embassy vehicle carrying the Japanese minister was attacked. A window was broken and other damage caused. The violent anti-Japanese sentiment stemmed from protests on the problem of awareness of historical issues in Japan and Prime Minister Koizumi's visits to Yasukuni Shrine. A number of incidents of excessive protest drew attention in the lead-up to the Beijing Olympics in 2008. In April 2005, anti-Japanese demonstrations took place in many parts of China to protest Koizumi's visits to Yasukuni and Japan's assumption of a position on the UN Security Council. A number of protests turned violent.

6. Quoted from the Japanese translation of the speech available online at the homepage of the embassy of the People's Republic of China in Japan (April 12, 2007). http://www.china-embassy.or.jp/jpn/zt/wjbzlfr/t311936.htm. All subsequent quotations from Wen Jiabao's speech taken from the same source.
   (English translation taken from the website of the Ministry of Foreign Affairs of the People's Republic of China. http://www.fmprc.gov.cn/mfa_eng/wjb_663304/zzjg_663340/yzs_663350/gjlb_663354/2721_663446/2725_663454/t311544.shtml)

From "Breaking the Ice" to a "Warm Spring": Hu Jintao and Wen Jiabao Break the Impasse

When the Sino-Japanese relationship had fallen into an impasse, Hu Jintao and Wen Jiabao carried on with the intelligent diplomatic strategy of the great patriots Deng Xiaoping and Hu Yaobang, turned the situation around, and opened the way to reconciliation between the two countries. This has brought great benefits not only to China and Japan but to the whole of Asia.

When the Sino-Japanese relationship had fallen into an impasse, Hu Jintao and Wen Jiabao carried on with the intelligent diplomatic strategy of the great patriots Deng Xiaoping and Hu Yaobang, turned the situation around, and opened the way to reconciliation between the two countries. This has brought great benefits not only to China and Japan but to the whole of Asia. Hu Jintao has left future generations a rich legacy of thinking on Sino-Japanese relations. He once said that developing a relationship of long-term stability and friendship between the two neighbors was a major responsibility and mission for the leaders of both countries.

In September 2006, Koizumi Jun'ichiro resigned as prime minister of Japan. During his time in office, he had visited Yasukuni Shrine six times. The temperature of Sino-Japanese relations had plummeted and the relationship was again plunged into a dark abyss. Abe Shinzo took office as the new prime minister on September 26. On October 8, he surprised many people by appearing in Beijing with a beaming smile on his face. Five full years had passed since the previous visit by a Japanese prime minister to China. Abe, despite being known as a "hawk," had broken with the convention that the first place a new prime minister visits should be the United States and was the first prime minister to choose China for his first foreign visit after taking office. This visit became known in both countries as the trip that "broke the ice."

Several years later, Abe looked back on this "ice-breaking" journey and spoke with a journalist from the Chinese newspaper *Huanqiu Shibao* (*Global Times*), which carried the interview on June 20, 2012:

> Japan and China are linked together by an unbreakable bond. The two countries are close neighbors and do not have the option of relocating. Developing better Sino-Japanese relations will bring benefits to both countries, will help boost the prosperity of both countries, and is also advantageous for the region and the world. I became prime minister at a time when relations between the two countries had reached an impasse. Based on the understanding I have just outlined, I resolved to work hard to change the situation and offered my own view of how we should position the relationship.

He also said: "Maintaining a balance with China is the foundation of Japan's East Asia policy." Abe faced an extremely sensitive problem as soon as he took office: whether to visit Yasukuni Shrine. This was without doubt a chief reason for the tensions in the Sino-Japanese relationship at the time. Taking into account the pressure he was under from some factions within the country and his own party, Abe adopted an ambiguous policy in front of the media and never said explicitly whether he would visit the shrine or not. But he did say that it was vital to act appropriately to overcome the difficult political situation. The international media analysis suggests that the Chinese side had been given to understand that there would be no more visits to the shrine. This explains not only why it was possible for Abe to visit China but also why he was treated so well during his visit.

On October 8, Abe met the top three members of the CCP Politburo Standing Committee. An Associated Press (AP) report noted that Abe's was the first visit by a Japanese prime minister to China in five years, suggesting that a turning point had been reached in Sino-Japanese relations. The report quoted Hu Jintao as saying he hoped the visit would become the foundation for a new improvement in the bilateral relationship. Agence France-Press (AFP) reported a statement by Wu Bangguo that developing friendly relations between the countries was the only option that accorded with the fundamental interests of the people of both countries. A report by the Central News Agency in Taipei carried a statement by Wen Jiabao saying he hoped Abe's visit to China would open a window for improving the bilateral relationship. Abe's visit achieved important results that went beyond dispelling the lingering effects of the previous prime minister's visits to Yasukuni. He obtained Chinese support for his proposal to build a mutually beneficial relationship with China based on shared strategic interests. This represented the "positioning" of the bilateral relationship he referred to.

The Hong Kong–based magazine *Asia Weekly* carried an article by the journalist Jiang Xun in its May 25, 2008, edition that traced the lineage of this new idea of building a strategic and mutually beneficial relationship. China had wanted to build a strategic relationship with Japan from an early stage, but the Japanese side was opposed to the use of the word "strategy," apparently believing that a "strategic relationship" was one that it could share only with the United States. Although the Chinese side referred to important meetings between the two sides as examples of "strategic dialogue," Japan preferred to call these meetings "policy discussions."

In the early summer of 2006, Yachi Shotaro, who was deputy minister for foreign affairs at the time, was worried that further deterioration in relations with China would imperil Japan's interests. With a change in prime ministers impending, major progress was vital. He decided to entrust an important mission to Tarumi Hideo of the Ministry of Foreign Affairs and asked him to draw up a blueprint for a new thinking on Japan's China policy that both countries would be able to accept. Tarumi traveled to Beijing alone, where he met with a wide range of important figures in various fields. Back in Tokyo, he reported to Yachi proposing that the two countries build a strategic relationship. Yachi approved this and the new concept of a "strategic and mutually beneficial" relationship was fleshed out in further discussions.

When they submitted the idea to Abe, who had only recently taken office, Yachi and Tarumi were surprised to find that the new prime minister—even though he had previously taken a hard line on China—was much more amenable to this plan than they had expected. On September 23 that same year, a sixth round of strategic dialogues was held in Tokyo between China and Japan. The Chinese delegation, led by Dai Bingguo, had received information that the Japanese side hoped to build a strategic and mutually beneficial relationship with the Chinese. Dai Bingguo felt that the prospects for improving the bilateral relationship were entering a new phase.

Tando Yoshinori, a Japanese China specialist and a visiting professor at Waseda University,[1] spoke to Jiang Xun for his article, saying,

> The strategy includes long-term elements and involves fixing a foundation for long-term mutual benefits to both countries. Its impact would be tremendous. Koizumi prioritized Japan's relationship with the United States, but Abe and Fukuda regard the relationship with China as important too, at the same time as valuing the relationship with the United States. This is why they have decided to position the relationship with China as one of strategic mutual benefit. Personally, I do not approve of the Japanese prime minister visiting Yasukuni Shrine. Abe hasn't made it clear whether he will visit or not, but so far he has been consistent in not visiting during his time in office. And Fukuda has a profounder understanding of the Sino-Japanese relationship.

Xuexi Shibao Study Times, the official organ of the CCP Central Party School, carried an article by Qin Zhilai on April 9, 2007, with the title "Sino-Japanese Relationship Led by Strategic Mutual Benefit." The article said that, compared to the impasse brought about by Koizumi's visits to Yasukuni Shrine, the idea of strategic mutual benefit had brought a new dawn to the Sino-Japanese relationship and gave grounds for hope. He explained that aiming for strategic mutual benefit meant a new roadmap for thinking about improving and developing the relationship. Of course, people in both countries were aware that even if the two countries succeeded in building mutual trust, there was still a long way to go. That said, *Zhongguo Xinwen Zhoukan* (*China Newsweek*) magazine opened its account of Abe's successful China visit by describing it as a "major U-turn in the Sino-Japanese relationship."

Wen Jiabao visited Japan from April 11 to 13, 2007, and continued to work hard to restore warmth to the bilateral relationship. This was the first visit by a Chinese premier to Japan in seven years, and people in both countries described it as "a visit that thawed the ice." *The Times* of London wrote on April 10 that if Abe's visit to China had been an ice-breaking journey, this visit by Wen Jiabao to Japan in April would be an ice-thawing one. In Singapore, the *Lianhe Zaobao* reported that Wen Jiabao had swept away the doubts of people in different fields in Japan regarding the prospects for the development of the relationship with his style, dialogue, and smile.

Early in the morning of April 12, after the sixty-four-year-old Wen Jiabao had gone jogging in Yoyogi Park close to his hotel dressed in sportswear emblazoned with the 2008 Beijing Olympics logo, he did stretching exercises with local residents. Through an interpreter, he spoke with a group of elderly women who happened to be nearby: "I'm Wen Jiabao." One of the women replied: "We've seen you on television." Then Wen Jiabao showed them some tai chi moves. Later, when Wen visited Kyoto, he attended a tea ceremony performance by a tea master, sat cross-legged with ordinary farmers to eat *bota-mochi* rice cakes, shared anecdotes with students at Ritsumeikan University, and enjoyed baseball with students.

The most important event on April 12 was the "For Friendship and Cooperation" speech Wen Jiabao gave to the National Diet. Kyodo News reported he was the first major Chinese political leader to give a speech to the Diet in twenty-two years.[2] The speech was interrupted eleven times by enthusiastic applause from the 480 members in attendance. When he finished speaking, he received a long and warm standing ovation from the entire audience. The warmth and enthusiasm of the applause was unusual for a speech by a foreign VIP at the Diet.

In his speech, Wen Jiabao drew upon his deep knowledge of history to speak eloquently about the friendship and exchanges between the two countries stretching back over 2,000 years. Two points in particular impressed the Diet members in attendance:

1. Since the normalization of diplomatic ties between China and Japan, the Japanese Government and leaders have on many occasions stated their position on the history issue, admitted that Japan had

committed aggression, and expressed deep remorse and apology to the victimized countries. The Chinese Government and people appreciate the position they have taken.

2. China has received support and assistance from the Japanese Government and people in its reform, opening up, and modernization drive. This is something the Chinese people will never forget.

Wen Jiabao spoke positively about the remorse the Japanese government has shown with regard to the war and about Japan's support for China's modernization and construction. This was extremely significant as the first time a Chinese leader had spoken in this way since the reform and opening up policy began, and it demonstrated clearly the Chinese government's determination to overcome difficulties and push ahead with friendship that would transcend the generations. Japanese Diet members were deeply impressed and moved by this.

In his speech, Wen Jiabao emphasized that, "Peace will bring benefit to China and Japan, while confrontation can only do harm to them." This is a truth that has been demonstrated repeatedly during the winding course that the relationship has followed. On the question of energy development in the East China Sea, Wen Jiabao put forward the principle of shelving the sovereignty debate and suggested the principle of joint development. Although this did not represent substantial progress, it did serve to soothe rising tensions over the issue. He said: "With regard to the issue of the East China Sea, our two countries should follow the principle of shelving differences, seeking joint development, and conducting active consultation so as to make substantive progress towards peaceful settlement of the differences and make the East China Sea a sea of peace, friendship, and cooperation." Speaking to a Kyodo News journalist on April 12, Chief Cabinet Secretary Shiozaki Yasuhisa said that Wen Jiabao's speech had been, "very forward-looking and made positive remarks on a broad range of topics. Japan will continue down the road it has walked since the war and will continue to contribute to peaceful development."

Wen Jiabao met with Prime Minister Abe on April 11, the day before his speech in the Diet, and the two leaders released a Japan-China Joint Press Statement.[3] The communiqué outlined the basic content of their efforts to build a strategic and mutually beneficial relationship as follows. "Both countries will mutually support their peaceful development and enhance mutual trust in the area of politics. They will maintain and increase mutual high-level visits. Both countries will deepen mutually beneficial cooperation and achieve common development. They will strengthen cooperation in the areas of energy, environmental protection, and more. Both countries will strengthen coordination and cooperation and tackle regional and global challenges together. They will work to improve the transparency of their respective policies." Wen Jiabao also met with the Japanese emperor.

The media in the two countries reported the visit on a positive note and took the view that Wen Jiabao had already achieved the primary objective of his trip by successfully thawing the ice. Although it was not possible to resolve all the issues in the bilateral relationship with this single visit, the thick ice had been broken and the road to exchanges reopened.

Ezra F. Vogel, Harvard University professor emeritus and a specialist on Chinese and Japanese issues, had high praise for Wen Jiabao's visit to Japan. He said that Wen's visit to Japan was very significant and compared it to the success of Deng Xiaoping's 1978 visit to Japan. Following Premier Wen Jiabao's successful visit to Japan, the *Southern Weekly* newspaper carried an article by Guo Guangdong in its April 19, 2007, issue that started off: "After this ice-thawing trip, we should learn from Japan and mark a new departure." The article argued that patriotism must not be allowed to become hot-blooded. Shifting from a position of implacable opposition to Japan to one of understanding Japan and learning from Japan will allow patriotism to thrive on a more rational and higher level. The idea that China and Japan must fight, the article argued, was past its sell-by date. As Deng Xiaoping argued, peace and development are the most important themes in today's world. Peace, freedom, democracy, human rights, and rule of law are increasingly seen as universal values, and the relationship between states is no longer one of life-or-death fights for survival but is one in which friendly relations and strategic mutual benefit are vital as the only path that can lead to a truly win-win relationship.

In May 2007, the Economist Intelligence Unit ranked various countries' ability to innovate and recognized Japan as the world's number one, placing it ahead of the United States, Switzerland, Sweden, United Kingdom, France, Germany, and everyone else.

Abe Shinzo resigned as prime minister on September 12, 2007, and was succeeded by Fukuda Yasuo. Will this change of prime ministers see the strategic and mutually beneficial relationship abandoned by the Japanese side? On September 29, Wen Jiabao sent a message of congratulations to Fukuda to mark thirty-five years since the normalization of relations between the two countries. In it, he said, "Today, the relationship between China and Japan has entered a new stage of comprehensively constructing a strategic and mutually beneficial relationship, and we face an important opportunity for further development. I sincerely hope that both sides will use this 35th anniversary of the normalization of ties as an opportunity to push ahead and ensure that the relationship develops in a healthy and stable manner in the long term." The message pointedly employed the phrase "strategic and mutually beneficial relationship" and represented an attempt to sound out the new government's attitude.

In crafting his side of the exchange of congratulations, Fukuda made it clear that the Japanese side had decided to strengthen its cooperation with China and work together to make a constructive contribution to building a mutually beneficial relationship built on shared strategic interests and to the development of peace and stability in Asia and the world. Fukuda too used the phrase "strategic and mutually beneficial relationship." On October 1, Fukuda gave a policy speech in the Diet and said: "With China, we will continue to work to establish a mutually beneficial relationship based on common strategic interests." Warmth was maintained in the relationship and conditions continued promising.

On December 27, Fukuda arrived in Beijing and began his itinerary in China. It was a cold winter's day, but Fukuda declared: "I want to call this visit one that will welcome the new spring." The Chinese people could hardly have been unaware of the Fukuda family. Yasuo's father, Fukuda Takeo, had been prime minister when Japan signed the Treaty of Peace and Friendship with China in 1978. Yasuo had witnessed that historic moment as his father's secretary. He had also visited China on the occasion of the 25th anniversary of the signing of the treaty and had taken part in the commemorative events.

In a speech he gave at Peking University, Fukuda acknowledged that there had been unfortunate periods in the 2000-year history of relations between China and Japan that Japan should look at squarely and with remorse. But Sino-Japanese relations were not about continuing to nurse the resentments of the past. Instead, the two sides should work to lift the relationship to a new level and move toward the future shouldering their shared responsibilities for Asia and the world—for the peace of the region and the world.[4] In his speech, he quoted Lu Xun, who studied for a time in Japan. "I thought: hope . . . is just like roads across the earth. For actually the earth had no roads to begin with, but when many men pass one way, a road is made."

On December 28, Fukuda met with Hu Jintao, Wu Bangguo, and Wen Jiabao. At his meeting with Fukuda, Hu Jintao said that developing good-neighborly and long-term stable relations between China and Japan and achieving mutual benefits through peaceful coexistence and friendship across generations was the major aim of joint development, the shared wish of the Chinese people, and the shared responsibility and mission of the leaders of both countries. The Chinese side will work with the Japanese side to increase mutual trust and understanding, to deal appropriately with sensitive issues in the relationship, to develop mutual benefits and strengthen exchanges, and to build and develop a mutually beneficial relationship based on shared strategic interests. Wu Bangguo said that the National People's Congress and the Japanese Diet, having established a mechanism for regular exchanges, must make full use of this channel to increase understanding and mutual trust. Wen Jiabao said that the two countries must work to strengthen and increase their economic and trade cooperation in fields such as energy, finance, environmental protection, high-tech industries, and information technology and should work to strengthen defense exchanges and dialogue in the national security field.

The two governments took the opportunity to sign a number of memoranda and communiques: a memorandum on activities relating to the China-Japan Youth Friendship Exchange Year, a joint communiqué on promoting environmental and energy cooperation, and a joint statement on further strengthening science and technology cooperation directed at the problem of climate change.

On December 29, Mrs. Fukuda visited a Japanese school in Beijing and an animation and manga exhibition featuring the work of young people from China and Japan, while the prime minister himself visited Binhai New Area, a new coastal development zone in Tianjin. On December 30, there was a visit to Qufu in Shandong Province and a visit to the Temple of Confucius. They were shown around the temple by Kong Fanpeng, a 74th-generation descendant of Confucius, and Fukuda showed great interest. As melodious ancient music was performed, Fukuda recalled that he had studied the *Analects* as a student in junior high school. On the journey, he quoted several of the best-known sayings from the *Analects*, including "What you do not want done to yourself, do not do to others" and "Of the things brought about by the rites, harmony is the most valuable." The musical and dance performance to honor Confucius lasted six minutes and twenty seconds, but Fukuda and his wife stood solemnly on the northern edge of the Xing Tan pavilion throughout. Fukuda was deep in thought as he listened to the explanations of his interpreter. When the music and dance came to an end, he said: "If Confucian thought became widely accepted and put down roots in all our hearts, the world would surely be a more peaceful place."

Later, Fukuda wrote his impressions of the visit in beautifully written Chinese calligraphy, writing: "wen gu chuang xin" or "remember the old, create the new." When the visit was over, he waved to fellow visitors and said: "I'll be back." This was the first time a Japanese prime minister had visited Qu Fu and paid his respects at the grave of Confucius. During this visit, Fukuda emphasized that the history and culture of the two countries shared a common source, reducing the cultural distance between the two countries and doing away with old resentments.

On December 31, the Chinese newspaper *Jingji Guancha Bao* (*Economic Observer*) carried an article by the journalist Lin Li: "Fukuda arrives in harsh midwinter, on a trip to welcome a new spring." The article said that the symbolic significance of Fukuda's visit to China was even greater than its immediate achievements in terms of encouraging economic cooperation and praised the far-reaching and strategic impact of these reciprocal visits of friendship. Although the East China Sea issue will require much time and deliberation, there was plenty of scope for cooperation between the two countries. Fukuda, who did not visit Yasukuni Shrine, valued cooperation between the two countries and, the article said, had certainly brought a breath of fresh new spring air into people's lives.

Hu Jintao's "warm spring trip" to Japan May 6 to 10, 2008, pushed the U-turn in the bilateral relationship to its zenith. This was the penultimate of the major visits between leaders of the two countries that took place in the period of a year and a half. The Japanese government accorded him the highest honors and the warmest welcome. Hu Jintao attended 55 activities in the space of just five days, and his visit resulted in important progress in Sino-Japanese relations.

He had a meeting with the emperor, and long meetings with Prime Minister Fukuda and House of Representatives Speaker Kono Yohei. He gave a speech at Waseda University, met with many people from various spheres of life in Japan, and made good connections and ties with a wide range of people, including the leaders of the main Japanese political parties, people from the private sector who had worked hard on Sino-Japanese friendship for many years, the leaders of a group of Diet members who had supported the Beijing Olympics, the former members of a Japanese delegation that had participated in youth exchange visits between China and Japan in the 1980s, several children of former prime ministers who had been active in promoting friendship between China and Japan, and business and media figures. He also visited a Chinese school in Yokohama, Panasonic Corporation in Osaka, and Toshodaiji temple in the ancient capital of Nara, where he visited the grave of the monk Jianzhen (Ganjin) who had served as an emissary in the early stages of exchanges between the two countries. He also had meetings with political leaders in Kanagawa Prefecture, Yokohama City, and Osaka Prefecture.

Hu Jintao regularly emphasized that China and Japan must walk a path of peaceful and friendly cooperation and constantly stressed that this was the only correct option for the two countries. He argued that there was a strategic and global significance to the Sino-Japanese relationship and made several new proposals regarding the relationship. These included maintaining high-level exchanges, boosting cooperation in such fields as the economy, trade, and science and technology, strengthening cooperation in the environmental protection field, expanding human exchanges, and beefing up defense exchanges. On the issue of the East China Sea, progress was made on high-level discussions that delved deep and Hu Jintao said that the two sides would reach an agreement as soon as possible. While the tainted *gyoza* dumplings Japan imported from China was a major issue at the time, he said that the Chinese side was taking the issue seriously, that the relevant departments were continuing their investigations, and that they would report the full story as soon as possible.

The Japanese media appreciated that Hu Jintao's visit expressed a warm vision for the future of the relationship that, while emphasizing the importance of looking squarely at history and looking toward the future, did not make excessive use of the "historical issues" card. In compiling the joint declaration, China did not even press for the inclusion of Japanese expressions of remorse or apology, and the media lauded the tenor of the visit as demonstrating the gravitas of a major power and showing concern for the feelings of the Japanese people.

The biggest achievement of the visit was the signing on May 7 by Hu Jintao and Fukuda Yasuo of the Joint Statement between the Government of Japan and the Government of the People's Republic of China on Comprehensive Promotion of a Mutually Beneficial Relationship Based on Common Strategic Interests. This was an important document with the power to move the relationship forward. Following on from the three political agreements signed in the past, this joint declaration embodied a new stage in the Sino-Japanese relationship, encapsulated a new shared understanding on both sides, set out clearly the new principles for development of bilateral relations, and contained an objective evaluation of Japan based on facts. Representing the fourth important political agreement between China and Japan, the joint declaration stated that:

> The two sides resolved to face history squarely, advance toward the future, and endeavor with persistence to create a new era of a "mutually beneficial relationship based on common strategic interests" between Japan and China. . . . The two sides recognized that they are partners who cooperate with each other and are not threats to each

other. The two sides again stated that they would support each other's peaceful development.[5]

The part of the joint declaration that attracted the most attention was the statement that: "The Chinese side expressed its positive evaluation of Japan's consistent pursuit of the path of a peaceful country and Japan's contribution to the peace and stability of the world through peaceful means over more than sixty years since the end of World War II."

In Hong Kong, the *Asia Weekly* published an article on May 25, 2008, with the title "A Warm Spring Visit: The Inner Feelings as Seen through Japanese Media Reports." The article said that this was the first time the Chinese government had evaluated postwar Japan positively in an important diplomatic document and argued that this showed the Chinese government's acknowledgement of the fact that Japan had constantly sought peace for the more than sixty years since the end of the war. With this, it added, the factually inaccurate judgment by some people that "militarism is reviving in Japan" was totally cleared up. On May 8, an AP analysis noted that the joint declaration did not explicitly mention the issues of war responsibility or apology but said that this was because these issues had already been resolved in the previous three political documents. Further, the joint declaration also clearly stated that: "The Chinese side attaches importance to Japan's position and role in the United Nations and desires Japan to play an even greater constructive role in the international community." In the foreign media, this was seen as suggesting that the Chinese side had changed its attitude, which had previously been to reject Japan's wish to become a permanent member of the UN Security Council, and saw China as implicitly suggesting understanding toward Japan's wish to become a permanent member of the Security Council.

On May 8, Hu Jintao gave a speech at Waseda University. He said: "The Japanese Government has played a positive role in China's modernization drive by making Japanese yen loans in support of China's infrastructure construction, environmental protection, energy development, and scientific and technological advancement. In addition, Japanese friends from various sectors offered warm-hearted help to China in its course of modernization. The Chinese people will always remember those Japanese friends who have devoted themselves to China-Japan friendship." For Hu Jintao to speak warmly like this after a period in which Sino-Japanese relations were frozen in ice was not easy. He embodied the courage to seek after true facts, as well as hopes that turned toward the future.

In this context, I would like to add that from 1979 to the present time,

Japan has provided China with a huge amount of low-interest yen loans and supported construction in China on more than 150 major important projects, including the Beijing-Kowloon railway and the second phase of the Beijing subway. Early on after the policy of reform and opening up was announced, China had limited funding resources and Japan's long-term, low-interest loans were a vital source of support. The annual rates of interest on these yen loans varied between 0.79 and 3.5 percent, with most of them actually falling between 1 and 2 percent. The repayment terms were from thirty to forty years, and Japan has also provided some grant assistance. Funding from the World Bank generally comes at a rate of 4 percent, on top of which the repayment term is normally three years. Policy banks in China itself charge interest rates of 4 percent and have repayment periods of ten years. All of this shows how favorable the terms of Japan's yen loans have been.

During Hu Jintao's visit to Japan, the two countries released the Joint Press Statement on Strengthening Exchange and Cooperation between the Government of Japan and the Government of the People's Republic of China which enumerated seventy items relating to cooperation between the countries. Little wonder Singapore's *Lianhe Zaobao* said that Hu Jintao's visit had brought the warmth of blossoming spring to the bilateral relationship.

On May 7, the *Southern Weekly* carried an article by Liu Ning with the title "Regarding Japan as a teacher and accelerating the speed of China's reforms." The article argued that there was nothing shameful or embarrassing about regarding Japan as a teacher and reminded its readers that Deng Xiaoping often used to say when welcoming friends from Japan that China should "learn from Japan." Another important result of this visit by Hu Jintao was to make reciprocal visits by the heads of government more systematic. Instead of merely coming together as if by accident on the foreign policy stage, they agreed to hold formal meetings at least annually in the expectation that they could thus avoid the possibility of a period with no exchanges and hence no progress in the relationship.

Japan played a leading role in providing disaster relief assistance in the wake of the Sichuan earthquake of May 12. On the 18th, a photograph of Japanese rescue workers standing in a line and paying their respects to the dead with a moment of silent prayer was prominently featured on Chinese websites. Chinese people said from the bottom of their hearts: Thank you, Japan. Japan was also the only country to establish a league of representatives in the National Diet to support the Beijing Olympics, in which more than 300 members of the Diet took part across party lines. Unusually, the *Global Times* carried an article calling on Chinese spectators to show support for Japanese Olympic teams.

On June 18, Ministry of Foreign Affairs spokesperson Jiang Yu announced that, following discussions, China and Japan had reached a basic shared understanding regarding the issue of gas fields in the East China Sea and both sides would cooperate in the transitional period before defining sea boundaries in a way that would not infringe on the legal position of either country. The two sides had agreed to take the first steps toward joint development within defined areas of the East China Sea.

All these signs of progress took place after Hu Jintao's successful visit to Japan. Of course, several difficulties and variables remain even with this progress toward better bilateral relations, and it is to be hoped that informed people in both countries will work even harder to overcome these difficulties.

NOTES

1. The text refers to him as a visiting professor at Waseda University, but he is also known as the former head of the Yomiuri Shimbun's Beijing bureau and a former professor at Toyo University.

2. Wen Jiabao was the third important Chinese official to give a speech at the National Diet, following Hu Yaobang, general secretary, in November 1983 and Peng Zhen, chairman of the Standing Committee of the National People's Congress, in April 1985. As the first Chinese official to speak at the Diet, Hu Yaobang had emphasized the importance of exchanges and cooperation between China and Japan and helped create a positive relationship between the countries in the 1980s.

3. The account here gives an excerpted summary of the basic content of the joint press release of April 11, 2007, and some of the points are given in a different order from that in which they originally appeared in the Japanese version on the webpage of the Japanese Ministry of Foreign Affairs (MOFA) as used for the translation. http://www.mofa.go.jp/mofaj/area/china/visit/0704_kh.html#a

4. This text quotes Fukuda's speech in a condensed, summarized form. The complete text can be accessed at the MOFA website. (December 28, 2007) www.mofa.go.jp/mofaj/press/enzetsu/19/efuk_1228.html
   Provisional English translation http://www.mofa.go.jp/region/asia-paci/china/speech0712.html

5. Translation quoted from the MOFA website. (May 7, 2008)
   https://www.mofa.go.jp/region/asia-paci/china/joint0805.html

TEN

How the March 11 Disaster Brought the Two Countries Closer

Good public diplomacy consists of finding points of similarity and continuity with foreign countries. Sino-Japanese relations are no exception. In the background to this natural disaster crisis are shared desires that can transcend local interests. Protecting lives, hoping for a stable environment, and giving thanks for sincerely offered help—these things too transcend national borders.

A major international conference—the Future China Global Forum—has taken place in Singapore every summer since 2010. Several hundred government workers, scholars, and businesspeople from Singapore, China, and other countries in Asia, Europe, and America come together for a free and frank exchange of views about changes and development in China. This makes it extremely interesting and impressive, with numerous lectures and discussions on political, economic, social, and cultural developments. It has been called the Davos of Asia; and Lee Kuan Yew, the senior statesmen and doyen of Singaporean politics, gives an address every year.

In July 2011, I was honored with an invitation to take part in the Forum, where I gave a lecture on the afternoon of July 11. There were four guest speakers on the panel. Besides myself, the other three were Supachai Panitchpakdi, president of the Thai Central Bank,[1] Tanaka Akihiko, executive vice president of the University of Tokyo, and Robert S. Ross, associate at the Harvard University Fairbank Center for Chinese Studies.

In my presentation, I argued that the positive development of Sino-Japanese relations had a key part to play in integrating China with the mainstream of a globalizing world. I opened by saying:

> Because the Beijing Subway does not have any safety gates on the Line 1 platforms, special staff are employed to maintain order by the doors and keep people from falling onto the tracks when it is crowded. One day in late June this year, I happened to take the subway at the height of the rush hour as people were making their way home from work and the system was extremely crowded. A middle-aged man who was obeying the rules by lining up in an orderly fashion next to me said: "If we're not careful there could be a major accident here. Why can't we be more like the Japanese—they always maintain order so sensibly?" Several people nearby overheard his remark and nodded in agreement. I was quite moved. Why did this apparently simple incident make such an impression on me? For an ordinary Chinese person to praise the Japanese in a crowded public place like this, and for the people around him to agree with his sentiments—this was something

that would have been difficult to imagine in the past. But since the March 11 earthquake, the Chinese media had sent hundreds of reporters to cover the story and many people in China had been impressed and moved by prominent coverage of the impressive levels of public morals and good order in Japan. It was this that had made the kind of scene I had just encountered possible.

One aspect that drew particular attention in China was the high praise given to the Japanese by Zhu Rongji, the influential and highly esteemed former premier. In issue 15 of the *Fenghuang Zhoukan* (*Phoenix Weekly*), dated May 25, 2011, an article appeared by the journalist Wang Dongya under the title "Zhu Rongji and a School Friend Discuss Current Issues." The article was a conversation piece with Zhu Rongji. In the course of the discussion, Zhu Rongji made the following point.

> The losses the Japanese people suffered in the massive earthquake and tsunami recently have been on such a scale that even we have been shocked by the terrible nature of the damage. But ordinary people in Japan have not panicked and have continued to prize good manners and public morals. This is something we could not do in China. If an earthquake of this scale struck in China, it would almost certainly bring confusion and chaos. Instilling these virtues in the national character is something that must start in the national education system.

China's leaders showed the highest levels of respect and goodwill toward Japan after the disaster. On March 18, Hu Jintao personally visited the Japanese embassy in China to express his condolences for those who had lost their lives. This act surprised many people, as it was something that had rarely been seen from a Chinese head of state before. On May 21, before taking part in a trilateral summit in Tokyo with Japan and South Korea, Chinese Premier Wen Jiabao went to Miyagi Prefecture, one of the worst-hit areas, to express his sympathies to people affected by the disaster. Some people in the affected areas said that Wen Jiabao had shown greater concern for the disaster victims than the Japanese prime minister had.

Hundreds of Chinese media outlets dispatched journalists to Japan to cover the story, and even some evening papers from medium-sized cities sent reporters. This too was unprecedented and shows clearly how important Japan is to the Chinese media. For approximately half a month, stories about the Japanese earthquake were prominent in the Chinese media. Among the many thousands of articles, one aspect that particularly stood out was reports of the high levels of public morality and orderly behavior among the Japanese people in the face of the disaster. For the Chinese media to go to such lengths to dig up stories illustrating the good points of Japanese society was another thing that was without precedent.

On April 3, 2011, Ye Qianrong, formerly an actor with the Shanghai People's Art Theater and now a professor at Tokai University, published a piece in the *Dongfang Zaobao* (*Oriental Morning Daily*) weekend supplement *Shanghai Review of Books*. He astonished countless Chinese readers with his detailed chronological account of his experiences on the day of the disaster. Ye Qianrong wrote:

> After the three strong shakings subsided, I left the underground carpark of the hotel and drove out onto the main road. People were streaming out of every building, and all the roads were locked with traffic. The sidewalks on both sides were crammed with jostling people. They were making their way forward at a slow pace, through a silence that was uncanny. It is not an appropriate comparison, but they reminded me of people walking in silent procession at a funeral. There was no sad music playing, but people's footsteps were synchronized as if walking to the same rhythm. Most of them had on a face mask, were wearing coats, and carried backpacks. They walked without talking to one another, without fighting for precedence, and without cutting in. Several million people were walking silently step-by step-toward their homes, and must have known beyond any doubt at this moment that they would have to walk three or four hours before they reached their homes in the suburbs. And yet they continued to walk unruffled and relaxed as before. The roads were jammed with traffic, but no one made to walk on the roads, and I found that I could drive faster than I had expected. At this instant when a colossal tragedy had struck, the scenery I was seeing was as if this nation's people had all suddenly started to mobilize and were marching off to battle. And from inside my car I posted my first comment on Weibo since the earthquake: "It's almost like a scene from a huge silent movie; like a scene from *Exodus*."

What explained this apparent calm? Ye says that although the Japanese adopted Confucian culture from an early stage in their history, the culture developed differently in Japan. In Chinese culture, utilitarian calculations are always present. The aims of Japanese morality, however, are quite different from those of China. He continues:

The Japanese have refined the objectives of morality to the status of a kind of aesthetic sense. This means that there is hardly any discussion of the benefits that might accrue to an individual as a result of following a certain kind of conduct. Instead, there is a constant focus on what kind of conduct is most pleasing and beautiful. The Japanese archipelago is situated at the meeting point of four tectonic plates, and its people have been forced by fate into a close acquaintance with four kinds of major natural disasters: earthquakes, typhoons, tsunami, and volcanic eruptions. This destiny has helped to shape a mentality dominated by ideas of impermanence. People have universally accepted that life and nature are transient and impermanent. Based on this understanding, consciously or otherwise, people seek a beautiful life, even if it must be short. They seek to make their lives bloom for a brief instant, like the petals of the cherry blossom. This pursuit of a moment's beauty and the objective of finite, limited beauty plays a crucial role in the Japanese subconscious. In fact, there must certainly have been some people (among those walking through the city streets in the hours after the disaster took place) who jostled for precedence and who considered leaving the sidewalks to walk in the middle of the street. But if even seventy percent of people continue to keep order and follow the rules, the rest of the people too will follow the example of the majority and exercise restraint and self-control. This is characteristic of the ideal of Japanese behavior. . . what is not beautiful is a source of shame, and to understand and avoid shame is to approach beauty. The pursuit of beauty is the driving power behind people's self-restraint—they wish to avoid being seen as not beautiful. Most people must surely realize the losses caused to them by their self-restraint. Probably many are quite aware that it would be more convenient and advantageous for them to escape from this self-control. But they nevertheless rise above utilitarian self-interest and suppress their wishes. For many Japanese people, this represents model behavior.

Xu Zhiyuan, a well-known media figure and author, published a piece in the April 3, 2011, *Asia Weekly* with the title "Dignity under Pressure." The article went as follows.

People affected by the disaster formed orderly lines as they evacuated; no one screamed or cried into the camera. Supermarkets distributed necessities at no charge, and there have been no reports of looting or similar crimes. One foreign journalist noticed that even in the midst of rubble, local people were apparently extending polite and well-mannered greetings to fellow residents and visitors. Another journalist noticed in Tokyo that taxi drivers were as courteous to their customers as usual, and that the interiors of the cars were decorated in white lace just as before. Toilet seats, of course, were warmed as usual, and store and restaurant managers still came scurrying over to provide excellent customer service. Company employees still worked diligently, putting in overtime to provide better service, and the faces of people on the streets were almost unbelievably calm beneath their masks.

The whole world has been astonished and impressed by the attitude and behavior of the Japanese in the face of this disaster. They are like characters in a story by Hemingway—displaying a certain dignity under pressure. And this surprise prompted a kind of mysticism. Is it possible that the Japanese really are different from other people? All people and all countries are constantly undergoing a process of ongoing self-discovery. Even without extreme experiences like natural disasters, national humiliations, or wars, it is always possible for the character of a person or country to be clearly revealed. Fear, powerlessness, and vulnerability press us to look closely at ourselves. This process of self-examination can sometimes have results that surprise us. Order and beauty are the most striking characteristics that Japan presents to the outside world. Following this colossal natural disaster, these characteristics have exerted a more powerful influence than in normal circumstances. A natural disaster is something that cannot be controlled, characterized by disorder and ugliness.

Study Times, the official organ of the CCP Central Party School, carried an article by the veteran *Xinhua* journalist Xu Boyuan in its April 25, 2011, issue with the title "Let Us Note the High Character Displayed by the Japanese People in the Midst of Disaster." The article made the following points.

Since the major earthquake in Japan, the Japanese people have displayed great character, moving people from this country who have witnessed it and experienced events for themselves. Discussion of this online has been heated. Many online commentators imagined how we ourselves would react if faced with a similar situation, and have felt that there is a sizeable gap between the Japanese behavior and the way people in this country might behave. These purely private actions are to be greatly welcomed.

In Japan after the disaster, telephone booths in the affected areas were made available free-of-charge, and vending machines and convenience stores offered daily essentials at no charge. There were no incidents of people competing to buy up limited supplies, looting, or other misconduct. Even so, in this country, although we are far away from the site of the disaster, from north to south people fought to buy all the salt[2] they could get their hands on, and some stores even took advantage of the situation to raise their prices. Immediately after the disaster, service on the subways was suspended, but people waited quietly at the stations. There was no pushing and shoving, and no confusion. On the escalators in supermarkets and other big buildings, people deliberately moved to the sides and left room for people to pass. People who have been evacuated to elementary schools, hotel lobbies, and other places, sit or lie quietly, and no one smokes or talks in loud voices. When morning comes and people move away from their evacuation places, they tidy up the trash around them and take it with them, so that the floors are always extremely clean, and it is almost impossible to imagine that anyone had spent the night there. In our place, there are very few people who have such self-awareness and self-respect even in normal times, let alone in emergency conditions following a natural disaster.

The late Ji Xianlin[3] wrote an essay about things he had seen by the Hou Hu Lake in the Langrunyuan Park at Peking University.[4] I was amazed when I read it. This piece, which Ji wrote in 2002, records that Ji visited the banks of the river and sat down for a while on a bench. In front of him, as always, were the discarded shells of sunflower seeds, cigarette butts, and all kinds of other rubbish. Sometimes he would find the leftovers of people's packed lunches, including chicken bones and spat-out fish bones. There were also lots of fruit peels. The state of chaos, with all kinds of refuse strewn about without any care, was enough to give him a headache and feelings of nausea. One time, Ji saw a foreign couple picking up rubbish with plastic bags and bamboo tongs in the area around a dormitory for foreign scholars. He and his assistant helped them and were astonished and ashamed to find condoms among the other trash.

Xu Boyuan continues:

Because Japan invaded our country, Chinese people still retain feelings of resentment in their hearts even today. This is a natural human reaction and is not something that needs to be criticized. But when this reaches such a level that people cannot even bear to hear people discussing Japan's good points, so that simply overhearing such a conversation is enough to put them in a bad mood and put a sour expression on their face, so that they start cursing such people as "betrayers of the nation" and "traitors"—this kind of behavior is simply immature and childish, and is both comical and sad at the same time. This kind of behavior is quite common online in recent years, and I myself have been the victim of curses based on this kind of immature patriotism. And now, because of these circumstances, people are consciously comparing the qualities and character of the two countries and their peoples. This is an extremely significant development that should be welcomed and commended.

Why do people in Japan have such a strong sense of public morals? My Japanese friend Oku Masafumi says it is something that has been cultivated as a result of many years of civics education. In Japan, this kind of education is provided and taken seriously starting in kindergarten. Children are taught to maintain social order and told that they must not throw litter on the ground or spit. The Japanese police visit kindergartens and show children how to cross the road safely. You must not cross when the light is red; you must wait for the light to turn to green. Look first right and then left before crossing the road. After many years of such training, people in Japanese society acquire a broad sense of public spiritedness that values the public space ahead of the individual's private individual interests. Oku Masafumi continued. "In Chinese subways and other public spaces, one often sees various rules posted, telling people not to do this or that. But, perhaps because of inadequate education, people just continue littering, making a lot of noise, and ignoring the traffic lights. In Japan, there are no posters in the streets or subways to tell people what the laws or rules are. But because they have had this kind of thorough-going education over many years, everyone keeps order without needing to be told. The differences between the countries boil down to the differences between the education of qualities in their respective peoples."

Xu Boyuan also expresses somewhat the same view in the essay. He says that in China, a small group of people who hold power and authority have coarsened the public property by refusing to abide by the laws and systems that are in place. The masses of regular people follow their example and act in a selfish and ill-disciplined way, failing to value public space and failing to treat it with respect

Economic Observer praised the quality of Japan's architecture and the strength of its media. Its March 21, 2011, issue carried an article by Zhang Hong called "Japan As Mirror." The article argued that the earthquake itself had not claimed many lives. It was the tsunami, reaching heights of up to ten meters, that caused widespread destruction and took tens of thousands of lives. Buildings in Japan were constructed so that even a huge earthquake like this did not cause major damage and destruction, and some schools and other relatively tall buildings became places of refuge after the quake when the tsunami surged in. People had been reminded of the true significance of homes as places of shelter. Zhang Hong wrote that NHK had continued to communicate information without pause during the disaster and had maintained an objective tone throughout, helping to keep people calm. This reporting had performed an important role in securing assistance from around the world.

The same day, the paper also published an article by Zhang Feifei with the title "Where Does Order Come From?" The article noted that at a press conference given by Tokyo Electric Power Co., Inc. (TEPCO) on March 15, the questions asked by journalists from NHK and other media outlets were extremely challenging and to the point, so that the TEPCO representative was discomfited and temporarily at a loss for words. The high level of freedom enjoyed by the media in Japan helped to ensure the transparency and communication of information and guaranteed the people's right to know.

Xinjing Bao (*The Beijing News*) carried an article in its March 19, 2011, edition with the title "A Look at What Weibo Can Tell Us About Public Diplomacy between China and Japan." The author was Zhou Qing-an, a professor at Tsinghua University, who wrote:

> Since the earthquake, tsunami, and radioactivity leaks in Japan, the general atmosphere on Weibo and the Chinese Internet has been fairly positive in terms of public diplomacy toward Japan. Immediately after the earthquake, some Weibo users expressed the view that "heaven has punished Japan," but expressions of grief and sympathy were more widespread. Even six days after the disaster, it is still possible to observe such mixed emotions.
>
> One Weibo user wrote: "When I first heard the news of the earthquake in Japan, I was inwardly happy that Japanese people were being forced to live through this bitter experience. But these thoughts only lasted a moment. They were immediately replaced by another thought, telling me that it was immoral to think like that and that the right thing to do was to pray for them."

Similar changes could be seen in many other Weibo users, suggesting that Chinese people were able to distinguish sensibly between historical issues and events happening in the present. Good public diplomacy consists of finding points of similarity and continuity with foreign countries. Sino-Japanese relations are no exception. In the background to this natural disaster crisis are shared desires that can transcend local interests. Protecting lives, hoping for a stable environment, and giving thanks for sincerely offered help—these things too transcend national borders. All form the foundations for important values in public diplomacy. As these shocking events unfolded, it became easier for people in China and Japan to share the same understanding. And this makes further improvements in the relationship possible.

The same day, *The Beijing News* carried Weibo postings by four ordinary Chinese citizens:

> In the face of a natural disaster, all that remains is our equality as human beings, and all prejudice or favor based on nationality or race disappears. Keep strong, Japan! I really wish some people would stop discussing everything through the lens of prejudice and bias. We should not forget history, but we also need to know how to value life.
>
> Ling Xian

> I sympathize with the people of Japan and believe we must do everything we can to extend a helping hand. This is based not only on human morals, but also on long-term interests. We must not lose this opportunity to improve our relationship with the people of Japan and must not be misled by hatred and let this chance for improving mutual understanding slip away.
>
> Ge Yancheng

> A lot of people online are happy about the huge earthquake in Japan, but personally I feel a deep pain in my heart. As a Chinese person, I think we should learn generosity and understanding. This huge natural disaster reminds us that we cannot hope to control the destructive force of nature and we should let go of hatred. Previously, I shed tears for Wenchuan and Yushu.[5] Now, I offer up prayers for the people of Japan. I hope they can rebuild their homes as soon as possible. We all live in the same global village.
>
> Feng Suiyue

> There is one ordinary Japanese citizen I will never forget. He saved

twenty Chinese trainees immediately after the earthquake struck. Sato Mitsuru[6] returned repeatedly to their housing, and the tsunami surged in when he was looking for his wife and daughter. He was unable to escape, and his wife and daughter are still missing. There is a saying that we should repay even the kindness of a droplet of water with gratitude like the gushing of a spring. I am hoping his family members are alive and safe. I express my gratitude and respect to Mr. Sato for what he did.

Caijing Shiping

Even in faraway Costa Rica, a Central American country of just 4.5 million people, the news of improving relations between the people of China and Japan following the earthquake attracted attention. The *Costa Rica Today* newspaper carried an article on March 19, 2011, under the title "Disaster Dissolves Historic Hatred" The article wrote: "The accumulated resentment of history runs deep between the two major nations of China and Japan, but Chinese people have shown sympathy for the victims of the recent earthquake and tsunami which claimed large numbers of fatalities in Japan. So far, these feelings of sympathy have been strong enough to overcome any other emotions."

In an online survey carried out by Sina Weibo and Kaixin Wang, a social network service, 68 percent of respondents said they had prayed for people who had been affected by the earthquake and tsunami, while 17 percent replied that they felt no particular emotions in regard to the disaster. Many netizens were able for a time to discard their differences of opinion and resentments about Japan and pray for the safety of people in the affected areas in the name of solidarity and brotherhood.

In Germany, *Die Welt* carried an article on March 20, 2011, with the title "China Projects an Image as Responsible Great Power." The article ran as follows.

On the day the earthquake hit Japan, Chinese Premier Wen Jiabao expressed his sympathies to Prime Minister Kan Naoto. On March 14, a team of fifteen Chinese rescue personnel arrived in Tokyo. This conduct is in line with the Chinese phrase that commands "li shang wang lai" (courtesy demands reciprocity). Previously, when the Wenchuan earthquake took place in 2008, Japan dispatched a team of rescue workers to China. On the 17th, a press spokesperson for the Chinese Ministry of Foreign Affairs said that China had already offered Japan 4.5 million dollars in material assistance and 20,000 tons of fuel, based on humanitarian principles. Activities to raise funds for Japan have taken place over the past several days in several Chinese universities and provinces. In the face of this colossal disaster, China has been moved by feelings of awe and humility and has demonstrated a foreign policy based on neighborly friendship and diplomatic courtesy. The emotional exchanges that have taken place between China and Japan may lead to an improvement of the bilateral relationship, at least temporarily.

In the middle of March 2011, a number of scholars including Wang Zhongchen, professor at Tsinghua University, Feng Zhaokui, vice director of the CASS Institute of Japanese Studies, Niu Dayong, dean of the Peking University history department, and Jin Canrong, associate dean of the Renmin University of China School of International Studies, started an appeal that was signed by 100 Chinese scholars extending a warm hand to Japan. This appeal marked the pinnacle of the goodwill and sympathy extended toward Japan by intellectuals in China. *Global Times* publicized the appeal in its March 16, 2011, issue under the title "Let's Extend the Warm Hand of Friendship to Japan—an Appeal by 100 Chinese Scholars." The appeal said:

> We have been shocked to hear the news that parts of eastern Japan have suffered the onslaught of an earthquake and tsunami on a scale rarely seen in human history. We offer our condolences to all those who have been affected by the Great East Japan Earthquake Disaster. We share the sadness of those who have lost their families, friends, and homes.
>
> A friendship exists between the peoples of China and Japan based on exchanges that date back more than 2,000 years. But there is also the pain of the deep wounds brought about by colonial wars. Today, the problems left by history are often the cause of political friction between the two states. But to overcome these difficulties bequeathed to us from the past, as the wisdom of our peoples grows, both sides must encourage each other and further strengthen these feelings of goodwill and sympathy. In both our countries, work is constantly ongoing among regular people at the grassroots level, intellectuals, entrepreneurs and businesspeople, and politicians.
>
> Natural disasters bring the morality of human beings into relief. Mutual assistance in the face of natural disasters can also become part of efforts toward historical reconciliation. Memories remain clear of the relief activities and fundraising carried out by Japan after the earth-

quake in Wenchuan in 2008. The Chinese government has already expressed its sympathy and support for Japan in this moment of its national calamity. Chinese rescue teams rushed promptly to the disaster area during the initial stages after the disaster struck. But when we see terrible scenes of the hellish conditions brought about by the earthquake and tsunami, and hear the terrible news about the explosion at the nuclear power plant, we cannot help but feel the fragility and hopelessness of human life in the face of nature and high technology. We experience these things as something that affects us directly. We must all work swiftly to take whatever action we can as individuals to help people in Japan withstand their suffering and overcome this natural disaster.

We make this appeal as ordinary citizens. Let us all act as quickly and effectively as possible via various fund-raising routes and by taking part in aid activities as international volunteers. Let us extend a warm hand of friendship and support and offer Japan our charity and sympathy as Chinese people. The people of Japan are strong. The thoughts and assistance we offer them from China may well give them more confidence and strength to stand up even more courageously in the face of this disaster.

This petition was open for anyone to sign. When the appeal was published online, many scholars were quick to sign it. Some netizens cursed the 100 scholars who had put their names to the petition appeal first, describing them as "100 traitors to the nation who want to extend a warm hand to the Japanese bastards," and "these people are all the spawn of Wang Jingwei."[7] Nevertheless, the appeal had a major impact as part of the exchange of emotions and support between the people of the two countries.

As Niwa Uichiro, the Japanese ambassador to China at the time, said in an interview he gave Guo Yina and Hou Lijun, two journalists from the Xinhua News Agency: "The assistance given to Japan by the Chinese government and people since this recent massive earthquake has deeply touched our heartstrings." (*Reference News*, April 25, 2011.) These demonstrations of friendship between the two peoples helped to resolve the tensions and strains brought about by the fishing boat collision in September 2010. This friendship reached new heights in the aftermath of the natural disaster. On March 12, 2012, *Global Times* ran an editorial marking the first anniversary of the Great East Japan Earthquake Disaster. It said, "China should wish sincerely for the development of neighboring states. This is the only way it will be possible for our own nation to continue to rise and prosper in the future." The process of reconciliation between China and Japan does not always run smooth and straight, and the process still has a long way to go, but the need is clear.

NOTES ──

1. Although Supachai Panitchpakdi is introduced here as president of the Thai Central Bank, the official forum website lists him as secretary-general, UNCTAD. Mr. Panitchpakdi received the Grand Prize at the Asia Cosmopolitan Awards Ceremony held in Japan in 2012 to commemorate 1,300 years since the establishment of the capital in Nara.

2. Following the accident at the Tokyo Electric Power Co., Ltd. (TEPCO) Fukushima Daiichi Nuclear Power Plant, there were rumors in China that contaminated sea water would mean that salt made from sea water would no longer be safe and that iodized salt helped to prevent an accumulation of radioactive materials, prompting a rush to buy salt.

3. Ji Xianlin (1911–2009), Chinese scholar, well known for his mastery of a wide range of scholarly fields, including history, culture, linguistics, Buddhist studies, and comparative literature.

4. Langrunyuan Garden, located in the northwest of Beijing, was originally a garden belonging to a residence owned by the Imperial Family. It was acquired by Peking University in the 1920s and converted into a residential area for the faculty. Hou Hu is one part of this area and is where Ji Xianlin had his residence.

5. Wenchuan was the center of the Sichuan earthquake that occurred on May 12, 2008. Yushu refers to the Yushu Tibetan Autonomous Prefecture, Qinghai Province, where a major earthquake took place on April 14, 2010.

6. Sato Mitsuru was the director of a seafood company located in Onagawa, Miyagi Prefecture, who evacuated 20 Chinese trainees to high ground ahead of his own family and fell victim to the tsunami when he went back to help his family. On March 16, Xinhua News Agency ran a detailed report on Mr. Sato and the people he rescued, which attracted widespread attention in China.

7. Wang Jingwei (1883–1944), better known in Japan as O Chomei (Wang Zhaoming), joined the Chinese Revolutionary Alliance led by Sun Yat-sen while a student of Hosei University in Japan, and contributed to the Xinhai Revolution. He cooperated for a while with Chiang Kai-shek after the death of Sun Yat-sen, but later split from him and founded the Reorganized National Government of the Republic of China based in Nanjing in 1940, in reality a puppet state controlled by the Japanese military. He died in Nagoya in 1944. In China, his name has become a byword for treason, largely because of his association with the Japanese, though some scholars have recently begun to reevaluate his reputation.

ELEVEN

What Is the True Nature of the Unrest Prompted by the Diaoyu/ Senkaku Islands Issue?

Seen from a broader perspective, the dispute over the Diaoyu/Senkaku Islands is a contest in which China and Japan are competing for Asian leadership. This is the true nature of the dispute.

The year 2012 marked the 40th anniversary of the normalization of diplomatic ties between China and Japan. Over the course of the year, however, bilateral relations worsened dramatically owing to the dispute over the Diaoyu/Senkaku Islands. Anti-Japanese demonstrations took place in 85 cities around China, the largest-scale demonstrations against Japan since the normalization of ties in 1972. The two countries had planned events to commemorate the anniversary, but almost all of these had to be canceled. One of my Japanese friends lamented:

> At a stroke, these disturbances canceled out the positive atmosphere that had been developed over the preceding years with reciprocal visits between the two countries' leaders and that had served to "melt the ice and welcome in a warm spring." It was as though the clock had been turned back and we had returned to the situation of a decade earlier, when the 30th anniversary of the normalization of diplomatic ties had been marred by an impasse in the bilateral relationship caused by Prime Minister Koizumi's decision to visit Yasukuni Shrine while in office. These vicissitudes in the Sino-Japanese relationship are truly regrettable.

The 2012 demonstrations were prominently covered around the world, with many media outlets featuring investigative reports on consecutive days as the story unfolded; because of this, I will not rehash the details of how events developed. The question that needs to be raised here is the question of why China and Japan have created such a stir over a collection of desolate uninhabited islands with an area of barely six km^2 where, to use a Chinese phrase, "no bird even bothers to lay an egg." In extreme cases, even previously moderate analysts have predicted that the two countries might go to war over the islands, and many expect that an economic war at least is a certainty at some stage. What are the problems that exist on a deeper level in the background to the dispute over the Diaoyu/Senkaku Islands?

Some people argue that territorial disputes must be tackled head-on and that letting go of any amount of territory, however small, is unthinkable. Others argue that the area is rich in fishing resources, that oil probably lies buried under the seabed, and that this means we must not surrender our right to the islands. Still others say that the islands represent a strategically important location on the shipping routes into the Western Pacific and therefore have a military importance worth fighting for. All these points are quite correct. Nevertheless, I believe, the tangled problem needs to be untangled.

Why do I say this? By way of comparison, consider the territorial dispute that exists between China and India—our country's Zangnan[1] region. This region covers an area of 90,000 km^2, roughly 15,000 times bigger than the Diaoyu/Senkaku Islands and roughly equivalent in size to Jiangsu Province. The Zangnan region is located to the south of the Himalayas, where warm air from the Indian Ocean comes into contact with the mountains. The region is blessed with a good climate, has a large population, and is rich and fertile. As a result, it is sometimes called a mini Jiangnan.[2] The natural resources of this region are far greater than anything to be found in the Diaoyu/Senkaku Islands. The region is under the de facto control of India, where it is known as Arunachal Pradesh. In the self-defensive counteroffensive of 1962, the People's Liberation Army seized control of the Zangnan region, but it was later returned to India on the orders of Mao Zedong. Despite this, to this day our country continues to insist on its sovereignty over the Zangnan region and remains strongly critical of claims that the region belongs to India. If territorial disputes must be tackled head-on, regardless of how small the territory in question, it goes without saying that we should tackle the issue of a territory as vast and fertile as the Zangnan region. However, when a military delegation led by Minister for National Defense Liang Guanglie visited India in early September 2012, according to a report in the *Xinjing Bao* (*Beijing News*), "the territorial dispute was not a focus of the talks." At the end of the talks, the two sides announced a decision to strengthen military exchanges. Given that some uninhabited islets with an area of just six km^2 have been such a focus of tension with Japan, why was this vast territory of 90,000 km^2 not a focus of these talks with India?

Or let us look at the case of Vietnam. Vietnam occupies twenty-eight islands of varying size in the South China Sea, which together make up an area many times larger than that of the Diaoyu/Senkaku Islands. Vietnam has carried out large-scale oil drilling in the waters around these islands, transforming itself from a country poor in petroleum resources to a net exporter. It even exports oil to China. In addition, Vietnam has repeatedly protested our country's public declaration of sovereignty over these islands and the establishment of Sansha City,[3] and has not only taken our fishermen prisoner but also used violence against them. On September 7, 2012, Hu Jintao met Vietnam's President Truong Tan Sang at the APEC forum in

Russia. Hu Jintao noted that the dispute in the South China Sea was causing difficulties in the relationship between China and Vietnam and said that both sides must exercise restraint. He went on to say that both sides must insist on finding a political solution to the dispute in the South China Sea, must shelve their differences, and must continue to work toward joint development and to maintain bilateral negotiations and dialogue. In China, the party and government both continued to value friendship between China and Vietnam under the guidelines of "long-term stability, future-orientation, good-neighborliness, and comprehensive cooperation." In the spirit of good neighbors, good friends, good comrades, and good partners, Hu said they would further strengthen positive relations with Vietnam and push for better development. Together with Vietnam, China wishes to deepen the traditional ties of friendship, expand practical cooperation, and promote an ongoing partnership of comprehensive and strategic cooperation.

Malaysia is another case. Malaysia occupies nine of China's islands in the South China Sea, including some of the richest in resources. Should China not attempt to get these islands back? The answer is clear. Nevertheless, when Wen Jiabao met Malaysian Prime Minister Najib Razak at the ASEAN 10+3 summit held in the Cambodian capital of Phnom Penh on November 19, 2012, he did not mention the territorial dispute. Wen Jiabao noted instead that China-Malaysia relations had continuously developed in recent years and were among the best bilateral ties China had developed with any ASEAN member. Both countries took the strategic perspective and attached more importance to mutual understanding and support in the political and security spheres. China is now Malaysia's biggest trading partner. The two countries had achieved outstanding progress in cooperation in finance and major projects and in human and cultural exchanges.

Wen Jiabao proposed that the governments of the two countries should collaborate even more closely and map out a five-year plan for cooperation to ensure the success of the industrial parks that China and Malaysia were building in each other's countries. He also said that the two countries should boost cooperation in tourism, education, finance, medicine, and telecommunications and should further promote the relationship of friendship and cooperation between China and Malaysia to a higher level.

A dispute also exists between China and the Republic of Korea over the ownership of a submerged rock, known as the Suyan Rock (Korean name: Ieodo; international name: Socotra Rock) located in Chinese territory in the East China Sea but currently under the de facto control of South Korea. In 2003, South Korea constructed an ocean research platform on Suyan Rock and conducts regular maritime patrols. Debates continue about the submerged rock in both countries, but despite this, the issue is not particularly important in the bilateral relationship.

Is the South China Sea strategically important? The answer is clear. All the resources required by the countries of Southeast Asia must be shipped through the South China Sea, particularly oil. The fact that the United States, despite the great geographical distance that separates it from the region, demands the maintenance of freedom of international navigation shows that the area is vitally important for shipping and transportation.

That the Diaoyu/Senkaku Islands have given rise to such heated antagonism and dispute is clearly a result of factors including disputes over territory, islands, and marine interests. But that is not all. What are the deeper issues? A French scholar has written with insight on this question and offers some clues.

Claude Meyer published a book in 2010 with the title *China or Japan: Which Will Lead Asia?* (The title of the Chinese version is *Shei shi Yazhou lingxiu, Zhongguo haishi Riben?*) The book's title hints at the underlying problem. A fluent Japanese speaker, Meyer obtained his doctorate at the Ecole des hautes études en sciences sociales, taught economics at the University of Tokyo and Keio University, and served as the vice manager of the Paris branch of the Bank of Tokyo-Mitsubishi. He has visited China on numerous occasions and has observed the country closely and in-depth. He has an impressive understanding of Japan and China, and is now a professor of international economics at Paris Institute of Political Studies (Sciences Po) in Paris. His book was translated into Chinese and published by the Social Sciences Academic Press in China in January 2011.

In the foreword to the book, Meyer writes:

> The 492-metre World Financial Center Building in Shanghai is the showpiece of the Japanese real estate developer Mori Building, and the optimist will be tempted to see in this the seeds of promising cooperation between China and Japan, the dominant powers in Asia. And yet, most unusually in international relations, their political relations have deteriorated profoundly since the turn of the century, even as their trade links have been growing at breakneck speed. The revival of national sentiment and memories of unhealed wounds partly explain these acute tensions, but their deeper cause lies elsewhere. The world's second- and third-largest economic powers are partners to form a cooperative relationship, but their rivalry and mutual mistrust springs from an identical ambition, namely to become the dominant force in Asia, to which the global economy's center of gravity is inexorably being drawn.

In his conclusion to the book, Meyer argues as follows.

> . . . the rise of nationalist sentiment on both sides, which goes hand in hand with their respective positioning in the new geopolitical context in Asia: "peaceful rise" for China, aspiration to "normalization" for Japan. In China, patriotism has become a kind of ideology and is being used by the government to reinforce its legitimacy . . . Japan is also experiencing a resurgence of nationalism. It wishes to enhance its international stature, and the "normalization" of its defense capability is no longer a taboo subject . . . [In this context] China's constant carping about the country's militarist past elicits only lassitude or denial . . . Chinese nationalism, fueled by its success and dislike of Japan, is answered by a strand of unapologetic national sentiment in Japan whose proponents, while very much in the minority, would like to see their country strong enough to counter China's growing influence in Asia. Even more than the weight of history, the two dominant powers are divided by competing ambitions. Their conflictual relationship with the past and antagonistic assertions of national identity are only surface-level symptoms. The real issue at stake is the battle for supremacy in Asia . . . because for the first time in their history China and Japan are both regional powers at the same time.

Meyer gets to the heart of the matter: Seen from a broader perspective, the dispute over the Diaoyu/Senkaku Islands is a contest in which China and Japan are competing for Asian leadership. This is the true nature of the dispute.

Let's look at how the situation appears to Chinese eyes. Territorial disputes exist between China and other countries, among them South Korea, India, Vietnam, Malaysia, the Philippines, and Brunei. In many cases the size of the disputed territory is quite substantial. But in comparison with China, these countries are relatively small and weak. They are not rivals for China. There is no sense of their competing with China for leadership in Asia. As a result, these disputes are not regarded as major issues, at least not for the time being.

But Japan is different. Japan was the first country in Asia to become a developed economy, and for many years it maintained a position as the world's second-largest economy. Japan's scientific research capability, industrial base, and manufacturing technology occupy positions of global precedence, and Japan has been the "lead goose"[4] in Asia for many years and has enjoyed wide influence both in Asia and around the world. These factors make it a powerful rival for China. Another factor is the complication of historical issues between China and Japan. Meyer writes that modern Japan has never been subordinate to China. As some Japanese themselves have pointed out, it is likely to take at least ten years for Japanese people to make the mental adjustment necessary to get used to a world in which China is strong and Japan weak.

As a result, Japan too has taken an inflexible position on the Diaoyu/Senkaku Islands. In the past few years, however, Japan has begun to feel the pinch of ailments common to developed economies and has seen a marked decline in energy as its economy has begun to atrophy. China, by contrast, is vibrant and optimistic. The latecomer has overtaken the pacesetter. Meyer writes: "The next twenty years will see supremacy in Asia shared between the two countries in an unstable and often conflictual configuration. . . . There are already so many bones of contention between the two countries that any such co-leadership is bound to be conflictual." One thing that needs to be added to this is the differences in values and ideology that exist between the two countries, which differences have also exacerbated the intensity of the conflict.

The dispute over the Diaoyu/Senkaku Islands that broke out in 2012 was fanned by provocation by the Japanese right wing. Many Japanese people also recognize this point. For example, Magosaki Ukeru, the former head of the Ministry of Foreign Affairs intelligence and analysis bureau, expressed his views in an article titled "The Diaoyu/Senkaku Issue—Japan's Misunderstanding," in the November 2012 issue of the monthly magazine *Sekai*. The article argued:

> The recent events were sparked by the actions of Ishihara Shintaro. On April 16, 2012, the then governor of Tokyo announced in a lecture in the United States that he was considering using part of the Tokyo Metropolitan Government budget to purchase the Diaoyu/Senkaku Islands. He then called on people to donate funds toward the purchase of the islands, and this met with a huge response.

A joint statement released on September 28 by 1,300 Japanese intellectuals, among them Nobel Prize-winning author Oe Kenzaburo, under the title "Japanese Citizens' Appeal to Stop the Vicious Cycle of Territorial Disputes"[5] made the following appeal.

> This year 2012 marks the 40th anniversary of diplomatic relations between Japan and China. Yet this friendship was changed into conflict

by Tokyo Governor Ishihara Shintaro's declaration that he intends to purchase the Diaoyu/Senkaku Islands and the Japanese Government's counter-declaration of its intent to nationalize the islands.

From the Chinese perspective, it is not surprising that these actions were seen as going against the tacit agreement to put the territorial issue aside and were regarded as acts of provocation. It must be said that domestic criticism of Governor Ishihara's acts was weak. Furthermore, Prime Minister Noda's announcement that the government intended to nationalize the islands was made on July 7, the anniversary of the Marco Polo Bridge incident and a sensitive date for people in China.

Yanai Tadashi, the richest man in Japan and the president of the leading clothing retailer Uniqlo, was also moved to comment on this turn of events in the November 23 issue of the weekly magazine *Shukan Asahi*. Ultimately, the actions of Ishihara Shintaro and other Japanese right-wingers demonstrate the truth of what Meyer wrote in his book: that a minority of Japanese nationalists will use any means necessary to check China's ever-growing power and influence in Asia.

In 2010, China's GDP surpassed Japan's. The relationship between China and Japan was one of two countries that were both strong at the same time—something unprecedented in history. In official Chinese histories, the first record of exchanges between the two countries comes in the Book of the Later Han, in the *Dongyi Zhuan* (Chronicle of the Eastern Barbarians), dating from the year 57 AD, nearly 2,000 years ago. (In fact, according to some accounts, the history of exchanges between the two countries dates back even further than this, for example the accounts that Xu Fu traveled from China to Japan.) During these two millennia, from the Han dynasty through to the Qing dynasty, the relationship was one in which China was strong and Japan was weak; during the Yuan dynasty, China even launched two invasions of Japan. But for 100 years from the beginning of the Meiji Restoration in Japan in 1868, lasting until the beginning of the period of reform and opening up in China, this situation was reversed, and the situation gradually became one in which Japan was strong and China was weak. The two countries had therefore never experienced a situation in which both are strong together at the same time. In Japan, for many generations, people had become used to a situation in which Japan was strong and China weak, and these people therefore tend to look down on China. This is true despite Japan's defeat in World War II, which is regarded in Japan as having been a war in which Japan was defeated by America rather than by China.

China's economic power has recently overtaken Japan's, and the difference between the two countries is growing all the time. This has had a great impact on many people in Japan. One has only to visit a Japanese bookstore to see numerous books discussing the pressure that will be brought to bear on Japan by China's military strength. In the discourse of Japanese right-wingers, it is often claimed that China is lording over Japan and making incessant claims and complaints. This is a constantly heard refrain. This fact reveals that some people in Japanese society, particularly right-wing elements, feel tense and even fearful in the face of China's rapid rise. Ishihara Shintaro's provocation over the Diaoyu/Senkaku Islands took place against this general background. It is fair to describe this as a reaction on the part of Japanese right-wingers to the fact that China has overtaken Japan. It was a reaction due to fear, a reaction to pressure. One person connected with the Chinese government who took part in drafting the political report published at the 18th National Congress said, "they cannot comprehend why so much pressure is being brought to bear against them by a foreign country." Which basically says the same thing.

Ishihara Shintaro was not the only one. On February 20, 2012, the mayor of Nagoya, Kawamura Takashi, made a mistaken statement about the Rape of Nanking. He said: "The Nanjing Incident, I believe, did not take place." Part of the reason for incidents like this is that some Japanese people are tired of being criticized for historical issues, as Meyer argues. Another aspect is that statements like this are prompted by fear of China.

One thing that should be noted is that this kind of fearful pushback against China among right-wing elements in Japan enjoys a good degree of support—something that can be explained by many Japanese people's dislike of the Chinese. In August and September 2012, anti-Japanese demonstrations took place in eighty-five cities around China, and a minority of the participants were guilty of violence including physical beatings, property destruction, looting, and arson. This unrest caused property damage to the property of Chinese people and Japanese companies alike. It had a serious impact. The Chinese media also exposed and criticized these acts of violence and some of the criminals responsible were arrested. Intellectuals at all levels of Chinese society lamented these incidents, criticizing the violence and calling on those responsible to be properly punished. The coverage of these acts of violence on Japanese television caused concern and distress in Japan. In a public opinion survey on diplomacy and foreign policy published by the Japanese Cabinet Office on November 24, 2012, some 80.6 percent of Japanese responded that they "felt no sense of closeness to China," an increase of 9.2 percentage points from the previous survey in 2011. The right-wing elements have used this discontent to stoke nationalism.

In addition, the recent actions of the Japanese right wing are closely connected to the turmoil in Japanese politics. For several years, Japan has had a new prime minister every year, causing chaos and stymying the government's ability to set and carry out its policies. This has distorted the political landscape and led to a situation in which the center is weak and the regions are strong. We are now seeing an unusual situation in which foreign policy is wrecked by regional politicians and in which the central government has lost the power to keep them in check. For example, Nagoya Mayor Kawamura Takashi's job is regional governance; there is no reason for him to get involved in foreign policy questions or international relations. These things are not his responsibility. But by getting involved in a sensitive question in Sino-Japanese relations and making his mistaken pronouncement, he went against the spirit of the Murayama Statement issued by the Japanese government, prompting criticism from China and putting Japan on the defensive. Three days after Kawamura made his remarks, Chief Cabinet Secretary Fujimura Osamu released a statement acknowledging that it was undeniable that the Japanese army had been responsible for the killing of non-combatants, looting, and other actions at the time. The *Tokyo Shimbun* newspaper later published an editorial calling on Kawamura to retract his remarks. Ishihara Shintaro has always been arrogant and unconcerned about other people's opinions. He caused serious damage to the Sino-Japanese relationship during his time as governor of Tokyo.

This loss of authority by the central government and unruly behavior by regional politicians has led to a splintering of Japanese political authority. In November 2012, politics were further divided due to the rise of "the third pole" when Ishihara Shintaro resigned his position as governor of Tokyo and formed the Sunrise Party, which then merged with the Osaka Restoration Association led by Hashimoto Toru, to become the leading right-wing party and an alternative to the Liberal Democratic Party and the Democratic Party of Japan. In December 2012, during his campaign for election to the House of Representatives, Ishihara shocked Japanese society by suggesting he was thinking of conducting simulations premised on Japan's possessing nuclear weapons. For the time being, the major variable in Japanese politics is Abe Shinzo, the new president of the Liberal Democratic Party. His statements during the election campaign were also right-leaning, proposing revising the Constitution and arguing that the Self-Defense Forces should be reorganized as a National Defense Army. In late December 2012, the Liberal Democratic Party took office after winning a victory in the election for the House of Representatives and Abe became prime minister for the second time. Many people in both China and Japan believed that the right-leaning statements he had made during the election campaign were only for show and that he would seek ways to break the stalemate after he rose to power. When he took office as prime minister for the first time in 2006, China was the first country he visited, and he used the visit to "thaw the ice," thereby easing the tensions in the relationship with China that had built up during the Koizumi era. People hope that he might do the same in his second stint in office. We also hope that will be the case, but we need to watch future developments carefully. On September 20, 2012, the *Washington Post* argued that "The shift applies strictly to Japan's foreign policy and military strategy, not social issues." On November 25, the *Nikkei* argued that "Nationalism and xenophobia are increasing in Japan today, but these tendencies also exist in other countries. International opinion sees this as a reflection of popular opinion in political policy-making, a view that will inevitably have some effect on how China and Japan influence and affect each other."

To return to our main point, the purchase of the islands prompted strong protests from China and gave rise to violent collisions. In this context, Deputy Prime Minister Okada Katsuya came forward with the following remarks.

> The purchase of the Diaoyu/Senkaku Islands by the Japanese govern-ment was an unavoidable and difficult decision, and one that was taken to avoid the islands passing into the hands of Tokyo Governor Ishihara Shintaro. If the islands had become his property, it is likely he would have sent people there to build a lighthouse, perhaps followed by a wind-break structure. And in that way he would have gradually started a succession of new projects, which could have become a major prob-lem. The Japanese government has purchased the Diaoyu/Senkaku Islands in order to preserve the status quo and maintain stability.

This interpretation is useful in terms of easing the tension and antagonism between the two governments, but clearly China cannot accept this kind of statement. The reason is that the Diaoyu/Senkaku Islands are Chinese terri-tory. How could China possibly accept someone else's buying them?

Despite offering this interpretation of events, the Japanese govern-ment did not acknowledge that a dispute exists over the sovereignty of the Diaoyu/Senkaku Islands. This is another point that the Chinese government cannot accept. Magosaki Ukeru's "The Diaoyu/Senkaku Islands—Japan's Misunderstanding" in the November 2012 *Sekai* argued:[6]

> From 1885, surveys of the Diaoyu/Senkaku Islands had been made several times by the Government of Japan through the agencies of

Okinawa Prefecture. Through these surveys, it was confirmed that the islands had not only been uninhabited but showed no trace of having been under the control of the Qing Dynasty of China. Based on this confirmation, the Government of Japan made a Cabinet Decision on January 14, 1895, to erect markers on the islands to formally incorporate them into the territory of Japan. How does China see this issue? In the *Beijing Zhoukan (Beijing Review)* issue 34, 1996, it is claimed that China discovered the islands first and incorporated the islands into its territory. There are mentions of the Diaoyu/Senkaku Islands in Chinese sources dating back to the sixteenth century. In the *Chouhai Tubian (Illustrated Compendium on Maritime Security)* compiled by Hu Zongxian during the Ming dynasty in 1556, the islands were included in the coastal sea defense region as belonging to Fujian Province in China. Based on this, the Chinese side believes that China has possessed the Diaoyu/Senkaku Islands since ancient times and that, accordingly, they are included in the territory that Japan seized from China during the Qing dynasty. . . . Under the circumstances, it is inappropriate from an international perspective to claim that the Diaoyu/Senkaku Islands are an integral part of Japanese territory and that no territorial dispute exists. . . . Previously, it was agreed to shelve the dispute, first at a meeting between Zhou Enlai and Tanaka Kakuei in 1972 and later at a meeting between Vice Premier Deng Xiaoping and Foreign Minister Sonoda Sunao in 1978. Today, the Japanese government takes the position that the Chinese government is speaking unilaterally of shelving the issue and that this is something that the Japanese side has never consented to. This position denies the historical facts. A look at the responses of Prime Minister Tanaka and Foreign Minister Sonoda at the time makes clear that they were quite in agreement. Mistaken interpretations are frequent regarding the idea of shelving the issue. For example, some people argue that the Chinese side has recently started to insist on its territorial rights over the Diaoyu/Senkaku Islands and that this means it has abandoned its policy of shelving the issue. But in fact, shelving the issue is premised on the idea that both sides assert their sovereignty. If both sides assert their rights and nothing is done to check this, there is a possibility that the situation might escalate into a military confrontation. Therefore, a proposal was made to shelve the dispute as a means of avoiding conflict before it occurred. What would happen if Japan distanced itself from the agreement to shelve the issue and tried to assert its claims to sovereignty over the Diaoyu/Senkaku Islands more determinedly?

Both sides would then push their competing claims and this could well escalate into a situation where the issue was settled by military means.

If no better way of resolving the issue exists at present, both sides should revert to the agreement to shelve the disagreement and look for a road to a peaceful solution. On October 26, 2012, Chinese Vice Minister for Foreign Affairs Zhang Zhijun held a press briefing on the Diaoyu/Senkaku Islands at which he said that China and Japan each had its own position on the issue and that the dispute was occurring because of differences between those two positions. He said that both sides should acknowledge this fundamental fact—negotiations and discussions were both possible. On December 15, 2012, *Reference News* carried a proposal by Shen Dingli, deputy director of the Institute of International Studies at Fudan University, who proposed that China and Japan jointly manage the islands and that patrol boats from the two countries carry out patrols alternately.

What the Japanese right wing could not have predicted was that by provoking the dispute over the Diaoyu/Senkaku Islands, Ishihara Shintaro gave China an ideal opportunity to publicly make its case for sovereignty over the Diaoyu/Senkaku Islands. Following this, China responded by increasing the frequency of its patrols of the islands with maritime surveillance vessels and aircraft, forcing Japan into an even more defensive position. What will happen if China and Japan continue this kind of antagonism? In *China or Japan: Which Will Lead Asia?* Claude Meyer offers two possible answers. The first is that Japan will ultimately accept the hegemony of an increasingly powerful China. He writes:

> The first would see China exercising sway over its neighbors—including Japan—in an avatar of the ancient tribute system. The fact that Japan has always refused to submit to Chinese domination in the past opens the way onto the second scenario, according to which confrontation would be inevitable and could result in violent or even armed conflict if their vital interests . . . were threatened.

The second possibility is that the two countries will cooperate as partners with complementary assets and form the foundation of cooperation and partnership for the establishment of an Asian community. Meyer writes that unfortunately, the two countries have not yet managed to overcome their painful memories of the past and that their destinies are caught up in a "dialectic of resentment." But Meyer also points out that the idea of an Asian Community has already been put forward. Shared needs exist among the countries of

East Asia and Southeast Asia in terms of economic development, the eradication of poverty, the prevention and cure of pandemics, disaster relief, and environmental protection, and this is one major trend making headway in Asia. This would have a similar effect, though with different means, as the ideals of pan-Asianism previously put forward by Tagore of India and the Asians' Asia advocated by Sun Yat-sen in China and Mahathir in Malaysia. In this scenario, China and Japan are likely to adapt to the general tide of the times and choose the path of cooperation. Having turned the page on militarism and no longer seeing its future in hegemonistic terms, Japan is likely to do its utmost to avoid a full-on direct collision with China. Japan may well combine economic power, financial wealth, advanced science and technology, and a strong manufacturing sector with conventional defense to carve out a distinctive position for itself. In a nutshell, Japan wants to make itself into a kind of Asian Switzerland—prosperous and pacifist. In the future, China, Japan, and India may compromise, seeking commonalities, putting their differences aside, and cooperating with the ASEAN countries to push forward with Asian unification over several decades.

On November 20, 2012, when the 18th National Congress had ended and the dispute over the Diaoyu/Senkaku Islands was gradually calming, China, Japan, and South Korea announced that negotiations would start toward a free-trade agreement among the three countries and that the first round of talks would be held in early 2013. This is good news indeed. Together, the three countries have a combined population of 1.5 billion people, equivalent to 22 percent of the world population, with a total GDP of 14 trillion dollars, or 20 percent of global GDP. If a free trade agreement can be successfully concluded, it will allow these countries to complement each other's strengths and become the strongest engine in the world economy, which would undoubtedly have a major impact on both the United States and Europe. Memories are still fresh of the agreement reached between China and Japan at the end of December 2011 on a dialogue regarding the reciprocal use of the two countries' currencies. This year, the value of trade between the two countries reached 350 billion dollars, but because dealings between them had previously been conducted in dollars, it was necessary for each country to convert its own currency into dollars before doing any trade. Following the conclusion of talks on reciprocal use of the two countries' currencies, it became possible to trade directly in their own currencies, thereby elevating the international position of the renminbi. Japan became the first developed economy to conclude an agreement with China regarding reciprocal currency use, and the agreement was highly significant in the context of the renminbi's increasing internationalization.

As a result of the agreement, the dollar got frozen out of trade between China and Japan. Negotiations on a free trade agreement among China, Japan, and South Korea took a major step toward a currency swap agreement. These interactions between the two economies worked as a buffer to reduce tensions in the bilateral relationship. At the same time, the Xinhua News Agency reported on November 25, 2012, that, although Japanese automakers had experienced difficulties in China as a result of the dispute over the Diaoyu/Senkaku Islands, sales were starting to recover. Toyota, Nissan, Honda, and other Japanese automakers regard the China market as an important priority and have made it clear that they will continue to invest in China. Honda even announced that it will establish a research and development center in China. Voices predicting that Japanese capital would retreat from China have gradually become less prominent.

These facts make it clear that both sides have begun to adopt a more restrained position in order to contain collisions and are working not only to avoid a military clash but also to lower the temperature of the economic competition and to gradually put economic and trade exchanges back on a normal track. This is a rational choice. From the perspective of seeking the greatest gains for both China and Japan, clearly both sides must work toward the peaceful resolution of conflicts.

People everywhere generally see a bright future for China's economic growth. China's economic power continues to grow rapidly, and it is expected that it will eventually grow to become two times, and even five times, larger than Japan's. The Chinese economist Zhang Wuchang says that the scale of China's economy could eventually grow to become ten times larger than Japan's. Against this general backdrop, if China implements its strategic plan thoroughly and adopts intelligent policies, the prospects for the development of Sino-Japanese relations are not altogether bleak. In times of difficulty, both sides should remember the words of Hu Yaobang: "Rational people take a long-term perspective and look at the overall picture."

If China takes advantage of its position in the world today and chooses the correct policies, it should certainly be possible to draw Japan to China's side. At the same time as defending the sovereignty of the state, it will be necessary to hold firm to the New Thinking on Relations with Japan. As the veteran commentator on Japan affairs, Feng Zhaokui, has noted, the New Thinking is the core of a foreign policy toward Japan that is suited to the needs of the times. The CCP Central Committee has recently been emphasizing the need to construct a new model of great power relations. This refers chiefly to the United States, but Japan is also undoubtedly a major global power. I believe that in terms of Sino-Japanese relations, it is only by holding firm to the New Thinking on Relations with Japan that it will be possible to build a new model of great power relations. We must work steadily on policies with ordinary Japanese citizens in mind and build a new model of great power relations. I believe that the New Thinking on Relations with Japan can be effective in the long term and may guarantee the next 100 years into the future. Ultimately, China and Japan will overcome their difficulties together, build a close and cooperative relationship of "Yiyidaishui" (meaning "so close that the two parts are separated only by a narrow river"), realize the hopes of Deng Xiaoping and Hu Yaobang for Sino-Japanese reconciliation, and together build an Asian Community.

NOTES

1. An area in southern Tibet, close to the border with India.

2. I.e. similar in characteristics to the warm and fertile Jiangnan area (the regions to the south of the Yangtze River).

3. An administrative district on the southernmost tip of China formed in July 2012, comprising several offshore regions that were previously treated as parts of Hainan Province: Xisha Islands (Paracel Islands), Zhongsha Islands (Macclesfield Bank & Scarborough Shoal), and Nansha Islands (Spratly Islands).

4. This refers to the so-called "flying geese" paradigm in which Japan played a leading role in Asian economic development.

5. The text of the Japanese citizens' appeal can be found online at: http://peace3appeal.jimdo.com

6. On the process by which Japan made the Daioyu/Senkaku Islands part of its territory, as detailed here, Magosaki's essay quotes from the Senkaku Islands Q&A, available on the Japanese Ministry of Foreign Affairs website.

CHAPTER TWELVE

Will China and Japan Come to Blows?

What is the most important thing for the Sino-Japanese relationship today? The most important thing is to continue to promote reconciliation and cooperation between the two countries and to advance a strategic relationship based on mutual benefits. This strategic relationship based on mutual benefits is the framework for a bilateral relationship of historical significance established as the result of a long-term process of seeking and discussions. Compared to this, the Diaoyu/Senkaku Islands issue is a small-scale problem whose solution can wait.

In the late summer and early autumn of 2012, popular unrest over the Diaoyu/Senkaku Islands issue reached fever pitch and seemed to exceed the stifling heat of the season. Angry youths took to the streets, pumped up and ready for a fight, while the media poured oil on the flames and repeatedly demanded the Chinese government resolve the issue by war if necessary.

On August 27, the headline on an editorial in the Beijing newspaper *Global Times* was one guaranteed to astonish readers who saw it. In a bold, oversized font, the headline read: "Naval Exercises by the People's Liberation Army (PLA) Navy Are Our Response to Japan." The editorial suggested that its author was hungry for war. "If China and Japan go to war, it will surely become a conflict that will sweep away more than a century of humiliation from the hearts of the Chinese people. No other war is as suitable to perform that role as a war between China and Japan."

For a time, things were on razor's edge, and it seemed that a single wrong step would be enough to set the situation aflame. An outbreak of war seemed imminent. Even Yu-chien Kuan, a famous China-born writer living in Germany, said in an article published in the *Hong Kong Economic Journal* on August 27 that: "If this uproar continues, I think war over the islands will be inevitable." At demonstrations to defend the Diaoyu/Senkaku Islands held throughout China in mid-September, participants carried banners inscribed with slogans saying: "Declare war on Japan!" The title of Yu-chien Kuan's article was "If China and Japan fall together, America will be the lucky fisherman who collects the prize." I will return to this subject a little later. For now, I wish to discuss the interesting fact that it was an American who first raised the possibility of war between China and Japan.

In the spring of 2012, not long after Tokyo Governor Ishihara Shintaro's provocative announcement that he intended to purchase the islands, the May 24 issue of *Time* magazine in the United States carried an article by Kirk Spitzer with the title "Clock Ticks on China-Japan Islands Dispute." The article argued that Japan had only a year or two to resolve the dispute over this tiny group of islands or risk the breakout of a war with China. Spitzer continued:

In recent weeks, Chinese officials have begun to refer to the Diaoyu/Senkaku Islands as a "core interest." That's the diplomatic equivalent of baring one's teeth and emitting a low growl. At the moment, the situation is this: Where China sees an unrepentant Japan clinging to a legacy of colonial expansion, Japan sees an arrogant and erratic China once again bullying its smaller neighbors. Chinese defense specialist Yang Yi worries that the dispute could trigger a military escalation, if not an outright shooting war. China's air and sea forces have increasingly encroached on territory around Japan's southwestern islands, while Japan has begun reinforcing those islands and building more mobile and flexible air and ground forces.

The article also quotes Yang Yi as saying: "We have much more urgent things to do. Let's not back each other into a corner." Spitzer writes that it is unclear whether a war between China and Japan over the islands would inevitably mean American involvement, but he suggests that the United States would probably find itself committed to come to Japan's defense under the terms of the US-Japan Security Treaty.

Two American military officials predicted that China and Japan would come to blows even earlier than Spitzer and wrote in some detail about how the war might play out. The first was Jed Babbin, who was a deputy undersecretary of defense during the first Bush administration. The other was Edward Timperlake, who was a mobilization planning official in the Reagan administration. Both are specialists in international security policy and Chinese military issues. In early June 2006, they jointly published a book with the title *Showdown: Why China Wants War with the United States*. The book novelistically predicts a major war breaking out between China and Japan in 2009.

Based on an analysis of the actual situation with regard to China's foreign policy strategy and the current state of the PLA, the book imagines that China, provoked by a number of issues—among them sovereignty over the Diaoyu/Senkaku Islands, Yasukuni Shrine, and oil resources—decides in 2009 to issue a series of tough demands to Japan. These are bitterly resisted in Japan. Ultimately, China launches a missile attack against Yasukuni Shrine and a major war breaks out. The *Sankei Shimbun* carried a review of *Showdown* in its June 27, 2006, issue and characterized the story as: "In 2009, China opens hostilities, leading to a full-blown war between Japan and China."

What might spark a major Sino-Japanese conflict like this? *Showdown*, published in 2006, describes the situation as follows. Not long after the Beijing Olympics in 2008, the first woman president takes office in the United

States in January 2009. A Democrat, her policies are friendly to China. Later, China conducts large-scale military exercises with Russia close to the Diaoyu/Senkaku Islands and brings pressure to bear against Japan. Japan asks the new president to issue a protest to China but she refuses.

According to the *Showdown* storyline, by 2009 the social disparities between rich and poor have become problems in China and the unemployment rate has shot up. To avoid a crisis at home, China foments nationalist sentiment and encourages people to direct their dissatisfactions at Japan. This seems to be the only way it can release the pressure caused by the contradictions and strains within the country. The Chinese government declares that the visits to Yasukuni Shrine by the Japanese prime minister are tantamount to a declaration of war. Anti-Japanese demonstrations break out all over the country, eventually involving 20 million demonstrators. A number of Japanese engineers are put on trial as spies. China demands an apology from the Japanese emperor and presses Japan to renounce its claims on the Diaoyu/Senkaku Islands. For a while, both sides refuse to give way. To increase the pressure, China sentences several Japanese to death and launches a cyber-attack on Japan, crippling the computer systems of the Tokyo Stock Exchange and Japanese airlines. In addition, China also launches several missiles, which fly over the Japanese archipelago and splash into the Pacific Ocean east of Japan. China also threatens to bombard the Diaoyu/Senkaku Islands.

Showdown continues. In August 2009, China launches a cruise missile that totally destroys Yasukuni Shrine. At the same time, China mobilizes its Navy and launches a formal invasion of the Diaoyu/Senkaku Islands, forcing Japan's Self-Defense Forces to respond. This marks the beginning of a major naval battle between the two countries. Japan asks the United States for urgent assistance, but the new president announces that her country does not want a war with China. The Japanese prime minister is forced to go to the United Nations for help and asks the UN to adjudicate fairly between the two sides in their conflict. In the end, having sustained major losses, Japan surrenders.

Global Times reported the publication of *Showdown* on June 28, 2006, and summarized the content of the book. The newspaper reported that some media outlets in Japan had been running special reports since the publication related to a hypothetical conflict and analyzing the possibility that the two countries might go to war. In one newspaper, it said, a column had debated the question: "Will the Diaoyu/Senkaku Islands become engulfed in fire?" Another person submitted a piece to a newspaper saying that a major conflict between the two countries was "just a matter of time." On the same day, *Global Times* commented that the vast majority of Japanese people loved peace from the bottom of their hearts and reminded readers that the aggressive tone of the debate in some outlets did not reflect the mainstream of Japanese opinion—that articles of this kind were extremely rare except in some right-wing publications.

Why was it that several American commentators separately forecast a major conflict between China and Japan and even wrote in detail about how such a war might unfold? Yu-chien Kuan's article offers one possible explanation. Kuan notes that China and Japan are two major global economic powers and, as such, pose a threat to the United States. If the United States does not deal with them fairly and impartially, there is a risk that they might become its most fearful adversaries in the future and threaten American economic interests. As the last few years have made clear, China, Japan, and South Korea are already cooperating and developing their economies and may one day become the strongest economic bloc in the world. This represents an enormous threat for the United States, which would be put in a difficult position by such a development. Thus the United States does not want to see this happen and sees squabbles and fights between China and Japan as very much to its own advantage.

Yu-chien Kuan continued by saying that he had recently discussed the tense situation in East Asia with a noted German political commentator named Müller, who pointed out that an armed clash between China and Japan over the Diaoyu/Senkaku Islands would only lead to further antagonism between the two countries. China has a huge territory and strategic depth. In contrast, Japan is a small island country without any nearby buffer land and nowhere it can retreat to. Its only option is to develop its economy through trade with the outside world. For the Chinese, war is a way to demonstrate determination and will. For Japan it is a question of life or death. Given this, the Japanese mobilize all resources in a war situation and throw themselves wholly into the fight, prepared to sacrifice their own lives. As a result, the war would inevitably become extremely brutal and would have a massive impact on both countries. On the other side of the Pacific, the global hegemon known as the United States naturally wants the two countries to be at loggerheads, since this helps it maintain its position as global hegemon. The more serious the animosity, the better for the United States. American intervention in a Sino-Japanese war is extremely unlikely; as soon as a war starts, the United States would withdraw its forces from Japan and sit back and watch the two countries destroy each other. The Chinese and Japanese navies would be destroyed and cities throughout both countries would suffer catastrophically. The United States would be able to reassert its control over the Asia-Pacific region at almost zero cost. As the Chinese proverb says, when the snipe and the clam fight, it is the fisherman who reaps the rewards.[1] Or the other old proverb: that the wise thing to do when tigers fight is to sit on a mountain and watch.[2] China and Japan should both see the truth of this, remain calm, and realize that fighting would be hugely disadvantageous to both sides. The two sides should do everything they can to ensure peace and to prevent nationalism from suddenly exploding in either country. With the advantage of distance, Müller proposed that China and Japan close the Diaoyu/Senkaku Islands off and agree that neither side will visit the islands for fifty to 100 years.

Yu-chien Kuan notes that some people have asked what they could do if the Japanese government took a selfish course. Kuan believes that the Japanese government will never lose its grip on rationality. Even if it did, China would probably not resort to force, since economic means would be more cost-effective. This would damage the Chinese economy as well, but it would be far preferable to a war, and the country would try to minimize the impact through subsidies and state spending. A little over a decade ago, the unemployment rate in Germany was nearly 10 percent and the economy was beset with numerous difficulties, but in the end the government succeeded in finding a way out of the impasse. This is how difficulties should be resolved and brought under control. If China cut back on the use of public funds by government officials, the resultant savings would likely be sufficient to cover the losses caused by an economic war between China and Japan. That said, Kuan was quick to add that he hoped the situation would not go that far.

Huang Mingjun, a Taiwanese military strategist and critic, ran a simulation of a war between China and Japan using geological models. The Hong Kong magazine *Asia Weekly* carried an article by him in its September 2 issue under the title "How Would a War Over the Diaoyu/Senkaku Islands be Fought?" He wrote: "The clouds of war now hang heavy over the Diaoyu/Senkaku Islands. War used to be unthinkable. Today it is a possibility that cannot be ruled out."

How would such a war be fought? Huang suggested that, from a military perspective, if continental China and Taiwan could cooperate, there is no doubt they would have the upper hand. This would make air-to-air refueling easier for the PLA and would make Japan more circumspect. If China acted alone, the first step in any military action would probably involve an attempt to seize "the three controls"—control of electronic networks, control of the air, and control of the sea.

Even before any official declaration of war, China would unleash a cyber-attack on US and Japanese information network systems. For China, to gain air supremacy would require aerial refueling for support operations. By contrast, Japan would be able to make use of the many airfields large and small that exist in the vicinity of the Diaoyu/Senkaku Islands and would be able to draw on assistance from US air bases in Okinawa and Guam, as well as US aircraft carriers. The United States and Japan would have superior air strength and would be able to counter the Nanjing Military Region air force and the East Sea Fleet naval air force.

As for control of the seas, the PLA Navy possesses a number of advanced submarines, destroyers, and ship-to-ship missiles, but naval control would be far from certain if the American and Japanese navies mobilized fully for war. Lacking numerical superiority, the PLA would have no choice but to engage in asymmetrical warfare and work to achieve even partial supremacy at sea.

If the PLA land forces were to attempt to land on the Diaoyu/Senkaku Islands when the Americans and Japanese had both air and sea supremacy, a sudden attack would be the only viable option. It would not be possible to engage in a large-scale joint land and sea campaign at the same time. Either a specially formed unit of crack troops would go ashore or elite units would parachute in, destroying the Japanese lighthouse and securing a defensive position in preparation for an attempt by the American and Japanese forces to take the islands back. The PLA would need to prepare a safe zone within the seas and air around the Diaoyu/Senkaku Islands first and hold this as a strategic priority for securing the safety of shipping and access lanes.

If the United States were to become involved in an armed confrontation between two foreign powers, the question "What are we fighting for" would become a sensitive one, since the purpose of the fighting would not be self-defense. The PLA would try to play on this. As well as fighting US forces, China would work to foment antiwar sentiment within the United States and eventually force America into a situation in which it had no choice but to withdraw.

Precision strikes by the PLA would require selecting and using the correct weapons, particularly for long-distance attacks at sea and in the air. China would have to paralyze the enemy's strategic priorities by "careful selection of targets and attacking the center of the enemy's power." If the PLA had to develop a campaign on the Diaoyu/Senkaku Islands, it is clear that it would have to choose an asymmetrical campaign to defend the Diaoyu/Senkaku Islands. With a large-scale conventional battle using all its military strength impossible, China's only options for gaining victory would be to launch a surprise attack or to strive to achieve partial superiority by taking advantage of the topography.

The very real gap that exists in military technology and military power between the PLA and the US-Japan alliance is something that must be squarely faced. Until the Beidou Navigation Satellite System is completed, China's ability to guide missiles is still problematic and fighting a war from a position of technical inferiority would involve major risks.

On September 11, 2012, the *Global Times* carried an account of a colloquium titled "Fighting a War with Japan to Defend the Diaoyu/Senkaku Islands." Dai Xu, a professor at the PLA National Defense University, said that China should prepare so that it can respond to Japanese provocations at any time by hitting and sinking Japanese ships. Xu Sen-an, a researcher at the State Oceanic Administration, said that China should aim to use a strategy combining political, economic, propaganda, and military means. Rear Admiral Luo Yuan said that guerilla operations at sea would be another possibility and called for China to fight a people's war at sea. If necessary, warships could be used to protect fishing vessels and sea lanes.

On September 19, the Russian online news site *Vzglad*[5] published an article by military strategists examining which side would have the upper hand in a war between China and Japan. Vasily Kashin, a researcher at the Center for Analysis of Strategies and Technologies, said that although China possessed a huge arsenal, Japan's resources were superior in terms of quality. Overall, the two sides' air and sea combat capabilities would be roughly equal. Konstantin Sivkov, first vice-president of the Russian National Geopolitical Academy, said that the presence of the United States made it unthinkable that China would initiate hostilities. Once the United States became involved, the Chinese Air Force would sustain serious damage in the first week or so, and the Chinese Navy would also inevitably sustain serious losses. America's Los Angeles class attack submarines would make short work of Chinese warships, and it is likely that China would abandon military action and switch to economic sanctions before it went that far.

While this has looked at the possibility that China and Japan might go to war over the Diaoyu/Senkaku Islands, many people think that such a war is impossible. In what follows, I want to introduce a piece written by Zhao Chu, a scholar from Shanghai. On July 14, 2012, the *Fengyun Guancha* section of the *WangYi* (NetEase) website carried an article by Zhao Chu with the title, "Will the Situation in the Diaoyu/Senkaku Islands Lead to a Military Confrontation between China and Japan?" The article argued:

> The Chinese media have recently carried increasing voices warning of a military crisis. Some scholars are implying that a war between China and Japan, or perhaps between China versus Japan plus the United

States, is posed to erupt at any moment over differences in the East China Sea. But this is not logical and fails to understand Japanese policy regarding the Diaoyu/Senkaku Islands. It also fails to understand Chinese, Japanese, and American strategic objectives in the context of a dispute over the Diaoyu/Senkaku Islands.

Zhao Chu continues:

> There are four reasons Japan has become more active with regard to the Diaoyu/Senkaku Islands. The first is that Japan is extremely concerned that China has overtaken it in terms of GDP and is afraid that a stronger China will adopt policies designed to put pressure on Japan. But in fact, the economic and trade relations between the two countries are deeply intertwined and Japan wants to use the advantage it has of exercising de facto control over the islands to apply pressure and increase the cards it can use in its relationship with China, on the condition that the overall picture of Sino-Japanese relations will not be destroyed. The second reason is that the confusion in Japanese politics has made the center weak while the regions are strong. In this context, recent events over the Diaoyu/Senkaku Islands are one more manifestation of the confusion in Japanese politics. The third is the Cold War era. During the Cold War, Japan's defenses were focused in the north and on the potential threat from the Soviet Union. When the Cold War came to an end, Japan was faced with the prospect of rapidly increasing Chinese military power. Japan therefore shifted the weight of its strategy to the south. The Diaoyu/Senkaku Islands fit this strategic shift perfectly. The fourth is the rebalancing of American strategy to the Asia-Pacific region and the fact that the bulk of American power in East Asia is concentrated in the Pacific. Japan must position its own strength in the southwest to fill in the resultant gap. The escalation of the dispute over the Diaoyu/Senkaku Islands thus suits Japan's strategic purposes.

Zhao Chu believes that China's strategic defense focus lies in the developed regions in the east of the country with their large populations and rich material resources. Defending these regions means China has to strengthen its air and sea defenses in the East China Sea and the coastal regions of the Western Pacific. In addition, a position of strategic defense also requires using conflict and strategic attack as methods, which has led China to act proactively in the East China Sea and has fomented strategic competition with Japan. This means that neither side can easily show any weakness over the Diaoyu/Senkaku Islands issue.

Zhao Chu asks: If this situation continue, will it lead to an armed confrontation between China and Japan? The answer, he says, is no or at least the probability of such a confrontation is almost nil. Even if Japan tries to play the Diaoyu/Senkaku card in its dealings with China, or even if Chinese defense forces project into the Western Pacific, the dispute over the Diaoyu/Senkaku Islands does not involve serious problems for either side with regard to the overall picture. Rather, it represents an area in which they can safely flex their muscles and demonstrate their power. But if shots were once fired, the Diaoyu/Senkaku Islands would lose their value as a card and it is very likely that the situation would develop into all-out war, something both sides want to avoid at all costs. In simple terms, so long as the dispute exists and is convenient for both sides, both should be able to score points free of catastrophic risk. Should a real catastrophe break out, however, the situation would mean a strategic defeat of unknowable proportions for both sides.

Zhao Chu argues that the dispute offers opportunities for both sides, but that both sides would inevitably lose if the situation were to escalate into a true crisis. He argues that the same applies to the United States. The United States has interests at stake in both China and Japan. Given this situation, the United States has pledged to absolutely support Japan in its defense of the Diaoyu/Senkaku Islands, this intended to maintain Japanese faith in the US-Japan Security Treaty. This puts it at odds with China. But at the same time, the United Sates wants to keep Japan from taking military risks and dragging America into an elective conflict, and it also needs to show appropriate concern for Sino-American relations. Accordingly, the United States wants to avoid making any clear statement regarding the rightful sovereignty over the islands. The dispute over the Diaoyu/Senkaku Islands is a headache for the United States, but that is all. The United States can step in at any time to mediate between the two sides or it can play them off against each other. But if a real catastrophe broke out, the United States would have to run real risks with unpredictable results and would be forced to choose one side or the other.

Also of interest in this context is an unsigned article online with the title "War over the Diaoyu/Senkaku Islands is impossible." The essay provides two reasons why the outbreak of war is supposedly unthinkable. One is the extremely close trade relationship between China and Japan and the scale of economic back-and-forth between the two countries. (In 2011, bilateral trade was worth 350 billion dollars.) This means that the economic losses that a war would inflict would be intolerable. The second reason is that, despite China's huge population and a GDP that now outstrips Japan's, Japan can still draw on an extremely rich and strong industrial base and manufacturing industries with some of the best technology in the world. Japan's military science and technology is also more advanced than China's. A maritime state, Japan has maritime self-defense forces and naval operations experience that makes it one of the world's leading naval powers in this sphere. It once sunk the Russian fleet. Japan's national power enables it to respond to a major large-scale war. Japan also enjoys the support of the United States, and the United States has repeatedly made it clear that the Security Treaty applies to the Diaoyu/Senkaku Islands. If China and Japan did come to blows, particularly over the Diaoyu/Senkaku Islands, it is impossible to say who would win the first naval confrontation. This makes it highly unlikely that the two countries would go to war rashly. Some angry young men talk big by urging the country to drop atomic bombs *in extremis*, but this is unhealthy thinking and totally out of proportion.

So far, my discussion has focused on either-or forecasts: either the two countries go to war or they do not. My own view is closer to the "do not" position. Although minor friction is unavoidable, the two countries must not allow a major conflict to break out over the Diaoyu/Senkaku Islands.

As noted above, the German political theorist Müller argues that the United States prefers to watch from a safe vantage point and would probably withdraw its troops if China and Japan came to blows. Müller's words must be at least partly in jest. Japan is an important ally for the United States, and the two countries have signed a Treaty of Mutual Cooperation and Security. If the United States, having given its word, were simply to flee once war broke out, how would any other ally ever trust it? How would it secure a position for itself in the world?

If the United States were so easily deterred—and if its words failed to be backed up by action—it would no longer be able to maintain its dominant position in the global community. Although the United States offers defense cooperation to Japan, this is not solely for Japan's sake. It is also for the sake of American interests in the Asia-Pacific. A long chain of interconnected American interests stretches all the way through the region, from Japan to the Philippines and on to Singapore. Doing everything it can to contain China, its chief rival, is an important part of America's global strategy to protect this chain of interests. This means that, setting minor friction aside, if China and Japan fight a major war, there is a better than 50 percent chance the United States would become involved. Indeed, as many commentators have argued, any major battle between China and Japan would need to take into consideration the likely timing of America's involvement. Failing to do so would risk a major error in judgment. Of course, the precise extent and nature of America's involvement would depend on conditions at the time.

The United States has large numbers of troops stationed in Japan. As the result of joint exercises and training over nearly seventy years of military alliance, the US armed forces and the Japanese Self-Defense Forces are for all practical purposes already one integrated force. In the 2012 movie *Battleship* about the US Navy,[4] audiences saw how US Naval officers and Japanese Maritime Self-Defense Force officers worked together to develop a strategy on the same ship—another example of how close the relationship is between the US Navy and the Japanese Maritime Self-Defense Forces. Even if Japan wanted to shake off American control, its military dependence on the United States is beyond dispute.

As noted above, if a major conflict did start between China and Japan, this would put the United States at serious risk of a major war. For the immediate future, the United States faces difficulties as its national strength declines. If it were to honor its promises under the Security Treaty with Japan, it would face a frontal military confrontation with a powerful China and would be forced into a position in which it had no choice but to accept the war's result. Policymakers in the United States have no wish to face such a situation, and accordingly, the United States does not want the dispute between China and Japan to escalate further. In mid-September 2012, at the height of the crisis over the Diaoyu/Senkaku Islands, US Secretary of Defense Leon Panetta visited Japan and China. He urged both countries to remain calm, exercise restraint, and do everything in their power to find a path to a peaceful solution; expressed his hope that Sino-Japanese relations would look forward and avoid getting caught up in the details of the past; and stated repeatedly that the United States takes no side in the dispute over sovereignty over the Diaoyu/Senkaku Islands. Panetta's stance reflected the American position.

What is the big picture for China at present? Modernization is still underway and continues to gain momentum. The most important challenges for China today are to seize the strategic opportunities of the moment, to accelerate economic development, to achieve advances in science and technology, to resolve the difficult challenges affecting people's livelihoods, to consolidate the social security system, to advance further social and political reforms, and to achieve the great rewards of modernization.

What needs to be made clear here is that the Diaoyu/Senkaku Islands are neither a core nor an overall problem within Sino-Japanese relations. The issue existed when Mao Zedong decided in favor of a normalization of relations with Japan, and it existed during the period when Deng Xiaoping pushed forward the policy of reform and opening up. Mao Zedong, Zhou Enlai, and Deng Xiaoping all argued in favor of shelving the dispute.

On September 1, 2012, in Singapore, the *Lianhe Zaobao* carried an article by the Singaporean-Chinese scholar Zhang Yun titled "The Re-Normalization of Sino-Japanese Relations." The article looked back at the time diplomatic relations between the two countries were normalized in 1972 and said that "Japanese materials on the Japanese side make it clear Prime Minister Tanaka brought up the Diaoyu/Senkaku Islands during his meeting with Premier Zhou Enlai and Zhou Enlai immediately stated that they should not touch on that issue during these talks."

Lin Xiaoguang, a scholar at the CCP Central Party School, published an article in issue 46 of *Leaders* magazine in June 2012 with the long title "Memories and Ideas: Looking Back at the Normalization of Sino-Japanese Relations 40 Years Ago through Declassified Diplomatic Papers of the Japanese Ministry of Foreign Affairs," which verified this view. Lin wrote:

> The Diaoyu/Senkaku Islands issue was raised by Prime Minister Tanaka toward the end of the third summit meeting, on September 27, 1972. Tanaka said: "There is one thing I want to say. I am very grateful for your magnanimous attitude. I want to take this opportunity to ask about the Chinese position with regard to the Diaoyu/Senkaku Islands." In response, Zhou Enlai answered that, "I do not want to talk about this issue now. There is nothing to be gained by discussing it at this point." Tanaka continued to insist, saying, "I will have trouble if I go home without even having raised it after having come all the way to Beijing. If I just raise the subject now, I will at least be able to give an account." To this, Zhou Enlai said: "This is understandable. Since oil was discovered on the seabed, Taiwan has taken the issue up and is making an issue out of it. Now the United States is trying to find fault and is making the issue into a big problem." Seeing that the Chinese side did not intend to pursue the problem further, Tanaka immediately said, "Very well, there is no need to discuss this further. Let us leave it for another time."

Even better known is that when Deng Xiaoping visited Japan in October 1978, he proposed the two countries shelve the question of sovereignty over the Diaoyu/Senkaku Islands. This is something I have already discussed elsewhere in this book. On October 25, Deng Xiaoping responded to a question about the Diaoyu/Senkaku Islands issue from a journalist at the Japan National Press Club in Tokyo by saying: "While it is certainly true that some people have used this issue to pour cold water on the development of Sino-Japanese relations, we believe it is better for the two governments to avoid discussion of this issue."

During this visit to Japan, Deng Xiaoping said that he wanted to learn from Japan and that both countries should work hard for the sake of friendship through the generations, for our children and our children's children. (*Deng Xiaoping Amid the Currents of Sino-Japanese Foreign Relations*, Central Party Literature Press, April 2002.)

When Mao Zedong and Deng Xiaoping governed China, the Diaoyu/Senkaku Islands issue did not have any impact on the normalization of relations between China and Japan and did not affect China's learning from Japan or Sino-Japanese friendship. We should note that both Zhou Enlai and Deng Xiaoping criticized the approach taken by people who wished to use the Diaoyu/Senkaku Islands issue to obstruct Sino-Japanese reconciliation. Today, it is essential both sides have a sense of proportion and balance on the issue and work to avoid overblown rhetoric and extreme policies.

What is the most important thing for the Sino-Japanese relationship today? The most important thing is to continue to promote reconciliation and cooperation between the two countries and to achieve a strategic relationship based on mutual benefits. This strategic relationship based on mutual benefits is the framework for a bilateral relationship of historical significance established as the result of a long-term process of seeking and discussions. In comparison, the Diaoyu/Senkaku issue is a small-scale problem whose solution can wait.

There are several points of comparison here. In the previous chapter, I wrote briefly about China's territorial disputes with India, Vietnam, Malaysia, and South Korea. The area of the territory disputed by China and India, China and Vietnam, and China and Malaysia, is much larger than that of the Diaoyu/Senkaku Islands. As is well known, the territorial dispute between China and the former Soviet Union, and later Russia, continued for a full eighty years. All of these cases show that a dispute over national borders or territorial waters need not be an insurmountable barrier to friendship and cooperation.

The important thing in the dispute between China and Japan over the Diaoyu/Senkaku Islands is to maintain the approach that says that, although it is Chinese sovereign territory, we should shelve the dispute and focus instead on joint development. In September 2012, Professor Zhang Zhaozhong of the PLA National Defense University made a similar proposal. Even within the PLA, many officers are opposed to the idea of rashly starting a war. Xu Yan, a major general with the PLA National Defense

University, published an article titled "On the Economic and Military Power Disparity between China and the US" in the August 2012 *Tongzhou Gong-jin* (*Advance in the Same Boat*). The article argues that, overall, China's industrial sector continues to be dominated by low-end industries while the United States and Japan are global leaders in high-end industries. There is a gap of 30-40 years between China and the United States in terms of military technology. Xu Yan continues as follows.

What we should note carefully is this: in recent years, some unbalanced people have come to feel skeptical about the peaceful development of our country, and we are seeing a phenomenon in which arguments propounded by angry young people are flooding the Internet. The arrival of prosperity is surely what the Chinese people have been looking forward to for many years, and a "harmonious" society is a slogan put forward by the Central Committee to encapsulate this in its social policies.[5] However, some people have deliberately gone against this path, making outrageous and exaggerated statements in the name of "patriotism," claiming that the region is at imminent risk of war, and attacking the country's foreign policy as weak and feeble. Even though Mao Zedong and Deng Xiaoping emphasized that the controversy should be shelved, some people nevertheless continue to fan nationalist sentiment and incite people by claiming that the issue should be resolved immediately by force. But if we deal with the problem this way, it will become quite impossible for us to achieve peaceful development. In recent years, a tide of frivolous, shallow-minded, and vulgar opinion has been rife in our country, and some corners of the media, whose chief aim is to attain popularity by sensationalism, have been perpetuating arguments based on inflammatory and excessive exaggerations. This has helped to further inflame the passions of young people and has produced extreme emotions. In this context, it is clear that a calm and objective account of the true extent of our country's economic and military power is more important than ever.

On September 5, 2012, the *Zhongguo Qingnianbao* (*China Youth Daily*) published an article by Xu Baike, editor-in-chief of *Bing Dian* (*Freezing Point*), its affiliated weekly paper, with the title "The Media Must Not Commercialize Patriotism," which criticized an editorial article carried in *Global Times*.

Xu Baike wrote that an old and aggressive way of thinking has deep roots in some parts of the Chinese media, and it now seems to be threatening to come out swinging at any moment. But an increasingly open society and liberation of minds and spirits are the true trends of the times. There are good grounds to hope and expect that rationality and logic will prevail. We need to be on guard against the way some media seek to make commercial use of patriotism to boost their circulations or audience ratings. This is the recent media tendency to enflame people's emotions with a shocking story and then use this to nurture market share. Such media continue to enflame the emotions with a succession of shocking stories and then attempt to win market success by catering to the emotions they have stirred up. Some print and broadcast commentators have made statements like the following about the Diaoyu/Senkaku dispute, suggesting that China and Japan would soon exchange fire. "If China and Japan do go to war, it will surely be a war that will sweep more than a century of humiliation away from the hearts of the Chinese people. No other war is as suitable for playing this role as a war between China and Japan."

Such talk is irresponsible. It fails to look at what is truly important, and hardly differs from the extreme attitudes of the foreign powers that we object to. I wish the media, grown accustomed to this style of discourse and this abuse of language, would discard this approach and look at the masses within the broader context. Whether on the pages of a newspaper or during a television broadcast, if media outlets that shape public opinion are constantly giving exaggerated and emotional information designed to fan animosity and war, the only possible outcome is a type of masochism based on these commentators' idle, self-serving conjectures or the commercial exploitation of nationalism and the transformation of patriotism into a product to be consumed. The first outcome would be lamentable; the second contemptible.

These articles by Xu Yan and Xu Baike both make extremely good observations.

NOTES

1. To the fisherman the spoils: that is, when two sides fight, a third party reaps the benefits.

2. To watch as a bystander, never to intervene.

3. An Internet news site.

4. In the text, this is described as an "American Navy movie," but in fact it is a science fiction movie based on the idea of joint military exercises between the US Navy and several countries from around the Pacific Rim. It was directed by Peter Berg. The original title was *Battleship*. In China, it was released under the title *Chaoji Zhanjian* (Super Warship).

5. The full formal name is "Socialist Harmonious Society" (Shehui zhuyi hexie shehui). This slogan, launched by the Communist Party in 2004, means aiming for a balanced and harmonious society. The slogan was put forward under Hu Jintao and Wen Jiabao to correct the inequalities that had increased as a result of rapid economic growth, but in fact these discrepancies in wealth have only continued to increase ever since.

THIRTEEN
Hatred Has No Future

In the case of the Sino-Japanese relationship, if we are to fulfill this solemn vow of peace, we must first get rid of hatred. Just as Deng Xiaoping said: We must not squabble over the rights and wrongs of history. We must do as the United States has done over its historical issues with Britain, and as France has done with Germany. This is the only rational choice, for hatred brings only narrow-mindedness, misunderstanding, and war. Hatred has no future.

Song Hongbing recently wrote a book called *Huobi Zhanzheng (Currency Wars)*.[1] Although I do not agree with everything he says in his book, the lecture he gave on the European Union on Phoenix Television's "The Forum" (*Shiji Da Jiangtang*) program on September 29, 2012, made a lot of sense. In summary, what he said was: For more than 300 years, European history was marked by war: religious wars, ethnic wars, political wars, and wars over sovereignty. These wars were more frequent, and cost more lives, than anything comparable in Asia. The two World Wars both broke out in Europe. Nevertheless, over the past sixty years, Europe has sought the path of peace through unity and community, first through the European Coal and Steel Community and later through the European Union. As a result, the continent has essentially been free of major conflict for more than six decades. When sovereignty disputes broke out between Germany and the Netherlands and Denmark over some islands, they were resolved peacefully through negotiations and compromise. Why has Asia not been able to seek peace the same way? In Asia, there have been numerous major wars in the past sixty years or more, and there is still a serious risk of war today. And this even though we have the advantage of several thousand years of political wisdom to draw on. It is incumbent upon us to think seriously about how we can prevent wars and walk the path of peace.

Song Hongbing gave his talk at a time when the anti-Japanese demonstrations were at their height across the Chinese mainland and their passion and fury showed no signs of subsiding. China and Japan were aggressively facing off over Diaoyu/Senkaku sovereignty and were on the brink of war. Countries around the world were trying to predict which side would win if war broke out. One thing is certain: if China and Japan did go to war, the fallout would be global and both China and Japan would risk being ruined together.

On October 4, the *People's Daily* carried a significant piece by Jiang Weiyu with the title "An Economist Looks at the Stars." The piece reminded readers of the writings of the British economist John Maynard Keynes as a way of encapsulating the lessons to be learned from European history and put forward a framework for peace based on the idea that the victors should not be too cruel or vindictive toward their vanquished foes after a war. Jiang's thesis was:

> After the end of World War I, the victorious countries of Great Britain, France, and the United States and the defeated countries of Germany and Austria-Hungary met in Paris for a peace conference to discuss, among other things, the reparations that the defeated nations should pay. Keynes attended the conference as a delegate for the British Exchequer. After running detailed calculations on Germany's ability to pay, he proposed that the amount of reparations demanded of Germany not exceed 2 billion pounds. In addition, Britain should renounce any demand that the reparations be paid in cash. Keynes argued that reparations should be realistic based upon ability to pay, and the purpose should not be hatred or retribution. The populace of the defeated country should be able to obtain consumer goods and should not be made to suffer from hunger and cold because of excessive reparations. Merciless demands for reparations would only leave the root of the evil intact and pave the way for the next round of reprisals and vengeance. He argued that, the prewar economic system in Europe having been built around German productivity, the aim after the war should be to rebuild this productivity peacefully, not to crush it. To crush Germany would mean nothing less than crushing Europe. But the leaders of several victorious countries ran their own calculations and claimed they could not ignore the national will of their peoples to punish Germany severely. As a result, when the Treaty of Versailles was signed, it committed Germany to pay reparations amounting to 11.3 billion pounds. Europe fell into an unprecedented economic crisis which exacerbated German resentment and eventually led to the worst possible payback—World War II. The final treaty terms drove Keynes to despair, leading him to resign his position with the Exchequer. After leaving his position, he published his "The Economic Consequences of the Peace,"[2] in which he argued that fools were more likely to destroy the world than evil men.

Song Hongbing worries that the conditions evoked by Keynes at the time of the Treaty of Versailles are in many ways similar to the situation we face today. Paris is a nightmare and the people there are sickly. The feeling that disaster is imminent runs rampant everywhere, and the populace cowers and panics in the face of impending disaster. Important decisions are confused by elements that have become detached from reality. Frivolity, blindness, arrogance, and confusion run rampant—all the elements of a classical tragedy are present.

Song Hongbing's intent is to wake us to the danger. Even though seventy years have passed since the end of the war with Japan, hatred for the defeated country is still rife. If people continue to long for retribution against Japan and continue to say things like "We must kill all the Japanese, even if China itself becomes a graveyard," Asia risks being plunged into an even greater tragedy—a tragedy from which it will never recover.

"Hatred has no future." These words were spoken by French President Jacques Chirac on June 6, 2004, at the ceremonies marking the 60th anniversary of the Allied landings in Normandy during the Second World War. On that day, leaders from 16 countries, including US President George Bush and Britain's Queen Elizabeth II, attended a ceremony held on the beach in France. Particularly notable was that German Chancellor Gerhard Schroeder was in attendance. Why, one wonders, has China made no attempt to invite Japanese politicians to attend events of this kind?

On June 6, 1944, as many as a million Allied troops converged on Normandy in a coordinated land, sea, and air attack—a campaign fought with extreme intensity and fierceness against German forces. In the midst of gunfire, bombs, and artillery fire, countless Allied soldiers lost their lives in the sea and on the beaches. Following an intense battle that raged for days and nights on end, the Allies finally succeeded in securing the beaches and took their attack to the Germans, eventually breaking through the German lines and achieving victory. On June 6, 2004, as the sun rose in the sky, several hundred veterans of that war stood on the beach at Normandy and offered up a solemn moment of silence in memory of their comrades who fell to the gunfire and bombardments.

President Chirac of France and Chancellor Schroeder of Germany unveiled a memorial plaque together. The inscription simply states that President Chirac of France and Chancellor Schroeder of Germany jointly attended a commemorative event on June 6, 2004, to mark sixty years since the Normandy landings. The text on the stone is simple and straightforward, merely recording a single historical fact. But the people who gathered at the ceremony that day felt sure this historical fact would have an impact that would stretch far into the future, would mark the end of an era, and would provide a shining example for the rest of the world and its future.

After presenting medals to veterans, President Chirac went out of his way to explain why he had invited the German chancellor to attend.

> Sixty years have passed, but none of us has forgotten these hours in which the destiny of Europe and the world was decided here. Sixty years ago, these beaches were strewn with blood and fire, but that

moment also marked a new beginning. It marked the beginning of the unification of Europe, of cooperation supported by peace, democracy, and freedom. It is my wish and hope that Germany should share with us this memory of the moment when the ideals of freedom returned to the European continent. We hold up the example of Franco-German reconciliation to show the world that hatred has no future, that the path of peace can free people forever. Your presence here, Herr Chancellor, is evidence once again of the long and patient work of reconciliation between our peoples, and of the fruit which it has borne.

In his own speech, Schroeder said that his presence was intended to engrave in the hearts of the next generation the responsibility of all Europeans to maintain lasting peace and work together to build Europe, as well as to remember the victims of Hitler's regime. He went on to say, "While we have different memories of the war, we have a shared conviction and a shared yearning for peace. There is no denying or refusing the painful historical responsibility that Germany bears for having failed to stop the war. We know who caused the war, we know our historical responsibility, and we take it seriously."

During the commemorative events, Schroeder was interviewed by the French newspaper *Le Figaro*. He revealed that his own father had died in combat in Romania during the war. For the generation that had experienced the war, he said, the suffering it had brought could never be forgotten. The media in several countries wrote that the presence of the German chancellor at these events was of epochal significance. The reconciliation was not for short-term interests and had not come about as a result of outside external pressure; nor had it come from any ideas of strategic balance. It was built on a shared resolution to renounce war forever.

Since the early modern period, the development of industrial civilization in Europe has brought great advances in civilization and improved productivity, but at the same time it also brought strong-eat-weak colonialism and war. Competition for resources, clashes of interests, inflamed nationalisms, opposing ideologies, deep-rooted centuries-old resentments, misunderstandings, and squabbles over infringed sovereignty condemned Europe to suffer through two major wars in less than half a century and came close to destroying European civilization itself. Even after the immediate pain and suffering passed, postwar Europe continued to remember the suffering and learn from it. Remembering those bitter experiences, Europe has not again fallen prey to ideology. Europe has believed in values and dialogue. By putting its faith in the construction of strong and dependable systems and a shared belief in the values of freedom, tolerance, and peace, and by using democracy to move forward with European unity, it has essentially succeeded in preventing further wars.

A French scholar has said that postwar Germany experienced a double liberation. Firstly, built on the foundations of remorse, Germany was liberated from the burden of history. Secondly, today's Germany, as a mature democratic state, shoulders an important responsibility to protect the values of peace and democracy in the international community. Johnny Erling, an old friend of mine and the China correspondent for the German newspaper *Die Welt*, experienced the process of Franco-German reconciliation himself. He told me that France and Germany have fought more wars in their history than China and Japan have. After the Second World War, President De Gaulle of France and Chancellor Adenauer of Germany understood that the relationship between France and Germany was at the very core of European relations and believed that if France and Germany were at peace, then the whole of Europe would know peace. De Gaulle and Adenauer dedicated themselves to Franco-German cooperation, casting aside the lingering resentments of history and building a new model for the Franco-German relationship. In 1963, the two leaders signed the Élysée Treaty establishing arrangements and targets for cooperation and pushing reconciliation and cooperation forward on a Europe-wide scale. France and Germany continue today to maintain a stable relationship of cooperation, cooperation that is vitally important. The relationship is so important, for example, that nothing can be done in the EU without these two countries' approval. EU expansion is making things increasingly complicated, but Franco-German cooperation continues to play a central role. It is fair to say that Europe as it exists today would not have been possible without reconciliation between France and Germany.

The ideals behind Franco-German reconciliation are peace, forgiveness, self-reflection, dialogue, and understanding. This means casting aside hatred and unraveling the resentments and entanglements of generations past. The violence, coercion, dictatorship, and lies fomented by imperialism, nationalism, totalitarianism, and extremism of various kinds were why Europe was continually troubled by the fires of war and a fundamental reason for global instability. Postwar Europe developed a new model of thought and systems based on reflection, and this development is of global significance. By the same logic, there cannot be stability in Asia without reconciliation between China and Japan. The important point in this context is not to allow hatred to drag on any further.

On March 13, 2007, Alexander Downer, then Australia's foreign minister, drew on the experiences of his own father to argue persuasively against those Australians who were opposed to the signing of a Joint Declaration on Security Cooperation with Japan. Since Australian troops had experienced harsh fighting with the Japanese during World War II, there were some people who were uncomfortable with the idea of developing close military ties with a former enemy. But Australians needed to show a tolerant forgiving mentality, he said. Downer went on to say that his father, Sir Alick Downer, had been a Japanese prisoner of war and had spent three long years in Changi Prison in Singapore, where he had suffered all kinds of torment. In the 1950s, when Downer Sr. was head of Australia's Asia bureau, he had conflicted feelings toward Japan. As foreign minister, Downer continued, "My father's thinking was that Japan had tortured him and almost killed him, but the world had moved on." In the end, he believed that Australia and Japan should move together toward the future.

The American author Hendrik van Loon says in his famous work *Tolerance* that tolerance and forgiveness is the highest human virtue.

> Tolerance can promote peace, rationality, freedom, democracy, and science and technology. Once the religious trials of medieval Europe no longer flaunted their authority, astronomy was finally able to develop in a normal and sound manner. The birth of the Magna Carta in England was the result of compromise between the oppressed people of the country and the king, and the results of tolerance gradually accumulated to establish a democratic political system in Britain at a relatively low cost.

To van Loon's way of thinking, being tolerant and understanding requires a relatively high intelligence quotient, and low-IQ people are always likely to be intolerant of others. He argues that tolerance in the broadest sense of the word has always been a luxury which could only be afforded by those endowed with a rich intellectual intelligence—by people who, mentally speaking, are far removed from the narrow prejudices of their less enlightened fellow-men and can see the bold and bright future possessed by all mankind. What kind of future is this? Van Loon continues, "If we look up into the sky we see the same stars, and we are all travelers together on our journeys on the same planet and live under the same sky. Why then do we always regard one another as enemies?"

George Orwell, the famous English author of *Nineteen Eighty-Four*, wrote in "The English People" that the English generally reject ideologies built on hatred and illegality, and that England's famous "insularity" and "xenophobia" are far stronger in the working class than in the bourgeoisie.

Van Loon's *Tolerance* was published in 1925; Orwell's essay in 1947. In the half century and more since then, science and technology have progressed, education has become widespread, and improved productivity and globalization have greatly changed people's thinking around the world. The idea of tolerance has become accepted by more and more people and is no longer restricted to a small elite.

On the issue of Sino-Japanese reconciliation, Zhu Xueqin, professor at Shanghai University, has expressed the hope that the two countries will cast aside hatred and achieve tolerance. On September 18, 2005—the anniversary of the Liutiaohu (Mukdan) Incident—Zhu Xueqin published an article titled "On the Sixtieth Anniversary of Victory in the War Against Japan" in the *Beijing News* newspaper in which he explained his thinking on tolerance in some detail. Zhu Xueqin writes that the Sino-Japanese relationship forms the very nucleus of politics within the Asian region. If relations between these two are stable, all of Asia will be stable; if the two quarrel, the natural state of affairs in all of Asia will be one of turmoil. Japan has its own issues, as does China. Japan has expressed regret for its sins of the past but lacks sincerity, and even now the ongoing problem of school textbooks still lingers. This is obviously something that China naturally criticizes. Yet China also has problems.

> The way we educate our young people still contradicts humanitarianism, democracy, and the facts in some respects. We must weed out and eradicate the exaggerated claims that have built up over the years and establish a sound civics curriculum. Good systems and good civics are the foundations of a modern major power. If the right systems are in place and civics are good, national power will naturally increase and become a power for peace. There is no need to continually boast of dominance or supremacy; the people of the world will deal with us as a democratic state and a civilized country. If there are no systems in place and no civics, then national power will be increasingly autocratic and no one will believe our claims are sincere and trustworthy. This will be a disaster for us. We will become isolated from other countries and will end up losing everything we have gained, eventually collapsing and falling in the blink of an eye. The lessons for our enemies are lessons for us as well. Prewar Germany and Japan transformed themselves from weak countries into strong powers, but no sooner had they achieved this than they plunged themselves into the disastrous abyss of war. After the war, after democratic reforms, they

made a fresh start with a new mentality and rose to prosperity a second time. Neighboring countries that had been victorious in the war merely stood by and watched as events quickly unfolded, until it was already too late. We can celebrate our victory as often as we like, but why is it that our enemy always recovers and prospers again despite defeat? History shows that while winners are able to rejoice and celebrate, what happens in the postwar years deserves careful thought and reflection.

Continuing, Zhu Xueqin uses the example of the American Civil War to elucidate the profound problems of tolerance. As is well known, the Southern states broke away and fought a war to validate their independence. Ultimately the North was victorious and succeeded in maintaining the country as one. Zhu Xueqin writes:

> Some 620,000 people lost their lives in the American Civil War. This was equivalent to one-sixtieth of the total population of the country at the time—but there were no war crimes trials, no purges, and not a single humble foot solider had his crimes totted up or was forced to make amends in the name of "historical issues." On the very day that the North accepted the Confederate surrender, President Lincoln himself requested the band play "Dixie" as the surrender was accepted. Lincoln's Gettysburg address has gone down in history as one of the all-time great speeches and Jiang Zemin recited it during his visit to the United States. Lincoln's speech simply reiterated the national founding principles of government "of the people, by the people, for the people," and did not contain a word of insult or disdain for the Confederate armies. Although Lincoln was assassinated by a Southern sympathizer, the Union government did not carry out any major operations to weed out sympathizers after this event. It had already broadened its aims. The political perspective of the novel *Gone With the Wind* could probably be described as reactionary. The novel sees events from the Southern perspective and denounces the Northern armies for arson, murder, and plunder, but the work was never censored or suppressed. It was reprinted many times and became famous around the world. President Jefferson Davis of the Confederate States lived out his later years in peace, until he died at the age of eighty-one. Vice President Alexander Stephens was elected to the federal United States Senate after the war, and his tombstone bears the simple epitaph, "patriot and statesman." Atlanta, Georgia, features a huge statue

of General Robert E. Lee, who was commander of the Confederate armies, on the outskirts of the city. Tourists look up at the statue, but the Northern government has never expressed anger at its existence.

In 2012, *Huanqiu Renwu* (*Global People*) issue 11 published an article by Zhang Xiaoping discussing the best way to part from hatred and citing the example of Nelson Mandela of South Africa. In 1994, a South African man, James Gregory, was extremely worried because Nelson Mandela, a man he had guarded for twenty-seven years as an important prisoner (serving a life sentence for sedition), had been elected president of South Africa.[3] Remembering occasions when he had tortured Mandela, Gregory was beside himself with anxiety. It had happened in the desolate prison on Robben Island when Mandela was kept isolated in a small cell, condemned to quarry and break rocks or gather kelp from an ice-cold sea during the day, all his freedom restricted and curtailed. Since Mandela was a political prisoner, Gregory often joined his fellow guards in insulting him, beating him with an iron shovel at the slightest provocation, and on some occasions deliberately contaminating his food with sewage water and forcing him to drink it.

In May, Gregory and two of his fellow guards received an invitation to the inauguration, signed by Mandela himself. The three men attended reluctantly. In his opening remarks at the start of the inauguration, Mandela said, "I am honored that I have been able to welcome so many distinguished guests here today. I am particularly happy that three of the guards who kept me company during my years of hardship on Robben Island are able to be here today." Then Mandela introduced the three men as guests and embraced them one by one. He said, "When I was young I had an impetuous temperament and a rough nature. It was thanks to these three men that I was able to learn to control my emotions." Mandela's words were discomfiting for the three men who had mistreated him in prison, but everyone in attendance was struck with awe and admiration. A flood of applause came from the audience.

After the ceremony was over, Mandela again walked over to where Gregory was standing and spoke to him in a calm voice, saying: "I knew that moment that I walked out of the cell toward freedom that I would remain inside the cell forever unless I was able to leave sadness and resentment behind." Gregory was unable to restrain his tears. In that instant, he finally understood. Tolerance is the best way to bid hatred farewell.

We should be relieved that, in the summer to autumn of 2012, when the confrontation between China and Japan over the Diaoyu/Senkaku Islands seemed to be moving to the brink of war, important reciprocal actions by ordinary people in the two countries demonstrated common sense rationality, tolerance, and mutual understanding. On October 7, 2012, *The Beijing News* reported that around 1,300 Japanese intellectuals, including Oe Kenzaburo, winner of the Nobel Prize for Literature, had released a joint Japanese Citizens' Appeal to Stop the Vicious Cycle of Territorial Disputes on September 28 calling on the Japanese government to reflect earnestly on history when addressing related issues. The text of the statement was carried widely and in full on numerous websites in China. Basically, the statement said:[4]

Tensions in the area around Japan are increasing through issues related to the Daioyu/Senkaku and Takeshima/Dokdo islands. This is particularly unfortunate and saddening in light of the sympathy and empathy extended to Japan following the March 11, 2011, Great East Japan Earthquake and Tsunami, when the Chinese and Korean leaders Wen Jiabao and Lee Myung Bak visited the disaster-striken areas and encouraged the survivors. Korea and China are both important friends for Japan and partners in the creation of peace and prosperity for the region. As citizens of Japan, we are deeply concerned at the current situation and make the following declaration.

Japan's claims to Takeshima/Dokdo began in February 1905 during the Russo-Japanese War at a time when the colonization of Korea was underway and Korean diplomatic rights were being lost. For the people of Korea, this is not an issue of a mere island but a point of origin and symbol of invasion and colonial rule. It is essential Japan understand this fact.

The Daioyu/Senkaku Islands were incorporated within Japanese territory in January 1895 as the outcome of the Sino-Japanese War was already evident, just three months before Taiwan and the Penghu Islands became Japanese colonies. Both of these territorial claims were made when Korea and China were at their weakest and when it would have been impossible for them to make diplomatic claims.

This year marks the 40th anniversary of the normalization of diplomatic relations between Japan and China. The events that changed this friendship into conflict were the declaration by Tokyo Governor Ishihara Shintaro that he intended to purchase the Daioyu/Senkaku Islands and the Japanese government's subsequent declaration that it would nationalize the islands. From the Chinese perspective, it should not be surprising that these actions were seen as going against the tacit agreement to shelve the territorial issue. It must be said that domestic criticism within Japan of Governor Ishihara's acts was weak. Furthermore, Prime Minister Noda's announcement of the intent to nationalize the islands was made on July 7, the anniversary of the Marco Polo Bridge incident and a sensitive date for the Chinese people.

Territorial issues are sensitive in any country, and action on one side leads to counter-action on the other. If this is allowed to escalate, it runs the risk of spiraling out of control and developing into a clash of arms. We oppose any use of violence and emphasize that the issue should be resolved through peaceful dialogue. Politics and media in both countries have a responsibility to curb nationalism and respond calmly. At times like this, when we are in danger of falling into a vicious cycle, the role of the media to stop the escalation of nationalistic sentiments, reflect upon history, and call for calm is more important than ever.

With regard to territory, consultation and dialogue are the only options. Japan must revise its position that "no territorial dispute exists." It is clear to one and all that a territorial dispute does indeed exist. No consultations or negotiations can take place unless this is acknowledged. In addition, it must be admitted that the concept of fixed "inherent territory" is not something that can really be true for either party.

At least during the consultation and negotiation, the current situation should be maintained and provocative actions should be curbed on all sides. Fundamental rules and action norms related to this issue should be created. On August 5, Taiwanese President Ma Ying-Jeou announced the East China Sea Peace Initiative. This Initiative called for shelving the dispute, dealing with it through discussion, finding a peaceful solution, and setting standards for activities within the East China Sea—extremely calm recommendations. Such voices should be further shared and strengthened.

The area around the Daioyu/Senkaku Islands has long been a place for fishing and exchanges—an ocean of production—supporting the livelihoods of the people of Taiwan and Okinawa. The Taiwanese and Okinawan fishermen do not want the Daioyu/Senkaku Islands to become the focus of a conflict between states. We should respect the views of those living and working in the area.

The most important point for Japan is to recognize and rue its own historical issues, respect the important documents it has signed with China, and reaffirm its statements of remorse about its history, including the 1993 Statement by Chief Cabinet Secretary Kono Yohei, the

1995 Statement by Prime Minister Murayama Tomiichi, and the 2010 Statement by Prime Minister Kan Naoto. It should show by its attitude how it intends to further reconciliation, friendship, and cooperation with its neighbors. The results of joint historical research between Japan and Korea and Japan and China should be recognized, as should the joint statement made between intellectual leaders in Japan and Korea in 2010 stating the invalidity of the 1910 Treaty of Annexation of Korea.

Joint development of the areas under dispute is the only way forward. While sovereignty cannot be divided, it is possible to jointly develop, manage, and distribute resources, including fishery resources. Rather than clashing over sovereignty, the countries involved should pursue dialogue and consultation to come to an understanding over resources and shared interests. We must shift the seeds of conflict which stir up territorial nationalism and use them instead as a foundation for regional cooperation.

The current situation should not mean an increased burden on Okinawa, either through the strengthening of the US-Japan Security Pact provisions or with the deployment of the V-22 Osprey, a new type of vertical takeoff and landing transport aircraft.

Finally, we propose the creation of frameworks for dialogue at the non-governmental, citizens' level between Japan, China, Korea, Okinawa, and Taiwan with a view to building good faith and mutual trust for the future.

This statement by Oe Kenzaburo and others met with a strong response in China. On October 3, people in mainland China, Taiwan, Hong Kong, and Macao responded to the appeal by publishing an online statement titled "Let's Restore Rationality to the Sino-Japanese Relationship: Our Appeal."[5] By October 30, a total of 785 people from all four regions had signed the appeal, including a considerable number of famous names such as Liang Wendao, Ye Tingfang, Chen Guanzhong, Yang Jinlin, Luqiu Luwei, Zhu Tianwen, Zhu Tianxin, Hong Ying, Cui Weiping, Li Yinhe, He Weifang, Qian Yongxiang, Cha Jianying, Su Xiaohe, Lu Yuegang, Tie Liu, Xu Xiao, Jiang Fangzhou, Gao Quanxi, Ye Kuangzheng, Zhou Shi, Zhou Baosong, Yan Bofei, Xie Xizhang, Xia Yeliang, Meng Mei, Du Xiaozhen, Lao Cun, Li Gongming, Hou Xiaoxian, Hu Fayun, Fu Guoyong, Ge Hongbing, Fan Hong, Chen Yizhong, Ai Xiaoming, and Wang Xiaoshan.

The main thrust of the appeal was:

The recent crisis in Sino-Japanese relations over the Daioyu/Senkaku

Islands and the disturbances it has brought to Chinese society are deeply upsetting. The Japanese Citizens' Appeal to Stop the Vicious Cycle of Territorial Disputes was a comfort and we were happy to feel the heartfelt goodwill of the Japanese people. The appeal does not try to avoid Japan's history of colonialization or the origins of the dispute over the Daioyu/Senkaku Islands; instead, it raises these issues from a perspective built on a relationship of friendly cooperation developed over many years. It looks in particular to a future of peaceful coexistence, and we believe this is a good way to turn the present crisis into an opportunity. In response we issue our appeal as follows.

The territorial issue over the Daioyu/Senkaku Islands is a problem left behind by history, but one for which our predecessors handed down a sound solution. In 1972, Zhou Enlai indicated his readiness to shelve the dispute, and in 1978 Deng Xiaoping made it clear that he intended to continue this policy. This was done to ensure the Daioyu/Senkaku Islands issue not be allowed to obstruct normal exchanges between the two countries. From today's perspective, we can see clearly how wise this decision was. In the present circumstances, any unilateral attempt to resolve the issue, no matter what kind of proposal it might be, is likely to result in a military collision or the obliteration of East Asian peace. Once the subject of the Daioyu/Senkaku Islands is raised, better dialogue and the possibility of discussion no longer exist. In such a situation, the first need is to return to the previous position.

The Japanese government has recently put forward a number of arguments and proofs on the subject of Daioyu/Senkaku sovereignty. We find these unsubstantiated and unpersuasive. What is undeniable is that postwar Japan failed to convince its neighbors of the sincerity of its apologies for its responsibility for the war, with the result that considerable resentment built up over the years, which resentment still remains strong among the Chinese people. The first priority should be to confront this accumulated resentment and find a way to exorcise it. To that end, it is vital Japan fully acknowledge its past and persuade people with virtue. In other respects, it is essential we not create new conflicts and stir up existing resentments.[6]

Rapid economic development has yielded dramatic lifestyle improvements on the Chinese mainland over the past thirty years. This is closely related to the fact that we have strictly adhered to the path of peaceful development. We must treasure the results we have achieved and value stable and harmonious friendly relations with our neighbors.

Accordingly, we hope both sides will work hard and use all possible means to achieve dialogue and discussion with regard to the current tensions, and we hope we can continue to maintain peaceful and stable relations with Japan and other neighboring countries. It is impossible for either state or citizens to prosper except in times of peace.

Japan's postwar political, economic, and cultural development has been astonishing. Looking at the changes in Japan's society and people today, we know that the majority of people in Japan are apologetic about the war and have worked nobly to build peace, and we also know of the strong support that Japan has given China during China's peaceful development. This is why, facing history directly and remembering the past, we need a new understanding and judgment that takes today's Japan into account.

We caution against and are opposed to any attempt by any interest group or political faction to stir up territorial disputes for their own purposes and interests, to manipulate popular sentiment for their own ends, and to inflame narrow-minded nationalism. The government itself has a major role to play in resolving the territorial dispute and bringing resolution to the issue. Once a crisis has arisen, it is the government's duty to take the lead so that people's behavior is based on a rational understanding of the issue.

The escalation resulting in acts of destruction and arson in some Chinese cities in mid-September 2012 is a source of great sadness for us, and something deserving of the sternest and most forceful condemnation. The acts of a small minority cannot represent the views on the Daioyu/Senkaku Islands held by the majority of the people who live in the four regions fronting on the sea. We hope these actions will not lead to misunderstandings in the international community, bring on economic recession, or have negative consequences in other fields.

Cultural exchanges between China and Japan have recently been curtailed and the publication of books on Japanese subjects has become a collateral victim of the dispute. This foolish behavior is extremely regrettable. Cultural exchanges between China and Japan have a long history and have produced impressive results. A disagreement over territory or politics must not be allowed to spread unchecked and cast a malign influence on other areas. Personal contacts have an important role to play in building and sustaining friendly relations. Normal cooperation and exchanges should be restored as soon as possible in the fields of economics, culture, and general life, and compensation should be made to the greatest possible extent for any damage and losses accruing from this dispute. Temporary measures likely to have a detrimental effect from a long-term perspective should be revoked.

All of us have the right to live where we were born, to work, to raise the next generation, and to participate in the business of society and the state. We have sovereign rights with regard to the state and the right to speak to state sovereignty. For these reasons, the government should listen to the opinions of the people when handling problems of sovereignty. We believe that the state must not disregard or ignore the masses or disregard their feelings.

Textbooks published in the four regions must include a record of modern history that is comprehensive and true to the facts. Chinese textbooks should put greater effort into educating children about exchanges and cultural blending with other peoples and educate children in a way that will be beneficial to the thinking and judgment of the next generation so that they can understand countries and peoples who are different from themselves with feelings of openness and can develop mutual respect between the peoples of China and Japan. This is essential if our young people are to grow up in a healthy way in the context of a relationship of partnership and friendship between the countries.

We believe that international problems regarding territory and state sovereignty are not merely the responsibility of the governments involved. We must work to develop conduits for more numerous exchanges between ordinary citizens, deepen mutual understanding, and create a peaceful future for our children and grandchildren.

This was the first meaningful bilateral exchange between ordinary citizens from the two countries on a scale large enough to attract the world's attention and have a rational reciprocal effect in the midst of this fierce territorial dispute between China and Japan over sovereignty. The leading media in Japan carried detailed reports on the Chinese appeal, and this had a positive impact in Japanese society. It is to be hoped the reciprocal effect achieved by this exchange will contribute substantially toward encouraging private citizens in both countries to cast off hatred and take the first steps toward forgiveness and generosity. To some extent, this exchange suggests the future of the bilateral relationship. Certainly, it indicates the direction in which my New Thinking on Relations with Japan is headed. Ups and downs will no doubt continue to be part of the Sino-Japanese relationship, but signs of hope are already appearing among ordinary citizens. This should become the foundation on which Asia can build a common community and become one family, and I am cautiously optimistic about our future.

Japanese and Chinese people alike eat with chopsticks, and the Japanese language uses thousands of Chinese characters. Even without any training in Japanese, a Chinese person can look at a Japanese newspaper or magazine and make a fair guess at the rough meaning of what the article is about. The Chinese character 駅 (*eki*) is still used today in Japan to mean "railway station," and this is clearly a straight adoption of the ancient Chinese term 駅站 (*yizhan*) meaning "staging point." Visiting Kyoto, you feel almost as though you have gone back to Tang China. It is quite different from anything I have ever felt on the streets of cities in the United States or Mexico. Japanese people study Chinese calligraphy and have achieved some outstanding results. In April 2010, when I was visiting research scholar at the University of Tokyo, I paid a visit to Kaieda Banri, a member of the House of Representatives who later became Minister of Economy, Trade, and Industry. He took up a brush and wrote neatly in my notebook in beautiful regular script the poem "Qing Ming," a quatrain in lines of seven syllables by the Tang dynasty poet Du Mu. He told me he has enjoyed classical Chinese poetry since he was in junior high school and still practices calligraphy today. It was at a bookstore in the Jinbocho area of Tokyo that I bought my copy of the *Nineteen Old Poems* (*Gushi Shijiu-shou*) primer edited by the Japanese scholar Kotaku Hosoi and written in semi-standard style. At the University of Tokyo Institute for Advanced Studies on Asia I perused works written by Japanese scholars focusing on China. In addition to the many studies published on such Chinese works as the ancient classics *Shangshu* (*Book of Documents*) or *The Four Dreams of Linchuan*, a drama by the Ming dynasty dramatist Tang Xianzu, there was also a detailed study on the life of late Ming dynasty scholar-officials. Chinese classics such as the *Analects*, the *Romance of the Three Kingdoms*, and *Journey to the West* are widely known in Japan and deeply rooted in the lives of Japanese people. If we take all this together, there is probably no other country in the world that has such a close and complex relationship with Chinese culture as Japan. In 2011, the value of economic and trade exchanges between China and Japan reached 350 billion dollars. It should certainly be possible for China to draw Japan to its side. There are four main points to note in this context.

One is to think strategically and overcome the immediate conflicts and entanglements. Several leaders, among them Mao Zedong, Zhou Enlai, Deng Xiaoping, and Hu Yaobang, have overcome the resentment accumulated over the years and have succeeded in seeing the bigger picture from a broader perspective. This has given them superior understanding and wisdom. On this subject, let me introduce an article published in January 2005 by General Liu Yazhou, political commissar at the National Defense University. He writes:

> The United States knows that, given the current circumstances, neither China nor Japan can undermine its position in Asia alone and that the only possible threat to American power would come if China and Japan joined hands. If China and Japan joined hands, they would be able to form an Asian community similar to the EU in Europe. The benefits from that would accrue not only to the two nations in question but to the entire world. The only loser would be the United States. A lot of people think that America's only rival in Asia is China and that the United States uses Taiwan to contain China—but this is too simplistic. The United States sets China and Japan against each other, encourages them to contain each other, and then controls each of them individually.
>
> It is not enough for the United States to contain China alone; it must also contain Japan. One step forward, it uses China to contain Japan. One step forward, it uses Japan to contain China. The United States manipulates both countries as it likes like pieces on a chessboard.

I wonder how readers feel about this analysis.

The second crucial point is to do away with hatred and develop the future in a spirit of generosity and forgiveness. Deng Xiaoping said: "In considering relations between countries, the main thing is to do it from the perspective of the strategic interests of the state . . . and not argue and bicker about the rights and wrongs of history." In a speech at Waseda University on May 8, 2008, Hu Jintao said: "We stress the importance of remembering history not to perpetuate hatred." Here again, let me quote Liu Yazhou's "The Grand National Strategy": "China and Japan both need a broad perspective. . . . If China and Japan cannot get over history and resentment and continue glaring at each other like this, neither will be able to become a great world power and both will continue forever to be second-rate Asian nations."

Third is to develop and implement focused efforts with regard to Japan. According to Zhu Liang, former director of the of the Central Committee's International Liaison Department, Zhou Enlai expended considerable energy on this aspect. Even when he was extremely busy with his political duties, Zhou Enlai remarkably set aside a whole six hours to talk with a single Japanese friend and to encourage Sino-Japanese understanding. How many people in Chinese government circles today are doing this much?

Fourth is to ensure that the entire range of the two countries' past and present is reflected in textbooks and political education. In addition to teaching about wars between the two countries, there should be increased teaching about the long-term friendly exchanges between the two countries, their history of learning from each other, the assistance that Japan has given to China's modernization and building, and the fact that the two countries' economies are joined so closely together.

In a report to the 18th National Congress of the Communist Party of China on November 8, 2012, Hu Jintao said:

> Peace and development remain the underlying trends of our times. To pursue peace, not war, to work towards development, not poverty, to aim for cooperation, not confrontation, in order to build a harmonious world of enduring peace and common prosperity—this is what the people of all countries long for. China is committed to peaceful settlement of international disputes and hotspot issues and opposes the wanton use of force or the threat of force. We will continue to promote friendship and partnership with our neighbors, consolidate friendly relations and deepen mutually beneficial cooperation with them, and ensure that China's development brings more benefits to our neighbors. The Chinese people love peace and yearn for development. We are ready to work with the people of other countries to unremittingly promote the noble cause of peace and development for all mankind.[7]

If we are to fulfill this solemn promise in the Sino-Japanese relationship, we must first exorcise our hatred. As Deng Xiaoping said, we must not squabble over the rights and wrongs of history. We must do as the United States has done over its historical issues with Britain, and as France has done with Germany. This is the only rational choice, for hatred brings only narrow-mindedness, misunderstandings, and war. Hatred has no future.

NOTES

1. Song Hongbing, born in Sichuan in 1968, writes about global financial history drawing on his experiences as a student in the United States and his time working in various financial institutions. His book *Currency Wars*, published in 2007, became a bestseller in China thanks to it being about a financial crisis and the publisher using a canny online sales strategy.

2. The Chinese translation of Keynes's work is *Heyue de jingji houguo*. It was translated into Japanese by Hayasaka Tadashi as *Heiwa no keizaiteki kiketsu* in volume two of the *Complete Works of Keynes*, published by Toyo Keizai Inc. 1977.

3. James Gregory was a prison guard under South Africa's apartheid system. He was appointed to guard Mandela because he could speak the local language. At first, he thought Mandela deserved the death penalty, but he gradually came to know Mandela and had considerable exchanges with him, as detailed in his memoir *Goodbye Bafana*. Various controversies surround the book, which is told from Gregory's perspective as a white man, but it has attracted considerable attention as a source for Mandela's prison years. The book was made into a film of the same name directed by Bille August and released in 2007.

4. Here the main content of the Joint Statement is quoted in excerpted form; the translation uses the original text, except in cases where the text differs from the original, which passages have been translated in line with the Chinese text. The original text in Japanese and English can be accessed at: http://peace3appeal.jimdo.com/

5. The text here gives the date of publication as October 3, but in fact the appeal did not appear until the next day. The appeal was uploaded along with the names of the initial 75 signatories to *Gongshi Wang*, a website influential among the Chinese intellectual community, at http://www.21com.net/articles/zgyj/gmht/article_2012100468733.html, following which supporters uploaded the appeal to their own blogs and websites. A central figure in the movement, who also wrote the draft of the appeal, was Cui Weiping, a former professor at the Beijing Film Academy, and among the initial signatories were famous writers, artists, scholars, and human rights activists. Petition movements were started by supporters in Hong Kong, Taiwan, and Macao in response to this call from intellectuals on the mainland, and signatures had been collected from 793 people by November 7 that year. One characteristic of the appeal was that the movement was not centered on well-known specialists on Japan. For more on Cui Weiping and the petition movement, see "Restoring Rational Dialogue into China-Japan Relations—the Reasons Why I Launched an Internet Petition," a record of a talk she gave at the Japan Foundation in Tokyo on January 29, 2013, published online at http://www.wochikochi.jp/english/relayessay/2013/03/japan-china-relations.php. See also Oikawa Junko, "Senkaku mondai o meguru Chugoku kara no 'kotonaru koe,'" in Nijuisseiki Chugoku Soken, ed., *Chugoku johogen 2013-2014 nenban*; *Tokushu: Senkaku-byo o sekkai suru*, Sososha, 2013.

6. This paragraph differs from the appeal as it was initially drafted. Some of the copies of the appeal that were circulated and reposted elsewhere on the Internet contain the appeal as it originally appeared before it was amended. A translation of the original version follows. "On September 27, 2012, Japanese representative to the United Nations Kodama Kazuo gave a statement to the General Assembly in which he offered the Treaty of Shimonoseki as proof of Japanese sovereignty over the Diaoyu/Senkaku Islands, but we believe that this represents an irresponsible attitude that attempts to conceal the facts, and cannot accept a starting point that places such weight on the ghosts of the unequal treaties. What cannot be denied is that territorial expansionism and militarism are currents of thought that have always been present in Japan, that the discourse of the extreme right is repeatedly made public, along with their understanding of the history of the invasion of China, and that none of this is any help in developing friendly and neighborly good relations."

   In fact, in September 2012, China's Foreign Minister Yang Jiechi gave a speech at the United Nations in which he claimed that the Diaoyu/Senkaku Islands belonged to China and that Japan had stolen them from China at the end of the Sino-Japanese War in 1895. The Japanese side responded by saying that Chinese territorial claims to the Diaoyu/Senkaku Islands only began in the 1970s, leading to an aggressive series of exchanges between the two sides. It is a misunderstanding of the facts to say that Japan's representative used the Treaty of

Shimonoseki as proof to back up Japan's territorial claims. The official view of the Japanese government is that the Diaoyu/Senkaku Islands were incorporated into Okinawa following a cabinet decision in January 1895, prior to the Treaty of Shimonoseki. After criticisms and corrections on this point, the people responsible for the appeal corrected it to the version translated in the main body of the text. There also seems to have been some debate about the references to militarism as an ever-present "current of thought" in Japan, and whether "militarism" was really an appropriate term for an understanding of modern Japan, regardless of any "shift to the right" that might be occurring in the country. This section was then rewritten, chiefly to correct these two points. But these corrections, made once the activities to petition collect signatures had already started, attracted fierce criticism, including from some people connected with the appeal. Here, the text has been translated as it appears in the Chinese.

7. This section is a partial extract from the section on international relations in part eleven of a report given by Hu Jintao to the 18th National Congress of the Communist Party of China on November 8, 2012. The complete text of the report is available in several places online, including at: http://www.china-embassy.org/eng/zt/18th_CPC_National_Congress_Eng/t992917.htm.
(Japanese text available at: http://news.xinhuanet.com/18cpcnc/2012-11/17/c_113711665.htm)

Index

About the Author

Ma Licheng was born in Chengdu, Sichuan Province, in 1946. After serving in such posts as vice director of the editorial department at the *China Youth Daily* and editorial editor-in-chief at the *People's Daily*, he moved to Hong Kong's Phoenix Television. A political commentator and scholar, he has been a University of Tokyo honorary member researcher, visiting scholar at Singapore University, and a Hokkaido University specially appointed professor. He has had a long career researching and commenting on such subjects as China's social transformation and nationalism, and he continues to be outspoken on both from his home in Beijing. Among his other publications is *Leading Schools of Thought in Contemporary China*, trans. by Jing L. Liu (Singapore: World Scientific Publishing, 2016). In 2000, he was made an honorary citizen of El Paso, Texas, U.S.A.

About the Japanese Translator

Oikawa Junko, PhD, Associate Professor, Chuo University, Faculty of Letters. Received her doctorate from the Nihon University Graduate School of Social and Cultural Studies. Her primary research focus is on the intersection of the intelligentsia and public discourse in contemporary Chinese society. Among her publications is "China's Social Divisions and the Search for a Common 'Baseline,'" The Tokyo Foundation for Policy Research, 2016.

（英文版）憎しみに未来はない　中日関係新思考
Hatred Has No Future: New Thinking on Relations with Japan

2020年12月15日　第1刷発行

著　者　　馬　立誠
英　訳　　公益財団法人日本国際問題研究所
発行所　　一般財団法人出版文化産業振興財団
　　　　　〒101-0051 東京都千代田区神田神保町2-2-30
　　　　　電話　03-5211-7283
　　　　　ホームページ　https://www.jpic.or.jp/

印刷・製本所　　大日本印刷株式会社